JOHN RUSKIN
AND THE LAKELAND ARTS REVIVAL
1880–1920

JOHN RUSKIN
AND THE
LAKELAND ARTS REVIVAL
1880–1920

SARA E. HASLAM

MERTON

First published 2004

Published by
Merton Priory Press Ltd
67 Merthyr Road, Whitchurch
Cardiff CF14 1DD

ISBN 1 898937 60 5

Printed by
Dinefwr Press
Rawlings Road, Llandybie
Carmarthenshire SA18 3YD

CONTENTS

LIST OF ILLUSTRATIONS

PICTURE ACKNOWLEDGEMENTS

Armitt Museum and Library Ambleside: Plate 2 (left), Plate 3 (top),
Plate 5, Plate 20; Ruskin Museum, Coniston: Plate 6 (bottom); Plate 23
(top left and bottom); Cumbria Record Office: Plate 4 (left), Plate 8
(top), Plate 9, Plate 14 (bottom), Plate 17 (top); Heaton Cooper Studio,
Grasmere (www.heatoncooper.co.uk): Plate 22 (top); Graythwaite Hall
Estate: Plate 14 (top); Kendal Town Council: Plate 22 (bottom); Abbot
Hall Museum and Gallery, Kendal: Plate 7 (bottom left), Plate 8
(bottom); Ruskin Library, University of Lancaster: Plate 3 (right), Plate
23 (top right); Simpson Family Archive: Plate 12, Plate 15, Plate 17
(bottom), Plate 18, Plate 12 (top); Malcolm Sisson: Plate 21 (bottom).
Other modern photographs are by the author.

CHRONOLOGY

This chronology gives the dates of Ruskin's writings from the time he purchased Brantwood until his death in 1900, and dates of events and publications concerning the revival of arts and crafts in Lakeland under his influence. It is a selective list which excludes some smaller texts and articles by Ruskin, Rawnsley, Collingwood and others.

c.1870	Two stained glass windows made for Lunefield, Kirkby Lonsdale, by Morris & Co.
1871–84	Ruskin publishes *Fors Clavigera* in eight volumes.
1871	East window made for St Peter's church, Kirkbampton, by Morris & Co.
1871	Ruskin buys Brantwood at Coniston.
1872	Ruskin moves into Brantwood.
1872	Ruskin publishes *Aratra Pentilici*.
1872	Ruskin publishes *The Eagle's Nest*.
1872	Ruskin publishes *Monuments of the Cavalli Family, Verona* (Arundel Society); reprinted in *On the Old Road* in 1885.
1872	Ruskin contributes a preface to *Christian Art and Symbolism* by the Revd R. St J. Tyrwhitt; reprinted in *On the Old Road*.
1873	Ruskin publishes *Love's Meinie* (Parts I and II).
1873	Ruskin publishes *The Nature and Authority of Miracle*, a paper for the Metaphysical Society, private distribution.
1873	John Ruskin publishes *Ariadne Florentina*.
1873	Albert Fleming publishes *In the House of Rimmon*.
1873	Stained glass window made for the Jesus Chapel, Troutbeck, by Morris & Co.
1874	Ruskin publishes *Val d'Arno*.
1874–8	St Martin's Church, Brampton, designed by Philip Webb.
1875	St George's Guild takes on a definite form.
1875	Susanna Beever edits *Frondes Agrestes*, selections from Ruskin's *Modern Painters*.
1875	Ruskin publishes *Notes on the Royal Academy*.
1875–7	Ruskin publishes *Mornings in Florence*.
1875–86	Ruskin publishes *Proserpina*.

1875–84	Ruskin publishes *Deucalion*.
1876	Ruskin contributes a preface to *A Protest Against the Extension of Railways in the Lake District* by Robert Somervell; reprinted in *On the Old Road*.
1876	Ruskin publishes *Letters to Young Girls* on the rules of St George's Company.
1876	Ruskin contributes a preface and notes to *The Art Schools of Mediaeval Christendom* by Miss Owen; reprinted in *On the Old Road*.
1876–8	Philip Webb designs Four Gables, Brampton.
1877	Webb designs Green Lanes, Brampton.
1877	Henry Holiday designs a window for St Bridget's church, Calder Bridge, the earliest known window design by Holiday in Cumberland or Westmorland.
1877	East window made for Ponsonby church by Morris & Co.
1877	Ruskin gives a lecture on 'Yewdale and its Streamlets' at Kendal on 1 October.
1877	Ruskin publishes his *Guide to the Principal Pictures in the Academy of Fine Arts at Venice*.
1877	H.D. Rawnsley publishes *A Book of Bristol Sonnets*.
1877–84	Ruskin publishes *St Mark's Rest*.
1877–9	Ruskin publishes *The Laws of Fesole*.
1877–1912	Stained glass windows made for Lanercost Priory by Morris & Co.
1878	Ruskin publishes *The Three Colours of Pre-Raphaelitism*, reprinted in *On the Old Road*.
1878–1920	Morris & Co. make stained glass windows for St Martin's church, Brampton.
1879–80	Ruskin publishes *The Lord's Prayer and the Church*, edited by the Revd F.A. Malleson; reprinted in *On the Old Road*.
1880	W.G. Collingwood starts work as Ruskin's secretary.
1880	Ruskin publishes *Usury, a Reply and a Rejoinder*, reprinted in *On the Old Road*.
1880	Ruskin publishes *Elements of English Prosody for use in St George's Schools*.
1880	Ruskin publishes *Letters on a Museum or Picture Gallery*, reprinted in *On the Old Road*.
1880	The Rawnsleys' Wray woodcarving class founded.
1880	The Laxey experiment begins on the Isle of Man.
1880	Ruskin publishes *Arrows of the Chace*.
1880–5	Ruskin publishes *The Bible of Amiens*.

1880–1	Ruskin publishes *Fiction, Fair and Foul*, reprinted in *On the Old Road*.
1881	Ruskin publishes Part III of *Love's Meinie*.
1881	Rawnsley publishes *Sonnets at the English Lakes*.
1881–1907	Stained glass windows made for St James's church, Staveley, by Morris & Co.
1883	The Lake District Defence Society is founded, with Fleming and Rawnsley as honorary secretaries and Ruskin as a member.
1883	Rawnsley becomes vicar of St Kentigern's Church, Crosthwaite, Keswick.
1883–4	First pieces of Langdale linen produced by Marian Twelves at Elterwater.
1883–4	Fleming and Marian Twelves join Ruskin's Guild of St George.
1883	The Keswick School of Industrial Arts is founded.
1883	Collingwood publishes *The Philosophy of Ornament: Eight Lectures on the History of Decorative Art Given at University College*.
1883	Ruskin publishes *The Art of England*.
1883	Ruskin contributes preface to *The Story of Ida* by Francesca Alexander.
1883	Ruskin contributes an introduction to *The Study of Beauty and Art in Large Towns* by T. C. Horsfall; reprinted in *On the Old Road*.
1884	Collingwood publishes *The Limestone Alps of Savoy*, with an introduction by Ruskin.
1884	First formal meeting of the Keswick School of Industrial Arts held in November.
1884	Home Arts and Industries Association founded. First exhibition held in 1885.
1884	Ruskin publishes *The Storm Cloud of the Nineteenth Century*.
1884	Ruskin publishes a *Catalogue of Minerals Given to Kirkcudbright Museum*.
1884	Ruskin publishes *The Pleasures of England* (four lectures).
1884–5	The National Footpath Preservation Society formed with Rawnsley as president and Ruskin as a member.
1885	Ruskin contributes preface and notes to *Roadside Songs of Tuscany* by Francesca Alexander.
1885	Ruskin publishes *On the Old Road* (three volumes, edited by A. Wedderburn).

1885–9	Ruskin publishes *Praeterita* in two volumes, his final work.
1885	Thomas H. Mawson acquires the Windermere site for his first nursery.
1885	Collingwood publishes *A Book of Verse*.
1885	Coniston woodcarving class founded.
c.1885	Burneside woodcarving class founded.
c.1885	Kirkby Lonsdale handcraft classes started.
1885	Keswick School of Industrial Arts holds its first exhibition.
1885	A.W. Simpson opens his first workshop in Kendal.
1885–1902	Collingwood exhibits at the Royal Academy.
1886	Simpson holds his first exhibition.
1887	John Ruskin publishes 'Arthur Burgess' (Century Guild *Hobby Horse* for April).
1887	Albert Fleming publishes *Hortus Inclusus*.
1887	Rawnsley publishes *Sonnets Round the Coast*.
1887–8	Stained glass windows made for St Paul's church, Irton, by Morris & Co.
1888	Rawnsley publishes *Five Addresses on the Lives and Work of St Kentigern and St Herbert*. Copies bound in Langdale linen.
1888	Ruskin publishes 'The Black Arts: a Reverie', *Strand Magazine of Art*, January.
1889	Marian Twelves moves to the Keswick School of Industrial Arts to teach spinning.
1889	Flax-bound copies of *Songs of the Spindle and Legends of the Loom* published, edited by H.H. Warner.
1889	Rawnsley publishes *Edward Thring Teacher and Poet*.
1889	Collingwood publishes *John Ruskin. A Biographical Outline*.
1890	Rawnsley publishes *A Coach Drive at the Lakes*, reprinted from *Cornhill Magazine*.
1890	Newlyn metalwork class founded.
1890	Rawnsley publishes *Poems, Ballads, and Bucolics*.
1891	Arts, Crafts and Loan Exhibition held in Kendal.
1891	Annie Garnett and the Brownsons found the Windermere Industry (The Spinnery).
1891	Heversham metalwork class founded.
1891	Collingwood moves into Lanehead, Coniston.
1891	Rawnsley publishes *A Skiddaw Shepherd's Life*.
1891	Collingwood edits *The Poems of John Ruskin*.
1891	Collingwood publishes *The Art Teaching of John Ruskin*.
1892	Rawnsley publishes *The Undoing of De Harcla. A Ballad of*

Cumberland.

1892	Rawnsley publishes *Notes for the Nile.*
1893	Rawnsley edits revised edition of *Jenkinson's Practical Guide to the English Lake District.*
1893	Rawnsley publishes *Valete, Tennyson and Other Memorial Poems.*
1893	Collingwood publishes *The Life and Work of John Ruskin.*
1894	Haslemere Weaving Industry founded.
1894	Rawnsley publishes *Literary Associations of the English Lakes.*
1894	Keswick School of Industrial Arts opens its new permanent building.
1894	Marian Twelves establishes herself independently in Keswick.
1894	Ruskin gives permission for the Keswick branch of the Linen Industry to be called the Ruskin Linen Industry.
1894	The first meetings of the National Trust take place.
1894	Landing window for Ambleside vicarage made by Morris & Co.
1894	Rawnsley publishes *Idylls and Lyrics of the Nile.*
1895	Collingwood edits *The Ruskin Reader.*
1895	Collingwood publishes *Thorstein of the Mere: A Saga of the Northmen in Lakeland.*
1896	Rawnsley publishes *Harvey Goodwin, Bishop of Carlisle.*
1896	Annie Garnett publishes *Notes on Hand-Spinning.*
1896	Rawnsley publishes *A Reminiscence of Wordsworth Day, Cockermouth, April 7th 1896.*
1896	Rawnsley publishes *Ballads of Brave Deeds.*
1896	Rawnsley publishes *The Revival of the Decorative Arts at Lucerne.*
1896	Collingwood publishes *The Bondwoman: A Story of the Northmen in Lakeland.*
1897	Rawnsley publishes *Sayings of Jesus.*
1898	C.F.A. Voysey's Broadleys and Moor Crag built on the Storrs Estate, Windermere, with garden designs for the former by Mawson.
1898	Mawson and Dan Gibson form a business partnership.
1898	Voysey designs a house at Kirkoswald for W.E. Rowley (unexecuted).
1898	Voysey designs a house at Windermere for H. Rickards (unexecuted).
1898	Rawnsley publishes *Henry Whitehead 1825–1896.*

1899   Rawnsley publishes *Life and Nature at the English Lakes.*
1899   Rawnsley publishes *Sonnets in Switzerland and Italy.*
1899   Collingwood publishes *Coniston Tales.*
1899   Collingwood publishes 'Notes on the Early Sculptured Crosses, Shrines and Monuments in the Present Diocese of Carlisle', *Transactions of the Cumberland and Westmorland Antiquarian and Archaeological Society,* ii.
1899   Kendal Exhibition of Pictures and Decorative Art.

1900   Baillie Scott's Blackwell completed.
1900   Ruskin dies.
1900   First exhibition held at Coniston Institute devoted to Ruskin. Preface to exhibition catalogue by Collingwood.
1900   Rawnsley publishes *Ballads of War.*
1900   T.H. Mawson publishes *The Art and Craft of Garden Making.*
1900   Rawnsley publishes *Memories of the Tennysons.*
1901   Rawnsley publishes *Ruskin and the English Lakes.*
1901   Robert Lorimer designs extensions for Brackenbrough, Calthwaite.
1902   Rawnsley publishes *A Rambler's Note-Book at the English Lakes.*
1902   Collingwood publishes *The Life and Death of Cormac the Skald* (Viking Club Translation Series).
1902   Collingwood publishes *The Lake Counties,* illustrated by Cuthbert Rigby.
1902   Rawnsley publishes *Gough and his Dog.*
1903   Rawnsley publishes *Lake Country Sketches.*
1903   Voysey designs a house at Windermere for G. Toulmin (unexecuted).
1903   Collingwood publishes *Ruskin Relics.*

1904   Lake Artists' Society co-founded by Collingwood.
1904   Rawnsley publishes *Flower-Time in the Oberland.*
1904   Gertrude Jekyll designs garden borders at Brackenbrough.
1905   St Martin's church tower completed by George Jack.
1905   Rawnsley publishes *A Sonnet Chronicle.*
1905   Beatrix Potter moves to Sawrey.
1906   Rawnsley publishes *Months at the Lakes.*
1907   Dan Gibson dies; his Birket Houses is completed by W.L. Dolman.
1907   Robert Lorimer designs church at Plumpton Wall.

1908	Collingwood illustrates *The Elder or Poetic Edda* (Viking Club Translation Series).
1908	Collingwood publishes *Scandinavian Britain*.
1908	Stained glass window made for St John the Evangelist, Plumpton, by Morris & Co.
1909	Voysey executes design for Littleholme, Kendal, for A.W. Simpson.
1909	Rawnsley publishes *Round the Lake Country*.
1909	Rawnsley publishes *Poems at Home and Abroad*.
1909–12	Carvings for St Mary's church, Urswick, carried out by Alec Miller and Ashbee's Guild of Handicraft.
1910	Collingwood publishes *Dutch Agnes Her Valentine, Being the Journal of the Curate of Coniston 1616–1623*.
1910	Baptistry west window made for St Cuthbert's Church, Cliburn, by Morris & Co.
1911	Rawnsley publishes *Pernicious Literature*.
1911	Rawnsley publishes *By Fell and Dale at the English Lakes*.
1912	Annie Garnett publishes *Spinnery Notes*.
1912	Collingwood publishes *The Roman Camp at Ambleside*.
1912	Collingwood publishes *Elizabethan Keswick* (Cumberland and Westmorland Antiquarian and Archaeological Society).
1912	Stained glass window made for Holy Trinity church, Ulverston, by Morris & Co.
1913	Rawnsley publishes *Chapters at the English Lakes*.
1915	Rawnsley publishes *The European War, 1914–1915*.
1916	Rawnsley publishes *Past and Present at the English Lakes*.
1916	Rawnsley's wife Edith dies.
1916	Rawnsley publishes *Shakespeare: A Tercentenary Sermon*.
1917	Collingwood publishes *The Likeness of King Elfwald*.
1917	Stained glass window made for the Wesleyan chapel, Arnside, by Morris & Co.
1919	Last exhibition held in Coniston.
1920	Rawnsley publishes *A Nation's Heritage*.
1920	H.D. Rawnsley dies.
1920	Stained glass window made for St Peter's church, Field Broughton, by Morris & Co.
1921	Collingwood publishes *Angles, Danes, and Norse in the District of Huddersfield*.
1922	A.W. Simpson publishes *Needleweaving* by Ann Macbeth.
1922	A.W. Simpson dies.

1923   Albert Fleming dies.

1925   Collingwood publishes *Lake District History*.

1926   East window made for the Church of Christ and Mary, Armathwaite, by Morris & Co.

1927   Collingwood publishes *Northumbrian Crosses of the Pre-Norman Age*.

1927   Mawson publishes *The Life and Work of an English Landscape Architect*.

c.1928 Ann Macbeth retires to Patterdale.

1928   W.G. Collingwood's wife Dorrie dies.

1929   Marian Twelves dies.

1929   Collingwood publishes *The Register and Records of Holm Cultram* (with Francis Grainger).

1932   W.G. Collingwood dies.

1933   T.H. Mawson dies.

1935   Cuthbert Rigby dies.

1938   Ann Macbeth executes the Patterdale embroideries.

1942   Annie Garnett dies.

1948   Ann Macbeth dies.

1951   A.W. Simpson's The Handicrafts closes.

1984   The Keswick School of Industrial Arts closes immediately prior to its centenary.

ACKNOWLEDGEMENTS

For assistance given during the research for this book, thanks go to Professor John Hannavy, James Dearden, Jean D. Simpson, Joan Downs, Dr Theo Cowdell, all the staff at Abbot Hall Art Gallery and Museum, the staff at the Kendal and Carlisle record offices (particularly Susan Dench), the staff of Kendal and Carlisle libraries, and all those who allowed access to their homes in Lakeland and the photographing of personal items or lent family photographs.

The author and publisher are greatly indebted to the Curwen Archives Trust of Cumbria County Council for a generous grant towards the cost of producing this book.

ABBREVIATIONS USED IN THE FOOTNOTES

AHM   Abbot Hall Art Gallery and Museum, Kendal

CROC   Cumbria Record Office, Carlisle

CROK   Cumbria Record Office, Kendal

HLC   Huntington Library, California

Works   Cook, E.T., and Wedderburn, A. (ed.), *The Works of John Ruskin* (George Allen, 1903–12).

YUBL   Yale University, Beinecke Library

PREFACE

Whilst this book is concerned with previously largely unresearched arts developments in the English Lake District during the years 1880 to 1920, the immensely hectic nature of that period in terms of art and design means that some reference must be made to broader developments and to associated literary studies. Arguably the most influential arts development of the late nineteenth century was the Arts and Crafts movement. In terms of literature, the movement has barely left the consciousness of the British mind since the founding of the Arts and Crafts Exhibition Society in the late 1880s. The movement itself was still exerting considerable and positive influence in the 1930s, with the 15th Arts and Crafts exhibition held in London in 1931, some 35 years after the death of one of its original founders, William Morris (1834–96). Having seen off a rumoured disbandment of the Exhibition Society in 1907,[1] and having continued to hold exhibitions (somewhat spasmodically) until at least 1931, barely had the term 'Arts and Crafts' slipped from widespread use when May Morris's *William Morris: Artist, Writer, Socialist* was published in 1936. Her substantial 24 volumes of *The Collected Works of William Morris* had already been published between 1910 and 1915 and, with other works, including Philip Henderson's *The Letters of William Morris* (1950) and Asa Briggs's *William Morris: Selected Writings and Designs* (1968) following, the Arts and Crafts, in the form of Morris at least, has been kept well and truly alive. The centenary of his death in 1996 generated more interest in the man and his work, one outcome of which was Fiona MacCarthy's biography *William Morris* (1994) which contains the expected references to the Arts and Crafts movement.

In recent years the movement itself, widely publicised by contemporary journals such as *The Studio*, has been subject to scrutiny on a more general level. Beginning chiefly with Gillian Naylor's *The Arts and Crafts Movement* (1971), this has resulted in a broader look at Arts and Crafts doctrine across Great Britain in the late nineteenth and early

---

[1] In reply to the rumour Walter Crane (1845–1915) denied that any such disbandment was to take place (*The Studio*, July 1907, 181).

twentieth centuries. Similar references to the spread of the movement have appeared in Fiona MacCarthy's *A History of British Design 1830–1970* (1979). Discussion of the movement across Europe and America can also be found in Isabelle Anscombe and Charlotte Gere's *Arts and Crafts in Britain and America* (1978) and in Elizabeth Cumming and Wendy Kaplan's *The Arts and Crafts Movement* (1991).

The sheer scale and density of the movement, however, has meant that much remains unresearched, particularly in relation to the origin of its theories, the application of those theories to the practical, and how successful that application was. Similarly, little detailed research has been carried out on the smaller, more provincial reactions to the Arts and Crafts in Britain. Cumming and Kaplan's study includes a wide range of brief references to some of those, including the Haslemere handcraft industries established in association with the Peasant Arts Society in the 1890s. Tanya Harrod's paper 'Reviving "peasant art" in Britain, 1880–1930' also offers some insight into Haslemere and the Peasant Arts.[1] But a comprehensive study of origin, history and development would prove most useful in creating a more detailed picture of the handcrafts in Britain during the period discussed here. A few other publications, such as Hazel Berriman's *Arts and Crafts in Newlyn* (1986) and Fiona MacCarthy's *The Simple Life: C.R. Ashbee in the Cotswolds* (1988), have already hinted that important developments were taking place other than in London in the late nineteenth century, but the finer detail of the outward spread of the movement remains largely uncharted.

In the case of women involved with the Arts and Crafts, in 1979 Anthea Callen made an important contribution to the understanding of their role in the spread of the movement with her *Angel in the Studio. Women in the Arts and Crafts Movement 1870–1914*. Little has been added, although in 1985–6 an exhibition on 'Women Stained Glass Artists of the Arts and Crafts Movement' at the William Morris Gallery in London added some knowledge on the period after 1900. Jude Burkhauser's *Glasgow Girls. Women in Art and Design 1880–1920* (1990) details the role of some of Scotland's leading female designers. But as far as other women of the Arts and Crafts period are concerned, few detailed individual biographies have been written, despite the recent publication of biographies of Clarice Cliff (1899–1972) and Barbara

---

[1] See David Crowley and Lou Taylor (ed.), *The Lost Arts of Europe: the Haslemere Collection of European Peasant Art* (Haslemere Educational Museum 2000), which includes Harrod's paper.

Hepworth (1903–75), who came just afterwards.[1] Comprehensive studies are still lacking of such leading Arts and Crafts figures as Walter Crane, W.A.S. Benson (1854–1924), John Hungerford Pollen (1820–1902), T.J. Cobden-Sanderson (1840–1922), Heywood Sumner (1853–1940) and Lewis F. Day (1845–1910). One of the most comprehensive and informative works on the crafts in Britain, Tanya Harrod's *The Crafts in Britain in the Twentieth Century* (1999), covers developments just outside the main period discussed here, beginning in 1916 with Morris's legacy to the arts world.

With other related and unrelated developments taking place in the late nineteenth century, including the formation of the Home Arts and Industries Association which held highly successful and long-running exhibitions of art and craft work, the period from 1880 to 1920 was undeniably hectic in terms of British art and design. As a result, other areas, including those not necessarily directly linked to the Arts and Crafts, have remained largely or wholly unresearched. One such case is considered here in an attempt to illustrate that not everything which occurred in the late nineteenth century in relation to the arts fits comfortably beneath the Arts and Crafts label. In some instances Arts and Crafts mis-labelling has been caused by the underlying presence of John Ruskin (1819–1900), whose exact role in the founding and development of the Arts and Crafts Exhibition Society (among other arts endeavours) has yet to be comprehensively considered.

This book is concerned with a particular group of artists, craftsmen and craftswomen based in the Lake District who, until now, have remained under the Arts and Crafts umbrella title, almost wholly because of links with Ruskin and lack of research into those links. Indeed, this study began as an examination of that specific group as an offshoot of the Arts and Crafts movement, but it quickly became clear that that was not the case. An examination of a large body of surviving papers, materials and specimens of art and design work showed almost immediately that the Lakeland group ran independently and was unique in its founding and approaches towards art and design. Indeed, if any comparisons are to be made, they should be with the earlier and similarly Ruskin-inspired Pre-Raphaelite Brotherhood, founded around 1848 and inspired largely by Ruskin's early volumes of *Modern Painters* (1843–60). The original Brotherhood consisted of the artists Dante Gabriel Rossetti (1828–82), William Holman Hunt (1827–1910) and John

---

[1] Leonard Griffith, Louis K. Meisel and Susan Pear Meisel, *Clarice Cliff: The Bizarre Affair* (1988); Anthony Adams (ed.), *Barbara Hepworth* (1970).

Everett Millais (1829–96). Influenced by those who worked before Raphael (1483–1520), the Brotherhood began to dissolve after 1853, and a second phase began around 1860, headed chiefly by Rossetti and William Morris. The original Brotherhood made a concerted effort to portray nature in all its detail in their works.

The Lakeland group deliberately restored respect for nature as the chief source of not only art but also design inspiration; but also expressed a concertedly more domestic and regional attitude towards art and design which had more definite links with the Home Arts and Industries Association. The association has also remained largely unresearched, yet it too is generally assumed to be derived from Arts and Crafts developments. Julian Holder has recently expressed the view that, far from being Arts and Crafts-based, the association was, in many respects, separate from the Arts and Crafts. It was rejected by them and the related Art Workers' Guild for being of an inferior and domestic nature.[1] Although sharing a number of common objectives, the Home Arts and Industries Association and the Arts and Crafts Exhibition Society ran their own independent exhibitions, the former on a more regular annual basis.

Since late nineteenth-century Lakeland arts have been largely unresearched and so have no comparative developed literary history, the sizeable quantity of surviving materials has provided much of the detail relating to origin and identity discussed here.[2] Although other contemporary material has provided evidence for the rejection of the Arts and Crafts title with reference to Lakeland, particularly the leading journals such as *The Studio* and the *Art Workers' Quarterly*, the bulk of the evidence comes from a local perspective. Much has been drawn not only from family papers but also from newspapers and journals. A thorough examination of the press between 1880 and 1920 has revealed a consistent view of Lakeland as something other than, or more than, Arts and Crafts, something which has been equally supported by the oral testimony of surviving family members and participants, which has offered additional insights. Other material consulted includes Harriet Jordan's Ph.D. thesis, 'Thomas Hayton Mawson 1861–1933. The English Garden Designs of an Edwardian Landscape Architect' (Wye College, London University, 1988), and Gillian Medland's BA dissertation 'Annie Garnett' (Manchester Polytechnic, 1979).

---

[1] Julian Holder, 'The Home Arts and Industries Association', *Sheffield Arts Review* (1993), 13–20; I am grateful to Mr Holder for discussing his ideas further with me.

[2] For the small number of pamphlets written on developments in late nineteenth-century Lakeland arts see below, Introduction and Bibliography.

INTRODUCTION

In the late nineteenth century south Lakeland experienced a strong return to pre-industrial arts and crafts.[1] The rejection of the machine in favour of the joys of hand labour in the arts was by no means unusual between 1880 and 1920, with a considerable number of successful art and craft communities, including Newlyn (Cornwall) and Haslemere (Surrey), forming around Britain, based on seemingly antiquated ideas in the arts. In the early 1880s Newlyn became a thriving artists' colony, attracting painters such as Stanhope Forbes (1857–1940), Elizabeth Forbes (1859–1912) and Walter Langley (1852–1922). Influenced by Ruskin's art teachings, they were drawn to the region chiefly because of its exceptionally rich subject matter, suited to their 'open air' or outdoors style of painting, but also because of the exceptional conditions of light and shade. In the early 1890s a metalwork class was also set up in Newlyn, run by J.D. Mackenzie. The class specialised in using local subject matter for design inspiration, including fish, coastal birds and flowers. Around 1894 Haslemere saw a similar arts colony evolve which concentrated more definitely on handcrafts. Under the influence of Mr and Mrs Joseph King, the Haslemere Weaving Industry was the first handcraft industry to begin there, followed by the St Edmundsbury Silk Weaving Works run by Edmund Hunter. Other industries founded and run at Haslemere around that time included the Green Bushes Weaving House, the Hammer Vale Pottery and the Pear Tree Press.[2]

Whilst it shared certain basic philosophies with both Newlyn and Haslemere, Lakeland stood apart from its late nineteenth-century contemporaries for two reasons. First, although for more than forty years it was based almost exclusively on John Ruskin's teachings, from 1883 until his death in 1900 it benefitted from his close presence and direct as well as indirect contribution in the application of those teachings. Second, under Ruskin's influence, it put a particularly strong and deliberate emphasis on the unique history and landscape of Cumberland

---

[1] The term 'south Lakeland' is used here to refer to the area stretching from Kirkby Lonsdale west to St Bees, north to Keswick and east to Appleby.

[2] See above, Preface.

and Westmorland, concentrating primarily on lost regional traditions in such things as textile production and woodcarving. Until now, the general view of the Lakeland revival has been that it was yet another offshoot of the then popular Arts and Crafts movement (which in fact it predates), chiefly because of links with Ruskin. The revival of handcrafts in late nineteenth-century Lakeland has been largely ignored by design historians, or has been regarded as a derivative of the Arts and Crafts movement. Thus Alan Crawford states:

> The Arts and Crafts was a metropolitan movement to the extent that the formative events in its history took place in London, and London was the home of its principal organisations and many of its leading figures ... It flourished early and independently in South Devon ... and on the banks of Lake Windermere, where the Ruskin Linen Industry was set up as early as 1883 ... for in the imagination of the Arts and Crafts, 'the countryside' wove spells only less potent than 'the Middle Ages'.[1]

Crawford makes no attempt to explain the three-year gap between the founding of the Langdale Linen Industry in 1883 and the founding of the Arts and Crafts Exhibition Society—from which the Arts and Crafts movement developed—in 1886, or why he believes the Langdale Linen Industry to be associated with the movement. Crawford's use of the name Ruskin Linen Industry is incorrect since the Ruskin Linen Industry was not officially founded until 1894, and it was never based on or near the banks of Lake Windermere.

The lack of research into the Lakeland revival of traditional arts and crafts has, until now, meant that its Arts and Crafts label has remained entirely unchallenged. This study argues that what occurred in the region was not only separate from Arts and Crafts developments, but was an independent and successful attempt to work closely to the theories of one of the most prolific writers of the nineteenth century. That independence is made more certain by the fact that Lakeland's rejection of the machine and simultaneous attempts to raise standards in the arts began at least three years before the founding of the Arts and Crafts Exhibition Society, and also by the fact that its origins and preliminary influences were of a quite different nature.

In terms of early (pre-1883) influences, Ruskin's associations with the

---

[1] Alan Crawford, *By Hammer and Hand* (Birmingham Museums and Art Gallery, 1984), 17.

Lake District were a key factor in the founding of its revival of arts and crafts, his early exposure to the region and its cultural heritage shaping much of what happened there between 1880 and 1920. Although born and raised in London, Ruskin travelled throughout much of his life, including visits to the Lake District. His first visit, which incorporated a trip to Friar's Crag, Derwentwater, took place in 1824. In *Praeterita*, his autobiography written between 1885 and 1889, he said of that visit: 'I have said somewhere that my first memory in life was of Friar's Crag on Derwentwater;—meaning, I suppose, my first memory of things afterwards chiefly precious to me'.[1]

Other visits took place in 1826, 1830, 1837, 1838 and 1847, during which he explored much of the area. His lifelong admiration for Southey and Wordsworth, who had particularly strong ties with the region, prompted the young Ruskin to begin writing his own poetry at the time of those visits, works including *Derwentwater* (1828) and *The Iteriad; or Three Weeks Among the Lakes* (1831), which reflected Wordsworth's own lyrical studies of the Lake District. He also executed numerous drawings of the region, including one of Carlisle cathedral (1838), from an early period. In 1848 Ruskin married Euphemia Gray (a short-lived marriage) and spent part of his honeymoon in Keswick, returning briefly to the town some nineteen years later. By 1872, when he finally moved to the Lake District, he was thoroughly familiar with the region and all that it represented, culturally and aesthetically.

Exposure to the Lake District and to Wordsworth's works meant that, at an early age, Ruskin formed a strong—and what would be a sustained and constant—impression of a region which blended dramatic scenery, extremes of climate, pre-industrial fell farming, rural isolation, poetic inspiration and the old village ways of life. Wordsworth was still living and working in the area when Ruskin first visited as a boy, and was already publicly denouncing the changes to the Lake District wrought by industrialisation. Most under attack were the local railways. In 1844 Wordsworth penned his *Sonnet on the Projected Kendal and Windermere Railway* in which he asked:

> Is then no nook of English ground secure
> From rash assault? Schemes of retirement sown
> In youth, and 'mid the busy world kept pure
> As when their earliest flowers of hope were blown,
> Must perish;—how can they this blight endure?

---

[1] J. Ruskin, *Praeterita*, i (1886), 154.

When similar proposals were put forward again in the 1870s Ruskin followed Wordsworth's example and headed the Lakeland railway opposition campaign. In 1871 he had already voiced his desire to see the destruction of 'most of the railroads in England, and all the railroads in Wales', and clearly now acted upon that.[1] It was no coincidence that, under Ruskin's influence, opposition to railways later became associated with the revival of local arts and crafts. The protection of the landscape in which the late nineteenth-century Lakeland artist, craftsman and craftswoman worked was held to be as important as the revival of the traditional arts and crafts practised within that landscape.

Whilst the condemnation of the Lakeland railways largely represented the defence of the natural landscape, or nature, the demise of other more physical aspects of Lakeland life was equally berated by Wordsworth and later Ruskin. Before industrialisation the region had a very distinct culture which revolved chiefly around its textile production. Hand spinning and weaving had been practised in the Lake District for centuries, with sheep farming and flax and hemp growing running alongside its history of cloth production since at least 1590. Kendal Green, a coarse cloth dyed with *Genista tinctoria* and mentioned in Shakespeare's *Henry IV Part 1*, written *c*.1599, was known far and wide by the seventeenth century, as were Lakeland hand-knitted stockings. When the abandonment of the Westmorland spinning wheels began in the late eighteenth century, Wordsworth questioned not so much the economic but the social and spiritual implications:

> Grief, thou hast lost an ever-ready friend
> Now that the cottage Spinning-wheel is mute;[2]

Hand spinning and weaving may no longer have been an economic necessity, but lost along the way was the recognition of the spinning wheel as the instrument of inner harmony brought about by individual creativity, and its deeper significance as the symbol of village and family life.

In 1865 Ruskin wrote his own poem, *Twist Ye, Twine Ye*, which clearly complemented Wordsworth's studies of the wheel:

---

[1] Extract from Letter I of *Fors Clavigera*, dated January 1871 (*Works*, xxvii. 15).

[2] Extract from Wordsworth's *Sonnet XIX* (1819) in *The Works of William Wordsworth* (1994), 255.

Twist ye, twine ye; even so
Mingle shades of Joy and Woe,
Hope and Fear, and Peace and Strife,
In the thread of human life.

While the mystic twist is spinning,
And the infant's life beginning,
Dimly seen through twilight bending,
Lo! what varied shapes attending!

Passion's force, by Patience knit;
Doubtful Reason reined by Wit;
Toil,—forgot in sighing Rest,
Joy,—we know not which is best.

Earnest Gladness, idle Fretting,
Foolish Memory, wise Forgetting;
And trusted reeds, that broken lie,
Wreathed again for melody.

Ah! the deep, the tender playing,
Worded Silence, unmeant Saying;
Ah! sweet Anger, insincere,
Trembling Kiss, and glittering Tear.

Vanished Truth, but Vision staying;
Fairy riches—lost in weighing;
And fitful grasp of flying Fate,
Touched too lightly, traced too late.

Graceful Pride, and timid Praise,
Love, diffused a thousand ways;
Faithful Hope, and generous Fear,
In the mystic dance appear.

Now they wax and now they dwindle,
Whirling with the whirling spindle:-
Twist ye, twine ye,—even so
Mingle human bliss and woe.[1]

---

[1] W.G. Collingwood (ed.), *The Poems of John Ruskin* (1891), ii. 328–9.

Although containing neither Wordsworth's literary genius, nor the signs of a burgeoning great poet, *Twist Ye, Twine Ye* does indicate a similar acceptance of the spinning wheel as an inextricable part of life itself, something which was to play a strong part in local events from 1883.

Although references to the Lake District and its culture appeared throughout much of Ruskin's literary work (which spanned the years 1834 to 1889), the purchase of Brantwood, a damp and decaying property set in some five acres of rocks and moors, was a more definite confirmation of his progressive absorption in things Lakeland. Overlooking Lake Coniston, the house was to be his retreat from September 1871 until his death in January 1900. In the preface to the rearranged edition of *Modern Painters* (1883) Ruskin wrote of Brantwood:[1]

> From my dining-room, I am happy in the view of the lower reach of Coniston Water, not because it is particularly beautiful, but because it is entirely pastoral and pure. Were a single point of chimney of the Barrow ironworks to show itself over the green ridge of the hills, I should never care to look at it more.[2]

This succinctly summarises its principal attraction, its largely unspoilt, natural Wordsworthian beauty. Ruskin's move to the relatively isolated house was in no sense a withdrawal from life, and from 1872 he entered another busy phase which would see the continued defence of Lakeland, and the arrival of one of his most loyal devotees, Albert Fleming (1846–1923) of Broxbourne (Hertfordshire). A learned and close follower of Ruskin's teachings, with an equally investigative mind, Fleming moved to the region with the express purpose of being closer to his mentor. Equally familiar with Wordsworth's writings, on his arrival in 1883 Fleming instigated the beginnings of the revival of local arts and crafts in the form of the Langdale Linen Industry. His return to the local spinning wheels then inspired other Lakeland-based devotees who collectively promoted a wider return to local, traditional arts and crafts which eventually spread across much of south Lakeland.

Although fed by local history and tradition, the Lakeland revival was a quite definite attempt by Fleming and his colleagues to work to Ruskin's theories. That in itself was not unusual: the Pre-Raphaelite Brotherhood had attempted to realise his teachings on art back in the late

---

[1] Ruskin began *Modern Painters* while still an undergraduate at Oxford. Published between 1843 and 1860, it was intended to be only a pamphlet, but eventually grew to five volumes of art criticism.

[2] *Works*, iv. 8.

1840s and early 1850s. Similarly, whilst the Lakeland revival was founded at least three years before any of its arts and crafts fellows (such as Newlyn and Haslemere), it was not the first endeavour to adhere to Ruskin's rejection of mechanisation. Three years before Fleming's revival of the Westmorland wheels, Egbert Rydings had been encouraged by Ruskin to attempt a similar experiment in the Isle of Man to save what Ruskin described as 'the venerable art' of hand spinning.[1] With its equally potent history of flax growing and spinning wheels, the Isle of Man proved a suitable place to attempt a revival of the wheels under Ruskin's guidance, following the traditions of the island. Ruskin provided the initial money for the scheme, and a water-mill, St George's Mill, was built at Laxey. Run without any unnecessary machinery, the source of power at Laxey was water rather than steam (which Ruskin regarded with concern), and a number of women were employed as spinsters. Laxey, however, failed where Lakeland succeeded, chiefly because the cloth was so durable that it was not a good prospect commercially. Nevertheless, Laxey had already introduced the Ruskinian concept of anti-mechanisation and pro-regional crafts to Britain just before 1883.

In contrast to Laxey, Fleming's hand spinning workshop survived for more than forty years. It was not, however, merely a better commercial prospect than Laxey, but a much clearer attempt to reintroduce the wheels with a view to developing an artistic side to local crafts not formerly associated with local textile production. At the time that Fleming began the local revival, Lakeland arts had slipped into something of a lull. Always a rich source of inspiration to the artist and writer alike, Lakeland had developed a strong tradition of landscape painting in the early eighteenth century, with the arrival of Matthias Read (1669–1747). Although born in London, Read established landscape painting in the Lake District, his most famous studies being his views of Whitehaven. In 1800 William Green (1760–1823), a friend of Wordsworth, moved permanently to the region to paint, continuing the tradition of Lakeland landscape painting.[2] A number of other Lakeland artists, particularly George Romney (1734–1802), helped secure the region's artistic reputation in the early nineteenth century, but did not prevent a lull occurring around 1850. The arrival of Ruskin, and later of his secretary, the artist William Gershom Collingwood (1854–1932), in about

---

[1] E.T. Cook, *Studies in Ruskin* (1890), 174. An outline of the Laxey project is given under the heading 'Some Industrial Experiments', pp. 161–83.

[2] M.E. Burkett and J.D.G. Sloss, *William Green of Ambleside* (1984).

1880, however, saw a resurgence in local art as well as handcrafts, the two running successfully side by side. Also as a result of Ruskin's influence, and directly attributable to his presence in Lakeland, a considerable number of other locally based artists followed Collingwood's example and returned to the Lakeland landscape for their initial inspiration. As for the Pre-Raphaelites before them, the natural environment became the focus of attention, now joined by the subject of country people at work.

Ruskin's role in the successful spread of the Lakeland revival of arts and crafts, and the intrinsic value of his presence to those who actually carried out the revival, is an important theme here, for its uniqueness and individuality hinged principally on the groundwork laid down by Ruskin. His interest in Lakeland from an early age, his lifelong admiration for Wordsworth in particular, the epitome of a lake poet, his eventual move to the region, his opposition to the Lakeland railways, his writings on Lakeland, and his direct guidance during the initial stages of the revival, all played a part in ensuring a strong resurgence in local arts and crafts. The histories of the individual workshops and industries which heralded the start of the revival form an equally important theme, their considerable achievements before and after Ruskin's death again being directly attributable to his early direction and presence in Lakeland. Although initially led by three individual craft endeavours—the Langdale Linen Industry founded and run by Albert Fleming and Marian Twelves (1843–1929), the Keswick School of Industrial Arts founded and run by Edith Rawnsley (1846–1916) and Hardwicke Drummond Rawnsley (1851–1920), and The Handicrafts founded and run by Arthur W. Simpson (1857–1922)—their influence inspired other changes in local arts and crafts after 1900 (when Laxey finally failed) which demonstrated that Lakeland had succeeded where Laxey had not. Surviving business and personal papers confirm that all those involved managed to run viable, artistic enterprises along comparatively antiquated lines, creating a high concentration of artists, craftsmen and craftswomen along the way.

Once well established in Lakeland, the Ruskinian revival of local arts and crafts began to display its distinctiveness in other more definite and significant ways. In the case of art, the work of a considerable number of local artists revealed a renewed respect for Lakeland as a rural environment still relatively unscathed by modern development. The concentration of artists working in accordance with Ruskin's teachings resulted in the formation of the Lake Artists' Society in 1904, in which Collingwood played a leading role. A long running and widely acclaimed school of art, the society cannot be omitted from any discussion of

Lakeland's artistic history between 1880 and 1920. The creation of a textile decoration unique to the Lakeland revival and named after its inspiration—Ruskin lace—takes an equally prominent place as another example of the region's artistic separateness. The simultaneous rise of the local exhibition, particularly the 1891 Kendal Arts, Crafts and Loan Exhibition and the 1899 Kendal Exhibition of Pictures and Decorative Art, and the development of the annual Coniston exhibition of local arts and crafts, has a similar place in a discussion of the artistic identity of Lakeland at the turn of the century.

The Lakeland revival, however, was not the only artistic development in the region between 1880 and 1920, particularly since the revival never practised exclusion or divorced itself from what was taking place elsewhere. Indeed, the artistically hectic nature of the late nineteenth century meant that the region was open to all manner of outside influences, evidence of which can still be seen today. Present in Lakeland in the late nineteenth century was George Howard (1843–1911), 9th earl of Carlisle and Royal Academy exhibitor. Howard associated with a number of those who were to contribute to the Arts and Crafts Exhibition Society from 1886, and encouraged several to stay at his home at Naworth Castle, near Brampton. Largely through Howard, design work was carried out in the region, by among others, Philip Webb (1831-1915) and William Morris. Other notable outside influences included Alec Miller (1879–1961) of the Guild of Handicraft, Henry Holiday (1839–1927), M.H. Baillie Scott (1865–1945), and Charles F.A. Voysey (1857–1941). The complexity of the period between 1880 and 1920 and the presence of Webb and his Arts and Crafts colleagues in Lakeland have previously contributed to the incorrect labelling of the Lakeland revival as Arts and Crafts, as has the lack of a detailed study of its origins and relevance to art, and more particularly design, history.[1]

To examine the background against which the Lakeland revival was set, it has been necessary to make reference to a small number of other individuals who, while lacking any strong links with the local revival,

---

[1] Very little research has been carried out on the individual workshops and industries discussed here. In the case of the Langdale Linen Industry, the first of the Lakeland Ruskinian experiments to be founded, only two pamphlets have been published, F.A. Benjamin, *The Ruskin Linen Industry of Keswick* (1974) and Marguerite Blake *Revival of Spinning and Weaving in Langdale* (1976), which offer a local viewpoint. More recently, Jennie Brunton has written on 'The late nineteenth-century revival of the Langdale Linen Industry' in E. Roberts, *A History of Linen in the North-West* (Centre for North-West Regional Studies, University of Lancaster, 1998). On Arthur W. Simpson's The Handicrafts there is only Eleanor Davidson's booklet *The Simpsons of Kendal* (Visual Arts Centre, University of Lancaster, 1978).

were a more permanent artistic presence in the region and had connections with Ruskin's Lakeland disciples. These include the craftswoman
Ann Macbeth (1875–1948), the artist Alfred Heaton Cooper (1863–
1929), the photographer Herbert Bell (1856–1946) and the artist and
writer Beatrix Potter (1866–1943). All have been discussed elsewhere as
isolated artistic figures, but there has been no previous attempt to assess
them as part of a broader picture which reflected a strong return to
regionalism instigated by Ruskin.[1] By assessing not only the revival, but
also what was happening immediately around it, the full extent of its
artistic as well as theoretical value can be better appreciated and its
rightful place in mainstream art and design history finally recognised.

---

[1] e.g. Jane Renouf, *Alfred Heaton Cooper Painter of Landscape* (1997); Anne
Stevenson Hobbs, *Beatrix Potter's Art* (1989).

1

THE BEGINNINGS OF THE LAKELAND HANDCRAFT REVIVAL

Although the revival of local arts and crafts did not begin until 1883, as far as the late nineteenth-century artistic regeneration of south Lakeland was concerned, Ruskin's first ten years at Brantwood (1872–82) were by no means unproductive. By the time Ruskin arrived in the region in September 1872 it had long since lost its most prominent early nineteenth-century artistic and literary figureheads. William Green died in 1823, followed by Southey in 1843 and Wordsworth in 1850. For local women in particular, there was a distinct lack of strong female role models around 1872, with only a small handful of relatively minor artistic figures, including Mrs O. Allen (active 1873), a watercolour artist from Grasmere, Harriet Anstey (1816–1903), a portrait painter from Sizergh, and Margaret Heathcote (active 1867–1913), a landscape painter from Keswick, active around that time.[1] Having also lost the opportunity to take part in domestic crafts (such as hand spinning), with productive home labour almost wholly superseded by mechanisation, the women of south Lakeland suffered a doubly discouraging blow to personal development. Even fewer strong female literary figures were active in Lakeland around 1872, while the number of male literary figures was noticeably smaller than in the earlier part of the century. By and large, the early 1870s represented an 'in between' period, where the nationally acclaimed local artistic figures had gone, and Wordsworth's place as the voice of the Lakeland people had yet to be filled. With Ruskin's arrival Wordsworth's successor had been found, and the lean years in the region's recent literary and artistic history were about to come to a close.

---

[1] Mrs Allen painted figure studies in watercolour, and exhibited *The Gentle Friend* at the Suffolk Street Gallery in 1873. Harriet Anstey was a copyist of portraits in oils and the daughter of Jarrard Edward Strickland. Mrs Heathcote exhibited her watercolour landscapes in London, where she lived from 1887 to 1913. She is believed to have lived at Keswick from 1867 until 1887.

Given his ardent lifelong admiration for Lakeland and for Words-worth, and the role of both in his own early development as a writer and an artist, Ruskin was perhaps the most fitting successor to Wordsworth. Given his additional, very public involvement with the opposition to the Lakeland railways in 1876, he not only set himself up as the defender of the Lakes, but secured a particularly favourable image for himself locally. So, whilst he showed no signs of personally instigating a revival of local arts and crafts between 1872 and 1882, and spent part of his time away from Brantwood, Ruskin would certainly have laid down much of the foundation which made local people particularly receptive to the realisation of his teachings after 1883. The eleven-year gap between his arrival and the beginning of the revival would have given the people of Lakeland a lengthy period in which to adjust to his presence, accept him as their new leading literary and artistic force, listen to his support for the region, and perhaps even familiarise themselves with his writings. Equally, it gave Ruskin the opportunity to involve himself further with the region and its people, and to assess their particular needs. Even before 1872, Ruskin had furrowed the ground for the Lakeland revival to some degree, with an extensive catalogue of writings (which eventually covered some 55 years), some of which had generally challenged nineteenth-century methods and systems from an ethical, social and economic viewpoint, and which were as relevant to Lakeland as to anywhere else in Britain. With the founding of the Pre-Raphaelite Brotherhood in the 1840s, the Ruskinian notion of a return to nature in the arts was already widely dispersed (and chal-lenged); but more significantly, by 1880 the Laxey project had begun to demonstrate the possibility of realising a given set of Ruskin's teachings on more practical (rather than artistic) grounds. Whilst the return to nature and the abandonment of machines were to play an important role in the Lakeland revival, its origins and the forces which influenced its growth into a strongly regional, Ruskinian exercise were entirely unique.

Although not directly indicative of the birth of a Lakeland arts and crafts revival, the preliminary stages of the late nineteenth-century return to regionalism began not in Lakeland, but with the growing friendship between Ruskin and Albert Fleming, an unmarried solicitor based in Hertfordshire but born in Camberwell, Surrey. Throughout his life Ruskin corresponded with many associates, admirers and friends in England and abroad, and Fleming was just one of those with whom he struck up communication by letter during his Brantwood years. Evidently an educated and well-read man who spent time in London, Fleming first took to reading Ruskin in the 1860s in a bid to find answers to a sudden dissatisfaction with life, and by 1873 had been sufficiently inspired to write *In the House of Rimmon* in imitation of Ruskin's *Fors Clavigera*. The first Letters of *Fors* appeared in 1871, with later ones, addressed directly to 'the Workmen and Labourers of Great Britain', published on an almost monthly basis until Christmas 1884. The book offered Ruskin the opportunity to explore various aspects of work and its condition in England. Originally published in eight volumes, it was later reduced to four, keeping the original letter format. Among other things, Ruskin contemplated the role of machinery in labour, man's need to work, women as workers, and the femaleness of *Fors*. As with his other writings, *Fors* contains a detectable sense of despair and resignation concerning the probable destruction of England under the rule of capitalists and machinery as it then was, but was not without some glimmer of hope for change, a change necessary in order to improve the spiritual, moral, and political climate of the age. The close similarity between *In the House of Rimmon* and *Fors* suggests that the former was based on the latter, as Ruskin recognised in a letter to Fleming of 29 October 1873.[1]

Fleming's similarly intense (if considerably shorter) *In the House of Rimmon* appeared in 1873 as a 38-page booklet and was his only separately published literary work.[2] Despite its small size, the essay is a clear testament to its author's total absorption in Ruskin's teachings by 1873, some ten years before he actually met the writer. Already he had cultivated a Ruskinian interest in pre-industrial village life, the ethics of John Stuart Mill, the loss of the handcrafts, and the worship of Mammon, all in relation to God and the Church. Clearly addressed directly to Ruskin ('I have no friend to whom I may so fitly address this letter as to you'), and presented in letter format like *Fors*, Fleming's essay was less political doctrine than philosophical debate, in which nineteenth-century moral and spiritual decline was closely linked to the progress of industrialisation. To Fleming modern life represented only immorality and 'shame' with 'rough horseplay, coarse jokes, singing prurient songs, semi-blasphemous ribaldry; in the morning gluttonous eating, and in the evening reckless drinking', whereas pre-industrial England represented only simplicity, innocence and a closeness to God, when a man's worth was measured chiefly in terms of his capacity for faith in God.[3] Such an

---

[1] Below, p. 15.

[2] In 1887 Fleming edited *Hortus Inclusus*, a collection of Ruskin's letters to Susanna Beever of The Thwaite, Coniston. He also wrote a small number of articles for *Cornhill Magazine*, including 'A Prodigal Son' (Sept. 1886), 'The Importunate Widow' (May 1887); 'Uncle Joe' (Feb. and March 1888); 'Hatesu' (Feb. 1893); 'Abu-Simbel' (Oct. 1894).

[3] A. Fleming, *In the House of Rimmon* (1873), 9–10.

age he discussed in terms of those things which had not been 'blown together by machines', clothes stitched by 'ready fingers', for example, being noted as 'valued and treasured as only home made things ever are'.[1]

The pleasures of those Fleming considered to be 'real workmen' and 'real workwomen' were 'leisure to serve your God, to see and know something of nature, to learn much that is noble of the past, and, if God will, to do something for the future'.[2] The true necessities of life were also outlined as 'Four, and four only: food, clothes, a dwelling-place and means of education',[3] Fleming adding that not one person in the nineteenth century knew 'how to use aright, a single one of God's free gifts, of fresh sweet air, green grass and herbs of earth, or bright sunlight and open sky.'[4] Maintaining that the nineteenth century had made progress only in the building of 'altars to Mammon' in 'all fruitful fields' and 'on every hill-side' in England, Fleming offered the example of an old man hoeing weeds as the antithesis to such evils.[5] Dignified labour he acknowledged as a sign of 'working hand-in-hand with God', money and the pursuit of it representative only of evil.[6]

Fleming concluded that work, to be true and useful, had to be one of two things: 'it must either help, strengthen, or teach, the people amongst whom we do it; or it must be useful and memorable for future generations'. Yet he readily admitted that his own work (principally as a solicitor) was 'hopelessly neither' of those, and that even his best efforts had had only 'entirely the worst results'.[7] Such deep philosophical questioning of his own value as a human being, and of his personal contribution to society, suggests that, as early as 1873, Fleming was analysing not only the faults of modern society, but his own contribution to those faults. Whether any one particular incident had sparked Fleming's self-analysis is unclear, but *In the House of Rimmon* clearly mirrored not only Ruskin's writings, but Ruskin's own similar questioning of what he himself could do to effect social as well as personal change. Under Ruskin's influence, to do something which would 'really benefit the community' and to 'leave work memorable and useful to

---

[1] Ibid., 6–7.

[2] Ibid., 31–32.

[3] Ibid., 23.

[4] Ibid., 10.

[5] Ibid., 11.

[6] Ibid., 13.

[7] Ibid., 13–14.

posterity' had now become Fleming's chief occupations of thought.[1] At first, such questioning provoked the desire in Fleming merely to 'draw back from the mid stream into some quiet inlet, and let the mad waters go tearing on blindly, to the Niagara Falls of Chaos'.[2]

At that stage he visualised his 'quiet inlet' as a cottage with 'an acre or two of land, fair facing to the south or south-east, of a good fruitful soil, and with sweet springs of water near ... and my garden shall be to me a place for refreshment and sweet honest labour'.[3] The cottage itself would be an example of good architecture (presumably vernacular) and its porch would invoke memories of 'Some Marguerite sitting spinning at her wheel, framed with overhanging masses of jessamine and roses'.[4]

Although he made his wants known publicly, he made no attempt to seek out such an inlet, or to make any radical changes to his life. With the publication of his essay, however, Fleming did make one important decision, which was to begin the chain of events which saw the revival of arts and crafts in the Lake District.

In October 1873 Fleming, then 27, wrote to Ruskin, enclosing a copy of *In the House of Rimmon* and asking his opinion. Ruskin replied:

> I had read your book from beginning to end, before I opened your letter ... Your 'letter' is so entirely in accordance with my Fors that I felt as if I had met a pleasant wraith of myself. You certainly have read some of my books—how is it you have not looked at Fors, the outcome of them all?[5]

Ruskin's letter may be seen as the beginning of Fleming's definite association with him, and of discussion of his *Fors Clavigera*. The indication that Ruskin himself believed *Fors* to be the 'outcome' of all his work (which indicates something of its importance) would certainly have been enough to encourage Fleming to continue reading the Letters; and Ruskin's reply evidently encouraged him to consider the possibility of cultivating a friendship. Their correspondence continued until at least July 1888 when it was curtailed by, among other things, Ruskin's

---

[1] Ibid., 16.

[2] Ibid., 25–6.

[3] Ibid., 26.

[4] Ibid., 27–8.

[5] YUBL, Ruskin to Fleming, 29 Oct. 1873, endorsed by Fleming 'The first letter I ever had from JR'.

worsening health.[1]

Although Fleming's essay revealed the extent of Ruskin's influence on his writings, it is from letters exchanged between the two that the depth of their friendship is apparent. So struck was Ruskin by Fleming's early letters that in December 1873 he told him that 'You are the first person engaged in the profession of law whom I have ever known express right feeling about it.'[2] In June 1874 Ruskin wrote to him from Assisi expressing a wish to include one of those letters in the August 1874 *Fors*.[3] Ruskin's letter concluded 'Please write to me as often as you can', indicating that, whilst they had yet to meet, he was as anxious as Fleming to maintain contact by letter. It is clear that the religious zeal shared by Fleming and Ruskin also drew them together, the title of Fleming's essay demonstrating that zeal. *In the House of Rimmon* is derived from the Old Testament, 2 Kings 5:18:

> In this one matter only may the Lord pardon me: when my master goes to the temple of Rimmon to worship, leaning on my arm, and I worship in the temple of Rimmon when he worships there, for this let the Lord pardon me.[4]

The correspondence was published as part of *Fors* with an additional note in which Ruskin urged 'I recommend the whole of the following letter to the reader's most serious consideration'.[5] Fleming's letter was probably a rejoinder to notes on law reform made by Ruskin, with particular reference to the Judicature Act which was to come into operation the following November. According to Fleming, the Act might halt the 'decrease in the estimate of human life' which he felt typified the nineteenth century. Fleming believed (by now) that two schools of thought were responsible for 'the decay of the national mind', the first teaching that 'man's primary object in life is to "get on in the world"', resulting in an exaggerated estimate 'of the value and sanctity of property', the second that 'love can exist without reverence, mercy

---

[1] Documents at YUBL and HLC show that the two exchanged letters (somewhat spasmodically) until at least July 1888.

[2] YUBL, Ruskin to Fleming, 4 Dec. 1873.

[3] See Appendix 1 for Fleming's letter of 11 June 1874, which was included in *Fors Clavigera* for August 1874: Cook and Wedderburn, *Works*, xxviii. 141–4.

[4] J. Hayman, 'John Ruskin's *Hortus Inclusus*: The Manuscript Sources and Publication History', *Huntington Library Quarterly*, lii (1989), 363–87.

[5] See note 3 above.

without justice, and liberty without obedience'.[1] Although a confirmed Ruskinian by that date, Fleming evidently held strong views of his own which, from time to time, he was moved to make more widely known.

For the next nine years the friendship between Fleming and Ruskin continued to develop, but always at a distance. Fleming spent much of his time commuting between Hertfordshire and Gray's Inn, and Ruskin continued to travel, lecture, entertain at Brantwood and write, including *Fors Clavigera*. In their letters the two men exchanged views on many subjects, including books, music, poetry and art, the 27-year age gap between them causing few problems. In 1883, however, a distinct change occurred, the details of which Fleming apparently never committed to paper. In the early part of that year he came 'into tenancy' of Neaum Crag, an eighteen-acre estate close to Coniston and Elterwater in the Lake District.[2]

Fleming's exact situation regarding Neaum Crag is unclear. Rawnsley's words suggest that he rented the house or inherited it, which would not have been improbable since he is thought to have had family connections with Lakeland, Fleming being an old-established Furness name. However, when the 1881 census was taken Neaum Crag was occupied by a Mr and Mrs Briscoe from Liverpool. This suggests that he followed the Briscoes as tenants, using the house as a summer retreat before choosing to move there permanently, and bought the freehold after his retirement. He certainly owned Neaum Crag when he died.[3]

Fleming continued to commute between Lakeland, Hertfordshire, and Gray's Inn until about 1903 when he would have been about 57. Like Ruskin, he died at his Lakeland home without children, after which the property was auctioned along with its contents. Although Fleming was thought to have had distant family connections with the region,[4] it seems that his principal reason for taking the property was to be closer to Ruskin, and to realise his earlier vision of a cottage retreat.

In many respects, Neaum Crag fulfilled all his wants, although at first it was only his summer residence. Set against a backdrop of Loughrigg and Little Langdale, the house was a typical Lakeland cottage, surrounded by woodland and fields, with Elterwater just over the hill and

---

[1] Ibid.

[2] H.D. Rawnsley, *Ruskin and the English Lakes* (Glasgow, 1901), 137.

[3] Sale cat. (1923) (copy at Armitt Museum & Library, Ambleside).

[4] According to a report of his funeral in the *Westmorland Gazette*, 31 March 1923, Fleming was a member of a well-known Lakeland family, the Le Flemings of Rydal, and belonged to the Rayrigg branch at Bowness, although no evidence has been found to support this.

Coniston easily accessible by road. It is probable that Fleming's first meeting with Ruskin took place on his arrival at Neaum Crag.

As a result of his years spent studying Ruskin, and exchanging opinions by letter, Fleming arrived in the Lake District with a preconceived notion of all that the region represented. An equally avid reader of Wordsworth, he was more than aware of Ruskin's hostility towards the Lakeland railways, and was well informed of what he regarded as other unwelcome regional changes wrought by industrialisation. It can only be considered as coincidence that, when Fleming moved into Neaum Crag, an old Westmorland spinning wheel—the very symbol of pre-industrial regional life to Wordsworth and to Ruskin—stood in the inglenook of his drawing room. The outmoded wheel was merely a decorative feature but, having spent at least twelve years 'pondering over Wordsworth's sonnets and Mr Ruskin's eloquent appeals in Fors', and also motivated by 'the homely speech' of one of his 'poor neighbours',[1] Fleming immediately resolved to revive 'the good old handicrafts of spinning and weaving'.[2] At Neaum Crag, he had inadvertently been presented with the opportunity finally to carry out the useful work he believed he had so far failed to do.

Although *Fors* was clearly Fleming's chief source of inspiration, precisely which aspects of that sizeable work particularly motivated him in his revival of the Westmorland wheels is less certain. *In the House of Rimmon* gives a general idea of his understanding of *Fors*, but its direct references to Lakeland's textile history must have played a dominant role in shaping his views. In Letter XL (written early in 1874), for example, Ruskin offered two letters, one sent to his friend concerning machine labour, the other concerning hand labour. The first was written by a woman mill worker who endured poor wages, poor working conditions and long hours tied to machinery, while the other was a recollection of hand spinning in Cumberland:

> My mother, a Cumberland woman, was a spinner, and the whole process, from the fine thread that passed through her notable fingers, and the weaving into linen by an old cottager—a very 'Silas Marner,'—to the bleaching on the orchard grass, was well known to my sister and myself when children[3]

---

[1] H.H. Warner (ed.), *Songs of the Spindle and Legends of the Loom* (1889), 15.

[2] Ibid., 14.

[3] *Works*, xxviii. 66.

Part way through the account Ruskin added: 'What factory, with its thousand spindles, and chemical bleaching powders, can send out such linen as that, which lasted three generations?'[1] Other discussions of labour in *Fors*, as well as references to the role of women in society, the need to respect God, and the need to return to nature, evidently also played a part.

Almost immediately, Fleming put his idea to revive the local spinning wheels to Ruskin, and received an instruction to 'Go ahead'.[2] Although at that stage Fleming was aware of the demise of other local crafts, including bobbin turning, charcoal burning, woodcarving and basket making, there is no indication that he intended to attempt more than the revival of the wheels, particularly since, away from Brantwood, his initial idea met with only 'a Babel of expostulation' as 'wild as a Parsifal chorus'.[3] Since neither Ruskin nor Fleming had any experience of what they saw as a traditionally female craft, Fleming arranged for his housekeeper, Marian Twelves, to take the first steps in learning to spin by hand, no teacher being available. Miss Twelves had moved from Hertfordshire with Fleming to look after Neaum Crag during his winter absences, and to run the house during the summer months. The daughter of William Twelves, a commercial clerk, she was formerly a private teacher who, while lacking any formal arts training, is reputed to have been a skilled needlewoman. It was entirely due to her practical efforts that the realisation of *Fors Clavigera*—in the form of the respected spinning wheel—was achieved. The enormity of the task in which she 'mastered the initial difficulties' of hand spinning were laid out by Miss Twelves a few years later:

> a by no means easy task in the absence of all technical knowledge as to why the wheels would turn the wrong way—bands fly off for no apparent reason—and yarn twist itself into innumerable kinks instead of winding in an orderly manner on the bobbin.[4]

A later description of Miss Twelves as the 'good genius of the household' by one of her Lakeland colleagues perhaps best indicates something of her capabilities on a practical level, and her persistence with the

---

[1] Ibid.

[2] E.T. Cook, *Studies in Ruskin* (1890), 166.

[3] Ibid., 165–6.

[4] M. Twelves, *The Ruskin Linen Industry* (Keswick, c.1900), 2 (copy in Sheffield Archives, GSG 21).

wheel ultimately brought only good results.[1]

While Fleming was a seasoned reader of Ruskin by 1883, the extent of Miss Twelves's knowledge of his writings is not clear, although in 1883 she joined Ruskin's Guild of St George with Fleming, and remained a Companion until her death in 1929. An exercise in social reform of sorts, the Guild of St George was formed in the early 1870s and legally constituted in 1878. In Letter LVIII of *Fors Clavigera* Ruskin presented the Guild's eight-point creed. Companions promised to trust God and to keep his law, to love their neighbours, to love themselves, to harm no living creature needlessly, to avoid deceit, to obey the laws of the country and the Guild, and to labour for their own daily bread. Machinery was done without, and the women carried out needlework by hand. With his already comprehensive knowledge, Fleming was able to guide more than adequately much of what his housekeeper did practically in Ruskin's name in the early stages, seeking advice directly from the Master (as the Master of the Guild Ruskin was often referred to thus) and ensuring that the revival of the wheels closely followed his teachings.

Once the art of hand spinning was mastered, a retired local weaver was asked to help produce the first pieces of cloth. An old loom in twenty pieces was found in a cellar in Kendal and given to the experiment for the purpose. Whereas almost every Lakeland village had once had its own weaver, no one knew how to assemble the loom, and so a photograph of Giotto's Campanile was consulted and the parts 'rightly put together'.[2]

Although lacking in practical skills, Fleming's business acumen was always faultless, and he ensured that there was national awareness of his work from the very beginning. In October 1883 he wrote to *The Standard* and explained:

> Many years ago Wordsworth lamented the disuse of the Spinning Wheel in the dales of Westmoreland. The poet says that the wheel was a cure for grief and care, that it composed the throbbing pulse, and had various other healthful influences, all of which you will find melodiously set forth in his XIXth Sonnet.
>
> I am trying in a small way to re-establish the industry in this quiet corner of the world. I shall lend the wheels to the cottagers and teach them how to spin, and (at first) give them the wool and

---

[1] Rawnsley, *Ruskin*, 137.

[2] Cook, *Studies*, 169.

flax, and buy it back when spun. I am aware that this method of business will not commend itself to the ordinary commercial mind. As a factor in cottage life nothing (Elias Howe to the contrary notwithstanding) has taken the place of the spinning wheel, and if we are able to brighten (not unprofitably) some weary hours, and to give work to some old hands, then we shall begin to think the good old influences yet linger round the Spinning Wheel. If any of your readers are old-fashioned enough to care for hand-spun and hand-woven linen, or unpractical enough in this utilitarian age to give us a good word and wish, let them write to me.[1]

Over the following years, references to his handcraft work were to appear regularly in other national newspapers and journals, including the *Pall Mall Gazette*, the *Architectural Review* and *The Studio*.[2]

To put his experiment on a more formal footing, Fleming rented a small cottage in nearby Elterwater as a workshop, which was named St Martin's by his and Ruskin's close friend, Susanna Beever (1806–1893) of The Thwaite, Coniston. It was assuredly Miss Beever who thought of the name (St Martin was the bishop of Tours who cut his cloak into two pieces, giving one to a beggar), given Fleming's reference to 'A wise friend, who keeps her mind nicely poised between sentiment and common sense, nominated St Martin's, and referred me to the first part of Mr Ruskin's *Our Fathers Have Told Us*'.[3] The cottage was deliberately chosen because it was situated 'half-way between Mr Ruskin's home at Coniston and Wordsworth's at Rydal'.[4] On either side were the homes of two of Lakeland's most influential literary figures whose work was to play a fundamental part in the revival of the region's pre-industrial heritage. After many experiments, by Easter 1884 the first pieces of finished cloth, made from flax imported from Ireland, had been produced at St Martin's. Fleming initially described it as 'terrible stuff', 'frightful in colour and of dreadful roughness, with huge lumps and knots meandering up and down its surface'.[5] From this description, the early cloth produced by Miss Twelves and her weaver appears to have been similar to the coarse linen made in the old days of the spinning wheel, prior to its demise in Lakeland in the 1830s and 1840s. Then, the

---

[1] *The Standard*, 30 Oct. 1883.

[2] See, for example, the *Architectural Review*, vii (1900), 93.

[3] *Westmorland Gazette*, 25 Oct. 1913.

[4] Cook, *Studies*, 167.

[5] Ibid., 170.

cloth, described as harden-sark and made of locally grown flax, was used mostly for outdoor garments. Undeterred, Fleming sought solace in Ruskin's *The Seven Lamps of Architecture* (1849) in which the irregular-ities of hand labour are seen as its merits:

> I said, early in this essay, that hand-work might always be known from machine-work; observing, however, at the same time, that it was possible for men to turn themselves into machines, and to reduce their labour to the machine level; but so long as men work as men, putting their heart into what they do, and doing their best, it matters not how bad workmen they may be, there will be that in the handling which is above all price: it will be plainly seen that some places have been delighted in more than others — that there have been a pause, and a care about them; and then there will come careless bits, and fast bits; and here the chisel will have struck hard, and there lightly, and anon timidly; and if the man's mind as well as his heart went with his work, all this will be in the right places, and each part will set off the other; and the effect of the whole, as compared with the same design cut by a machine or a lifeless hand, will be like that of poetry well read and deeply felt to that of the same verses jangled by rote. There are many to whom the difference is imperceptible; but to those who love poetry it is everything — they had rather not hear it at all, than hear it ill read.[1]

In accordance with both local tradition and Ruskin's teachings, once the linen had been improved (by mixing it with such things as silk, depending on the quality of linen required), it was sun bleached. In an account of those early stages of linen production written in 1890 Fleming noted:

> Having got our linen, the next process was to bleach it. I read various treatises on bleaching, and discovered that all the processes were more or less injurious both to workmen and to stuff; so, as Giotto fixed our loom for us, Homer taught us the true principles of bleaching, and we adopted the simple method described in the 'Odyssey'. Sun, air, and dew were our only chemicals: potent magicians they, changing by their sweet alchemy our coarse brown

---

[1] *Works*, viii. 214.

stuff into soft white linen.[1]

The need for old spinning wheels was then made widely known, with some coming from Stornoway and the Isle of Man, probably from Laxey which, by 1900, had been acknowledged a failure. In 1900 Egbert Rydings wrote to Mrs Talbot (an associate of the Guild of St George) discussing the St George's Mill at Laxey on the Isle of Man, which was run on similar lines to Langdale, and concluded:

> I am quite of your opinion 'that the whole concern is a total failure'—I am quite certain so far as I am myself concerned it has been so. I have worked the Mill on the lines laid down by Mr Ruskin when the Mill started 20 years ago and I find myself at least *£200 poorer* than I was when I commenced the business.[2]

An additional fifteen wheels were made by a local carpenter, not without some difficulty. The demise of the spinning wheel across Britain meant that the iron fittings needed, once made extensively in Birmingham and Sheffield, were almost—but not entirely—impossible to find. Finally, in honour of the picturesque valley in which St Martin's sat, the project was named the Langdale Linen Industry, another strong indication of its regional significance.

With its fully equipped workshop, by mid 1884 the Langdale Linen Industry set its first spinsters to work. Numbering at least fifteen, they were taught by Miss Twelves and, when ready, given a wheel and flax to take home. Each Saturday the spun flax was brought back to St Martin's where it was weighed, tested and paid for, initially at the rate of 2s. a pound. It was expected that the largely uneducated and poor spinsters would earn an average wage of 5s. a week from work intended to be carried out only in their spare time. Since the Industry was never short of willing workers, it evidently offered much-needed additional income. Once the flax had been spun, it was woven by a local man, one of the few males (aside from Fleming and Ruskin) directly involved in the Industry. For his troubles he was given a 'fixed wage' of 16s. a week

---

[1] Cook, *Studies*, 170.

[2] John Rylands University Library, Manchester, Ruskin Collection, No 1164 (R.99552), Letter No 10, 1900.

and 'a good cottage rent free'.[1] At that stage Marian Twelves worked without payment, her efforts on behalf of the Industry given 'purely out of friendship' to Fleming and 'devotion to Mr Ruskin's teachings'.[2] As recreation and reward, Miss Twelves held 'spinster tea-parties' at Neaum Crag where the accounts were read out, the works of Wordsworth and Ruskin were read aloud, and music and dancing were carried on with young men invited from the village. Rawnsley notes that the spinster tea parties 'were not allowed to degenerate into mere gossipings, for many a passage from the poets and from Ruskin were read aloud, and the aims of the Brantwood prophet and his good wishes to the adventure were spoken of'. According to Rawnsley the first gathering of 'would be spinsters' took place at Neaum Crag on Christmas Eve 1883.[3] The tea parties were also reported in the local press:

> On Tuesday evening, the Langdale spinners and weavers held their annual tea and dance at Neaum Crag. About thirty members assembled. The accounts for 1885 were passed and audited, and Mr Fleming and Miss Twelves gave a general review of the work done in the year. It seems that there is a real demand for genuine homespun goods, for £220 worth of Langdale linen has been sold during last year. Constant work has been given to a large number of women, and whatever truth there may be as to the depression of trade in general, it has not affected this little industry, for not only has it proved to be self supporting, but after wages, rent, and all other outgoings had been paid, there remained a little profit in hand, which was divided amongst the workers. The business part of the meeting was thus concluded. After tea, the spinsters were pleasantly reinforced by the arrival of some of the young men from the village, and dancing was begun and carried on with great spirit. We believe dancing forms an important part of Mr Ruskin's scheme of education, and we think the Professor's heart would have been gladdened if he could have seen the way in which his workers addressed themselves to reels, cottagers, and other good

---

[1] Cook, *Studies*, 172. The lack of surviving papers for 1883-4 means that total wages, total costs of materials, and other expenses incurred in the very early stages are not clear. It has been assumed that, by 1884, when St Martin's was being used, Miss Twelves was no longer acting as Fleming's housekeeper and presumably lived at the cottage, but used Neaum Crag for social gatherings.

[2] *Westmorland Gazette*, 25 Oct. 1913.

[3] Rawnsley, *Ruskin*, 140, 142.

old fashioned dances.[1]

On a practical level the Langdale Linen Industry appeared comparatively straightforward to organise and run, using largely tried and tested ancient methods. Theoretically, however, it was much more complex than anything witnessed by Lakeland before 1883. Since Laxey, the nearest similar Ruskinian textile experiment in the early 1880s, failed within twenty years, and Langdale survived commercially for at least 40 years, it can only be that Fleming's understanding of Ruskin's writings, Miss Twelves's application of those writings, and Ruskin's direct contribution were the elements essential to success. Laxey followed the same three basic Ruskinian principles as Langdale—it questioned the use of machinery, rejected any unnecessary and harmful processes in textile production, and ensured that working conditions were conducive to a harmonious atmosphere. It was not the theories themselves which brought failure, but the conditions under which they were applied. In the case of Langdale, that application took place under Ruskin's direct guidance, with Fleming consulting the Master on every detail of his writings from 1883, as far as Ruskin's health permitted. Fleming also had the benefit of at least ten years spent studying Ruskin's works before 1883, and in *In the House of Rimmon* had already encapsulated his own understanding of those works, creating an almost formulaic recipe which condensed what were for him the most critical aspects of his mentor's writings.

It is also apparent that the Langdale Linen Industry thrived because of the additional influence of Lakeland's history and tradition. Its unique regional character helped to shape what was to become increasingly a Ruskinian exercise. The spinning wheels used by the Langdale spinsters were either old ones which had been recovered, or new ones based directly on old Westmorland wheels; no machinery other than that driven by the hand was ever used; local, traditional methods of treating the cloths made were applied; the Westmorland cottage became the focal point of industry once again; and attempts were even made before 1900 to revive flax growing in south Lakeland. With the demise of the wheels, flax and hemp growing, once concentrated around Crook, Preston Patrick, Farleton, Milnthorpe and Lambrigg, had largely died out by the mid nineteenth century. When the wheels were revived, unsuccessful attempts were made to reintroduce flax as a local crop, which might have helped to revive pre-industrial Lakeland farming methods in certain

---

[1] CROK, DB 111/93, unidentified newspaper cutting, 19 Feb. 1886.

areas. Attempts to grow flax in the late nineteenth century on behalf of the Langdale Linen Industry failed for a number of reasons, including bad weather conditions. The experiments were, apparently, never recorded, but are remembered locally.

For the Langdale Linen Industry, the growing of flax was the only piece of the jigsaw of traditional textile production missing, and one which could not be retrieved. Laxey, by contrast, was based in a specially built mill, a picture of which hung in Ruskin's drawing room. Although some spinsters were employed and steam power (which Ruskin questioned) was forbidden, the bulk of the carding and spinning was carried out by water-powered machinery. For this reason Laxey could not be described as a true domestic industry, and its speedier production of cloths (chiefly wools) was carried out on a larger scale than Langdale.

Starting with Fleming's original proposal in early 1883, Ruskin was directly informed of every aspect of the Langdale Linen Industry's growth and development, and was given gifts of linen in the form of sheets and towels. In June 1883, before the first pieces of cloth had been produced, Ruskin wrote to Fleming, 'Be of good courage—you cannot possibly be engaged in a work of purer wisdom and benevolence'.[1] Such support undoubtedly made Fleming's and Marian Twelves's seemingly impossible task somewhat easier, although Miss Twelves did not meet Ruskin until 1884. Their first meeting took place at Susanna Beever's home, The Thwaite, and until then she took Ruskin's advice solely through Fleming. Ruskin's interest in the Langdale Linen Industry, however, went beyond the mere realisation of his theories. Over his lifetime he had developed an interest in textiles which extended to collecting laces and embroideries on his travels abroad. In his collection were samples of Persian embroidery bought in Paris, Italian Greek lace bought in Lucca, and Italian embroidery bought in Venice, some of which were as much as four hundred years old. Some items from Ruskin's textile collection appeared in several of the Coniston exhibitions of arts and crafts which were held annually from 1900 to 1919.

His interest appears never to have transferred itself to the practical, and even his ideas for a set of embroideries, originally suggested by his close friend Edward Burne-Jones (1833–98) and based on Chaucer's *The Legend of Good Women*, never reached full fruition. The designs were completed, but the embroideries remained unfinished. His respect for textiles was probably initially fired by his mother's and grandmother's needle skills, both of whom executed fine needlework to an exceptional

---

[1] YUBL, Ruskin to Fleming, 26 June 1883.

standard.[1] His work as an artist only exacerbated his interest, his close observation of the nature of fabrics creating an additional awareness in him of fabric-like qualities in nature, for example in sheets of water and blankets of ferns. The study of great works of art also played its part, as he revealed in an inaugural address delivered at the Cambridge School of Art in 1858:

> Well, one of the most notable characters in this picture is the splendour of its silken dresses: and, in particular, there was a piece of white brocade, with designs upon it in gold, which it was one of my chief objects in stopping at Turin to copy. You may, perhaps, be surprised at this; but I must just note in passing, that I share this weakness of enjoying dress patterns with all good students and all good painters ... the queen is one of the loveliest of Veronese's female figures; all the accessories are full of grace and imagination; and the finish of the whole so perfect that one day I was upwards of two hours vainly trying to render, with perfect accuracy, the curves of two leaves of the brocaded silk.[2]

A textile workshop such as St Martin's, which concentrated on producing high quality fabrics (often bought as a base for embroidery), later joined by lace and embroideries, thus appealed to Ruskin's personal and artistic as well as practical and theoretical interest.

In his writings too, Ruskin demonstrated an unequivocal appreciation of hand-produced textiles, with particular reference to the significance of the spinning wheel and the needle. Over a number of years he adopted a series of complex images linked to embroidery, tapestry, lace and what he described as the 'silk and purple', relating to productive and unproductive labour.[3] Most relevant to Fleming were the images of the ancient spinning wheel, the symbol of dignified domestic labour, and the antithesis of nineteenth-century industrialisation. The needle too Ruskin frequently linked to dignified labour, describing it as the 'feminine plough' and the provider of clothing as well as the vital partner to the masculine plough used in the field to provide food.[4] Of lace, he expressed similarly strong views, contemplating not only its use and its aesthetic value but its design. In 1857, in *A Joy For Ever*, he wrote:

---

[1] M.B. Huish, *Samplers and Tapestry Embroideries* (New York, 1970). pl. X.

[2] *Works*, xvi. 185–6.

[3] Ibid., 129–39.

[4] J. Ruskin, *The Two Paths* (1859), 223.

The real good of a piece of lace, then, you will find, is that it should show, first, that the designer of it had a pretty fancy; next, that the maker of it had fine fingers; lastly, that the wearer of it has worthiness or dignity enough to obtain what is difficult to obtain, and common sense enough not to wear it on all occasions … But I return to my point, of cheapness. You don't think that it would be convenient, or even creditable, for women to wash the doorsteps or dish the dinners in lace gowns? Nay, even for the most ladylike occupations — reading, or writing, or playing with her children — do you think a lace gown, or even a lace collar, so great an advantage or dignity to a woman.[1]

On a number of occasions he also discussed the religious significance of, in Isaiah, 'the great family of the lints and flaxes',[2] and employed the image of the 'perfect economist' (or 'mistress of a household') holding in her right hand 'food and flax', the 'objects of utility'.[3] Even the Langdale Linen Industry's use of flax, therefore, had much deeper theoretical significance than at first might be assumed.

Arguably the most powerful textile imagery used by Ruskin appeared in *Fors Clavigera*, the foundation text behind Fleming's Langdale experiment. There, Ruskin visualised *Fors* as a female text and himself as the embroiderer of the Letters: 'but I must put a stitch or two into her work'.[4] Similar imagery had already appeared some years earlier in 'The Cestus of Aglaia' (nine papers printed in the *Art Journal* between 1865 and 1866) in which he had written:

I can't give you any detail, yet; but, not to drop a stitch in my story, I want to say why I've attached so much importance to needlework, and put it in the opening court of the six. You see they are progressive, so that I don't quite put needlework on a level with painting. But a nation that would learn to 'touch' must primarily know how to 'stitch'.[5]

In that respect, Ruskin freely expressed the feminine side to his nature, calling for a renewed respect for needle skills and an upgrading of

[1] *Works*, xvi. 157–8.

[2] J. Ruskin, *Modern Painters* (1897 edn), iii. 242.

[3] J. Ruskin, *Deucalion, Arrows of the Chace* (Boston, Mass., n.d.), 339–40.

[4] *Works*, xxviii. 68, extract from Letter XL of *Fors Clavigera*.

[5] Ibid., xxxiv. 257.

embroidery to an art.[1]

In response to Fleming's successful realisation of some of the more complex as well as more basic aspects of his writings, in Letter XCV (October 1884), one of the last of *Fors Clavigera*, Ruskin praised the Langdale Linen Industry:

> Very thankfully I can now say that this vision of thread and needlework, though written when my fancy had too much possession of me, is now being in all its branches realized by two greatly valued friends,—the spinning on the old spinning wheel, with most happy and increasingly acknowledged results, systematized here among our Westmorland hills by Mr Albert Fleming; the useful sewing by Miss Stanley of Whitelands College.[2]

This passage was the earliest clear public acknowledgement by Ruskin that he recognised Fleming's work as the realisation of his own writings, with no reference to any other influences than himself. Letter XCV also contained sections of 'The Cestus of Aglaia' referring to the respected arts of spinning, dyeing, weaving and embroidery which made up his own particular 'vision of thread and needlework'. The Letter immediately prior to that contained the illustration by Kate Greenaway (1846–1901) *Neither Doth She Spin* (July 1883), executed after her visit to Brantwood between April and May 1883, when the Langdale Linen Industry had just begun. Given Ruskin's lyrical descriptions of his 'vision of thread and needlework', it was not long before Fleming and Marian Twelves began to consider employing the 'feminine plough' or needle in their work. As a result, the revival of the Westmorland wheels began to take on a design identity not known in the former days of spinning and weaving in Lakeland, and one which further highlighted its individuality.

---

[1] *Works*, xxxiv. 81, where Ruskin notes that the critics talked of 'the effeminate sentimentality of Ruskin'.

[2] Ibid., xxix. 511, extract from Letter XCV of *Fors Clavigera*.

2

THE LANGDALE
LINEN INDUSTRY
UNDER MARIAN TWELVES

From his reading of the works of Ruskin, Fleming was clear that an *absolute* return to lost ways and methods was not possible. The old ways had died out chiefly because they were no longer relevant to modern life, and so to return to making the old coarse harden-sark which was no longer needed would have been a mistake.[1]

Initially Fleming and Miss Twelves attempted to overcome such difficulties first by ensuring that the linens made as St Martin's were much improved, and second by broadcasting the work at Elterwater far and wide. To compete in the modern market, by 1889 the Langdale Linen Industry was producing at least seventeen types of linen of various widths and qualities, each of which was given a number. The cheapest were sold at 2s. a yard and the most expensive at 6s. The widest measured 44 inches and sold at 5s. 6d. a yard. As well as being suitable as a base for embroidery (bought by the likes of Susanna Beever), St Martin's linens were bought for use as towels and sheets, some of the first of which were sent to Ruskin in January 1884. According to St Martin's order books, Susanna Beever bought Langdale linen in 1884 and was probably one of the Industry's earliest customers.[2] In January that year Ruskin thanked Fleming for a present of linen sheets, adding: 'I am sure I shall find the sheets full of happy dreams'.[3] It was also used for making curtains, portières, tablecloths, chair-backs, a wide range of other, mostly domestic, items and occasionally clothing.

Fleming made sure that the linens were familiar well outside the

---

[1] In *Ruskin and the English Lakes* (Glasgow, 1901), 135, Rawnsley describes Langdale linen as: 'Not harden-sark as of old, nor blue bedgown material truly, but honestly hand-spun and hand-woven linen, grey as the skies are grey, or golden yellow as the waning larches upon Latrigg-side'.

[2] CROK, WDB 73/1.

[3] YUBL, Rusking to Fleming, 2 Jan. 1884.

Lakeland region, and was determined to create as wide a commercial market as possible. As with *The Standard*,[1] he used newspapers and journals as a means of advertising, unashamedly exploiting the novelty of hand-spun, hand-woven cloths created by poor women, as well as the names of Ruskin and Wordsworth, two of Lakeland's best known literary figures. Enquiries were always encouraged from interested parties, and a mail order service was available for those who could not call at St Martin's in person. In more practical terms, however, Marian Twelves was solely responsible for the further development of the linen into a successful artistic product which eventually achieved for the Industry the description of 'art industry', and which reaffirmed the venture's uniqueness.

Given the conditions of late nineteenth-century England, in which the London Royal School of Art Needlework (founded in 1872) in particular had made considerable attempts to restore needlework to its rightful place in the decorative arts, the introduction of embroidery at St Martin's comes as little surprise.[2] As devout Ruskinians, in which their mentor had long made similar calls for a reassessment of needlework as a valid art form, and a reappraisal of the ancient needle as the feminine plough, they were also aware of the theoretical and historical significance of the needle and the 'laudable mystery of embroidery', as Fleming described it.[3] Having mastered the art of hand spinning (and Ruskin, Fleming and Miss Twelves surely saw hand spinning as an art as much as a craft), for which she had no formal training, the introduction of embroidery in which she was already accomplished can have presented Miss Twelves with few difficulties. On three counts, therefore, the Langdale Linen Industry had already surpassed its local predecessors: it had become a better commercial prospect; it was making a wider range of linens than witnessed in the Lake District in the past; and it was now decorating those linens. The exact date of execution and sale of the first embroidered linens at St Martin's is unclear; but it was probably early in 1885, once the demand for plain linen had become evident. Fleming admitted that the fashion of the day for hand-produced embroidery helped to sell the Industry's decorated linen products which were mostly

---

[1] Above, pp. 20–21.

[2] The Royal School of Art Needlework was founded in 1872 by, among others, Lady Welby Gregory. Initially based in Sloane Street, London, its president was Princess Christian of Schleswig-Holstein. The school's dual purpose was to provide paid and suitable employment for middle-class women, and to restore needlework to its status of 'art'. It continues today as the Royal School of Needlework.

[3] E.T. Cook, *Studies in Ruskin* (1890), 172.

household such as napkins, teacloths and tablecloths.[1] Although detailed records of wages and sales for the period 1883 to 1889 appear not to have survived (or were not kept), the steady growth of the Industry suggests that, even before the introduction of embroidery, St Martin's was running at a small profit.[2] With the addition of embroidery and of selling skeins of flax, sales and profits appear to have increased.

After the introduction of embroidery an additional 40 'poor ladies' were employed.[3] Before 1889 there were at least 70 women working in the Langdale area, all earning additional income by producing high quality, sought after textiles. The younger generations of Westmerians may have migrated to the towns and factories, and rejected the local arts and crafts once carried out in villages whose population had fallen, but their mothers and grandmothers proved to be a valuable work force. Not only had Fleming returned to them the 'venerable art' of spinning which Wordsworth saw as 'torn from the poor', but he had offered them a means of increasing their income.[4] On the other hand, the Industry never aimed to make the women financially independent. Thus Anthea Callen criticises the Langdale Linen Industry for paying its workers some 60 per cent less in the 1890s than those at Morris & Co.,[5] although the Industry was run on two important Ruskinian lines. First, all profits were paid into a bank and distributed among the workers at the end of each year; second, because it was a true Ruskinian industry, strident efforts were made to ensure that the workers remained at home (rather than be moved into large studios, mills or factories), so that they worked in the best possible conditions. Incomes were 'topped up' by dividing the profits, and the women remained the true queens of domesticity which Ruskin—however rightly or misguidedly—held them to be:

> Whereupon, you are to note this, that the end of all right education for a woman is to make her love her home better than any other place; that she should as seldom leave it as a queen her queendom;

[1] Ibid.

[2] CROK, WDB 73, unidentified local newspaper cutting (Feb. 1886), reporting total sales for 1885 of £220 and that a 'little profit' had been made that year. 1885 was the first full year in which the Industry ran. Since the first pieces of usable linen were woven by April 1884, the Industry ran commercially for a maximum of eight months or less in 1884.

[3] Cook, *Studies*, 172.

[4] H.H. Warner (ed.), *Songs of the Spindle and Legends of the Loom* (1889), 13.

[5] A. Callen, *Angel in the Studio. Women in the Arts and Crafts Movement 1870–1914* (1979), 117.

nor ever feel entirely at rest but within its threshold.[1]

Returning the Langdale spinsters to the home was therefore not a concerted effort to restrict their activities necessarily born of patriarchal rule, but an attempt to restore them and the craft they practised to what Ruskin regarded as their rightful place. For its workers to be freed from the ties of machinery, to produce what Fleming described as 'valued' home-made things, and to be given a sense of control over what they made, was the Industry's answer to nineteenth-century disease.[2]

An equally important effort was made to increase individual creativity. Although local arts had diminished with the demise of the wheels in the 1830s and 1840s, and hand spinning might best be described as an art, there is little evidence to suggest that Lakeland linen production had once been an artistic activity. Previously, the main object had been to produce plain, undecorated cloth which fulfilled Lakeland man's fundamental need to be clothed and protected. Under the influence of Ruskin and his two devotees, a distinctly new creative edge soon revealed itself, with embroidery transforming even the simplest of household linen items—such as tea cloths—into art products. From 1885 the Langdale Linen Industry developed its own distinct embroidery style which was largely created in the cottages of its workers and always executed by hand. Every one of the embroiderers was encouraged to create her own designs, many of which were based on nature. Like the Pre-Raphaelites before them, the Langdale women followed Ruskin's recommendations—either recounted by Miss Twelves or read aloud at the spinster tea parties—and resorted directly to their natural Lakeland surroundings for inspiration.

Since Marian Twelves sought Ruskin's advice in person from 1884 onwards, and given his interest in textiles, there can be little doubt that he also played a direct as well as theoretical role in design. His influence filtered down from Miss Twelves to the workers, with she and Fleming consulted on, and authorising, every design executed. Not only did sales increase as a result of the encouragement of individual creativity, but so too did personal talents in certain women. By the 1890s one invalid girl (formerly employed by Ruskin as a copyist) had developed a form of linen decoration in which parts of the design were stained before being

---

[1] Extract from Letter XXXII of *Fors Clavigera* (*Works*, xxvii. 619). George Thomson of Huddersfield, also a follower of Ruskin, ran a woollen and worsted factory around the time that Laxey was running. Thomson also aimed to divide some of his profits among his workers.

[2] A. Fleming, *In the House of Rimmon* (1873), 6–7.

subjected to fast dyes. Other workers developed a skill for flax thread and silk embroidery worked on linens woven with silk, and some became proficient in copying antique embroideries. In 1900 it was noted that:

> One of the home workers, an old lady over eighty years of age, does the most beautiful embroidery in fac-simile of old French brocades. She also works a kind of glorified darned netting, which is a marvel of skill and delicacy.[1]

As an admirer of brocades, Ruskin would have approved of such work. The additional use of vegetable and plant dyes, at a time when anilines were widely accepted, added to the Industry's reputation for using tried and tested ancient methods, and also increased design possibilities for the workers.

Whilst all this gave the Langdale Linen Industry a distinct identity, its associations with Ruskin's Guild of St George further shaped its individuality. To understand the Guild was to understand the Linen Industry, the one being an ever-present force, albeit at first very discreet, in the life of the other. Fleming and Marian Twelves were Companions of the Guild from around the time of the first experiments in linen production at St Martin's. Miss Twelves in particular was as fervent a devotee of the Guild as of Ruskin, and was a member for some 46 years. Callen neglects to acknowledge the Guild as the force behind the Langdale Linen Industry, or to explain how it shaped the way it ran, its philosophical approach to dignified domestic labour, its attitude towards wages and the division of profits, and the very careful rejection of all machinery other than that driven directly by the hand, all of which held little interest for the likes of Morris & Co. in their production of fabrics and embroideries. The Industry's basic working practices were a deliberate attempt to follow Ruskin's teachings, and also Ruskin's credo for the Guild which was signed by every member. The creed covered eight points which advocated in members a fundamentally Christian approach to life and work which encouraged thought and consideration.[2]

In proposing that they should live a life of truth and love, the Guild aimed to make its Companions more answerable for their actions, and more aware of the consequences of those actions. Whether members or not, the Langdale spinsters and embroiderers were encouraged to live and

---

[1] *Country Life*, 24 Feb. 1900, 233–4.

[2] The Guild's rules were set out in Letter LVIII of *Fors Clavigera* (*Works*, xxvii. 419–20).

work by such principles, with respect for each other and their environment as important as their respect for what they made. The Guild's outright rejection of machinery in favour of hand labour was carried through with a stringency not even attempted by the Laxey industry, and was successfully adhered to well beyond the 40 or so years in which the Industry ran commercially.

To some the lack of machinery at St Martin's may make the Langdale Linen Industry seem akin to a sweatshop, using drawn out, antiquated methods instead of speedier mechanised processes. But the removal of machinery, regarded by Ruskin, Fleming and Miss Twelves as a barrier between the maker and the product, did appear to increase worker satisfaction, which was also aided by a division of labour where necessary. No worker was expected to become proficient in spinning, weaving, dyeing and embroidering her own linen, since each specialised in one field. Thus several women might work on one piece of linen as it passed through its various stages. All had a direct hand in its creation, each experiencing the personal satisfaction of contributing to what was made and sold in the workshop. Interest was further increased by the division of profits among the workers. Far from deterring the women from joining the Langdale Linen Industry, the abolition of machinery and the application of other Ruskin or Guild principles concerning 'individual effort' seemed to attract workers, with about a hundred women associated with the Elterwater workshop by 1900.[1] Whether any were influenced to join the Guild of St George as a result is not clear, but Fleming and Miss Twelves never made any rules which coerced workers into following practices with which they were not entirely happy. Nor was there any compulsion to join either the Industry or the Guild.

Although the Guild of St George and Ruskin were two powerful forces behind the Langdale Linen Industry, it always maintained its equally important and strong identity as a Lakeland industry. Whilst new practices such as embroidery were introduced under Ruskin's influence, the basic nature of the Industry stemmed just as much from its very particular regional history and tradition. According to Ruskin, the fundamental role of the Guild of St George was to demonstrate the 'rational organization of country life, independent of that of cities', which Fleming understood as best done not by creating industrial villages but by reviving village industries such as linen production by

---

[1] Marian Twelves, *The Ruskin Linen Industry Keswick* (*c*.1900), 5 (copy in Sheffield City Archives, GSG 21). The phrase 'individual effort' was of considerable importance to Miss Twelves and appeared in several of her leaflets and articles concerning her Lakeland work.

hand in Lakeland.[1]

However idealistic and impracticable such notions may have been at the peak of industrialisation, the Langdale Linen Industry succeeded admirably as an example of the revival of a village industry. Initially, the Guild probably provided assistance in covering the costs of rent and materials, and the Industry was one of the very few Guild-related art and craft projects to thrive. The choice of Lakeland as the site of a revival, and its particularly potent textile history, however, had as much to do with its success as its Ruskin foundation, as did its associated literary traditions. The links between the Industry and Wordsworth were never lost amidst the drive for artistic and commercial success. Ruskin's admiration for, and frequent references to, the poet added fuel to Fleming's desire to revive the local spinning wheels, even affecting his choice of Elterwater as a suitable site for a workshop. Wordsworth's lament over the demise of the wheels then appeared in virtually every account of the Industry by Fleming.[2] In 1889, in *Songs of the Spindle and Legends of the Loom*, he gave a similar account of the early days of the Industry which included further references to the role played by 'Wordsworth's sonnets and Mr Ruskin's eloquent appeals in *Fors*' in his work.[3] Produced entirely by hand, bound in Langdale linen, and with flax paper, the book also included Wordsworth's *Spinning Song* and *Sonnet*, along with other writings appropriate to the spinning wheel.

More specifically, a concentrated effort was made to use old spinning wheels traditional to Westmorland, or copies of the traditional Westmorland wheels (some of which were later made by Arthur W. Simpson of Kendal), and a new loom was made in imitation of the Westmorland loom given to the Industry in its early days. How precisely such wheels and looms differed from those used outside Lakeland is not entirely clear. But Fleming and Marian Twelves, and later Annie Garnett of The Spinnery, were always most specific that they were using traditional Westmorland wheels and looms, or direct copies. Based in a traditional seventeenth-century Westmorland cottage (rather than a purpose-built mill like Laxey), and adhering to local practices in linen production, including bleaching by 'the pure mountain air and sunshine', the Industry promoted every aspect of Lakeland, even using the local environment as a design source.[4]

---

[1] Cook, *Studies*, 161.

[2] e.g. the *Standard*, 30 Oct. 1883, and the *Pall Mall Gazette*, 8 Feb. 1886.

[3] Warner, *Songs*, 15.

[4] Ibid., 7.

Socially too the Langdale Linen Industry had a role to play. To Fleming, the restoration of the wheels at Elterwater helped to bridge the gap wrought by mechanisation between the generations. In Lakeland the demise of the wheels had left a generation of women unable to spin, and forced a break in what had been for centuries a sustained tradition of passing on the local craft of spinning flax from mother to daughter. At St Martin's, mothers and daughters, and even grandmothers, were once again working side by side, and traditional Westmorland domestic life had been partially and temporarily restored. The linen produced was once more passed on through the generations as 'treasured'[1] family heirlooms which, according to Fleming, 'rust and moth could not corrupt'.[2]

Had attempts to reintroduce flax growing in Lakeland been successful, the Langdale Linen Industry might have returned local textile production to its full original status as a family industry in which all the members took part in the various processes. As it was, the first stage could not be revived, the flax was imported from Ireland, and only the local women were employed by the Industry in any numbers. In the case of weaving, which was formerly done by men, the Industry appears never to have employed more than two weavers at its peak, with the women carrying out some of the weaving themselves.[3] There was never any question of employing the number of men once associated with old-fashioned spinning in the Lake District. Inventories made before 1800 suggest that some Lakeland cottagers, particularly farmers, grew their own flax and owned a spinning wheel and loom, and so were able to complete all the processes involved in linen production themselves. In other instances, certain villages had an allotted weaver or weavers who would carry out the task for them. How many could actually be classed as employed as weavers is not clear. But, given the area's strong textile tradition, the number would have been significant for the Lakeland area.[4]

The revival of linen production by hand had a new significance for Lakeland not contemplated by previous generations of Westmerians. With the growth of industry in the nineteenth century, the threat of environmental pollution had begun to rear its head, even in Lakeland. As a Ruskin disciple, Fleming had already read of his mentor's concern at the polluting of the Derwent, and of the waters at Coniston being

---

[1] Fleming, *House of Rimmon*, 7.

[2] Cook, *Studies*, 171.

[3] J. Satchell, *The Kendal Weaver* (Kendal Civic Society, 1986), 49–50.

[4] Mr John Dawson, author of *Torver* (Chichester, 1985), kindly passed on information concerning the local textile industry. Spinning wheels, wool, hemp, frames and woollen wheels were common household items from at least the 1680s.

'seriously diminished in purity and health' by waste from the copper mines.[1] Having also already expressed his own concern in 1873 that no one knew how to use aright 'God's free gifts' of 'fresh sweet air, green grass and herbs of earth, or bright sunlight and open sky', Fleming was only too aware of the environmental risks involved in the further spread of industry in Lakeland.[2] The best way to minimise the risks was to abandon all unsound practices in linen production which might pollute the region's land and water, and replace them with 'God's free gifts' (for example, by sun bleaching linen). The rejection of machines was to become a particularly potent symbol of Fleming's life in Lakeland, and his concern for the preservation of the region took other forms, chiefly in taking up Ruskin's fight against local railways. Immediately on his arrival at Neaum Crag in 1883, Fleming had become acquainted with Canon Hardwicke Rawnsley, another Lakeland Ruskin devotee whose work in reviving local arts and crafts is discussed later. Under Ruskin's influence, Rawnsley instigated a series of Lakeland railway opposition campaigns, beginning with the proposed Buttermere to Braithwaite line in 1883. Ruskin offered written support, and Fleming pledged his help, becoming honorary secretary of the Borrowdale and Derwentwater Defence Fund, despite his frequent absences from the region on business. This defence work continued throughout much of Fleming's forty years in Lakeland and, as an associated aspect of the Lakeland revival, became yet another trait which marked the district's separateness. The protection of the pre-industrial Lakeland landscape ran hand in hand with the revival of those ancient arts and crafts once practised within that landscape.

Although Ruskin remained less optimistic about the possibility of halting the spread of the Lakeland railways, and even regarded the Guild of St George as (somewhat pessimistically) 'mere raft-making amidst irrevocable wreck', he always maintained a most positive as well as supportive attitude towards the Langdale Linen Industry.[3] Throughout its first seventeen years, whenever his health permitted, he played a direct as well as theoretical part in its founding and running. It must be said that his initial enthusiasm when Fleming first broached the idea of reviving the Westmorland spinning wheels was important in encouraging Fleming to put his thoughts into action. Ruskin was consulted on the detail of realising his theories whenever possible, and between 1883 and

---

[1] *Works*, xxvi. 122, extract from *Deucalion*.

[2] Fleming, *House of Rimmon*, 10.

[3] *Works*, xxviii. 264, extract from Letter L of *Fors Clavigera*.

1888 Fleming visited Brantwood frequently. Ruskin also sent letters to Fleming, some containing messages of support and approval, others thanks for gifts of linen—or 'love gifts' as Ruskin described them—sent to Brantwood.[1] Whether Ruskin actually visited St Martin's remains open to question, although it seems likely that he would have at some stage in the early days; but he certainly visited Fleming's home (the 'Dark Tower of Neaum' as he called it), detailing some of those visits in his diary.[2] On 30 April 1885 he recorded: 'Yesterday delicious afternoon at Albert Fleming's. Never saw Langdale so lovely', the Langdales being the backdrop to Neaum Crag.[3] On 26 May 1886 he wrote:

> This bad languor on me bothers and frightens me, always glad to lie on sofa or go to bed. Yet walked well with Albert F. in afternoon of real blue sky for once, (yesterday), and showed him things.[4]

This particular extract suggests not only something of the paternal role of Ruskin in Fleming's life, but that the real difficulty was Ruskin's deteriorating health. At times, he was completely unable to take any part in Fleming's and Miss Twelves's work: early in March 1886, for example, Marian Twelves called at Brantwood, but Ruskin was too ill to receive her. On 28 April 1888, however, he was well enough to send her his love via a letter to Fleming.[5] As a result, there were periods of apparently no communication with Fleming or Miss Twelves, and other periods in which numerous letters were exchanged on almost trivial matters. This indicates something of the variable state of Ruskin's mental and physical health. This is not to suggest that his presence in Lakeland grew any less important to the Langdale Linen Industry, since papers belonging to the Industry from the years of Ruskin's illness (which worsened markedly after 1889) show only the ever-constant value of the writer as both theoretical source and close presence.

Although Fleming initially acted as a 'go between' and a more heuristic influence, consulting Ruskin in person and then passing on

[1] YUBL, Ruskin to Fleming, 2 Aug. 1884.

[2] YUBL, Ruskin to Fleming, 20 March 1886, in which he calls Fleming's home the 'Dark Tower of Neaum'.

[3] J. Evans and J.H. Whitehouse (ed.), *The Diaries of John Ruskin, 1874–1889* (1959), 1107.

[4] Ibid., 1128.

[5] YUBL, Ruskin to Fleming, 28 April 1888.

advice to Marian Twelves, from 1884 Miss Twelves struck up her own friendship with Ruskin, and began to seek advice directly from him. Whether their first meeting at Susanna Beever's home in 1884 was accidental or engineered is not clear. But from then on she became an ever more devout Ruskinian, calling at Brantwood, writing to Ruskin, developing a friendship with his second cousin Joan Agnew Severn (1846–1924), living strictly by the laws of the Guild of St George, reading *Fors Clavigera* (upon which much of her work in Lakeland was based), and continuing her friendship with Miss Beever, whom all of Ruskin's Lakeland circle admired. The depth of her devotion, and the place of Ruskin in her life and work, was perhaps best perceived by Canon Rawnsley who in 1901 wrote of his much admired colleague and her spinning industry:

> But what had Ruskin to do with this work? He had everything to do with it. It was the kindly message sent now and again of heartfelt thanks to his tireless worker, it was the handshake and the 'thank you, thank you,' and the smile of his face whence the faithlessness of lack of obedience of others had driven the smile, that encouraged her as it encouraged others to determine to carry out the known wishes of the Master and to do what in her was possible while health and strength were hers to add to the mind's content of her friend and teacher.[1]

More important still, as a result of Ruskin's direct guidance and influence, in the late 1880s Marian Twelves was inspired to create a new form of linen decoration which emphasised the Linen Industry's independence and uniqueness, and complimented Ruskin's own interest in textiles.[2]

With the successful introduction of embroidery at St Martin's, other possibilities in textile decoration soon became apparent. Elsewhere, traditional handmade lace was already enjoying something of a revival, for example, at Paulerspury and elsewhere in Northamptonshire. The Paulerspury industry was revived in 1880 by Isabella Harrison, the wife of the rector. She sought to provide suitable employment for women, making lace which was sold through the Ladies' Work Society in Sloane Street, London, and elsewhere. Like the Langdale Industry, Paulerspury

---

[1] Rawnsley, *Ruskin*, 144.

[2] Hereafter the term Langdale Linen Industry is also abbreviated to the Linen Industry.

was supported by Princess Louise.[1] Lacking any knowledge of the art of traditional lace making, however, Marian Twelves attempted (most successfully) to create her own form of decoration which she named Ruskin lace in honour of her mentor. In design terms Ruskin lace was an important step which gave the Linen Industry an even stronger independent identity, taking the linen further beyond its original use and contributing to the Industry's reputation as an 'art' industry. As with the embroidery, the exact date of its creation and commercial introduction is not clear, but appears to have been 1889 or just before. The lace combined a number of techniques including drawn thread work, needleweaving and embroidering with flax thread, either worked directly onto the linen or made into strips of varying widths and complexity of design which were added as edgings.

To begin with, the patterns and designs used were based on traditional Sicilian and Greek laces which were probably lent by Ruskin from his textile collection, as contemporary catalogues, which contain descriptions of several pieces of Ruskin lace whose designs were directly copied from textiles lent by Ruskin, indicate.[2] But it was also probable that, given Ruskin's associated interest in drawing textiles and dress patterns, he also lent some of his drawings to Miss Twelves to use as inspiration. If that was the case, it would add weight to the argument that what occurred in Lakeland between 1880 and 1920 was unique, and depended heavily not only on Ruskin's writings but on his actual presence and direct contribution.

Because Ruskin lace was inspired by, among other things, Sicilian and Greek laces and embroidery, it also acquired the name Greek lace. Present-day Ruskin lace maker Elizabeth Prickett believes that the 'Greek' title was sometimes used to make the lace more commercially desirable outside Lakeland.[3] Since the technique of Ruskin lace making was an entirely original invention, however, there appeared to be few hard and fast rules established for the workers to abide by, and their individual creativity was given more opportunity to develop. How many additional women were originally employed to make the lace is not clear; but Miss Twelves provided the initial tuition, and later ran a special class in 'Greek lace' for five years at Coniston at the expense of the Guild of

---

[1] *VCH Northants.*, v. 271.

[2] Ruskin Museum, Coniston, annual exhibition catalogues, 1900–19.

[3] Elizabeth Prickett is the author of *Ruskin Lace and Linen Work* (1985), a manual devoted to the techniques and designs of Ruskin lace. Her views on the naming of Ruskin lace as 'Greek' lace were passed directly to me.

St George.[1] Like the embroidery, lace making was undoubtedly a time consuming activity, but one which quickly began to develop its own identity, with individual workers becoming skilled and proficient enough to introduce their own designs and techniques. At the same time, traditional designs suggested by Ruskin were also used. Each lace maker was encouraged to keep a notebook recording her designs, and was permitted to introduce additional techniques such as crochet.

Because of the nature of the lace, which was built up on a basic grid of threads constructed on the linen by each individual worker and then executed to her own particular tension, and given the individual preferences expressed by each worker for certain patterns and techniques, no two pieces of Ruskin lace ever turned out quite the same. Mass production, therefore, was never possible, and any attempt to produce the lace by machine was liable to eradicate the very individuality on which it clearly thrived. The name Ruskin lace was not merely a selling ploy but an apt description of something which, in essence, represented Ruskin's support of anti-mechanisation and individual creativity. Unlike Devon, Buckinghamshire, Nottinghamshire and other counties, the Lake counties had no history of lace making, yet they clearly took to it with great skill and aplomb, and began a tradition which is still practised today by a few dedicated individuals. Since Laxey concentrated chiefly on cloth production in a water-powered mill, it never developed any form of textile decoration such as Ruskin lace, and (despite their shared Ruskin and Guild of St George origins) never attempted to adopt lace making.

Much of the success of the Langdale Linen Industry clearly lay in Marian Twelves's natural ability to realise the written word, her practical skills amazing even Ruskin at times:

> Dear Miss Twelves, It is terribly difficult for me to understand how the more or less visionary talk of my books can have been of use to a mind so practically and cheerfully strong as yours. But I am deeply thankful in my wonder that it has been so.[2]

Whatever her formal artistic shortcomings, she had a natural ability to digest and interpret Ruskin's often complex writings, and a keen

---

[1] Twelves, *Ruskin Linen Industry*, 7.

[2] Sheffield Archives, GSG 21, Ruskin to Miss Twelves, 16 Jan. 1884. Miss Twelves has added a note to the letter stating that it was the first she received from Ruskin. Presumably the letter would have been sent after their first meeting at Susanna Beever's home, which would place that meeting in early January.

judgement for good, basic design. By 1889 that discretion had resulted in the Langdale Linen Industry producing an even wider range of goods, some decorated with embroidery, and others with Ruskin lace, sometimes with the addition of natural dyes. Generally, however, the linen was most often used in its natural colour, and was rarely decorated with lace and embroidery together, or in any way overworked or over ambitiously designed. Diversity might have increased, but simplicity was always observed, lavishness being a trait of Victorian decadence not recommended by either Ruskin or the Industry. Goods for sale also included pincushions, bedspreads, napkins, doyleys, sideboard cloths, slippers, book covers, children's pinafores, various mats and other items of clothing such as linen dresses, modesty vests and dress collars, the last two of which often included a combination of more traditional decorative techniques such as bobbin lace or finer Ruskin lace. The linen dresses were available either plain—the linen having been bleached outdoors—or dyed. The dyeing was done by Harris's of Cockermouth and later by Pullar's of Perth. There are also indications that, under Marian Twelves's influence, the Industry moved into another area of Lakeland's traditional textile past—the production of woollen cloths using wool from the sheep on nearby Wetherlam. Some production of silks also appears to have been carried out on a small scale.

In terms of business acumen Fleming played a considerable part in ensuring the Langdale Linen Industry's success over the first six years of its life. From 1885 both he and Miss Twelves sent samples of the Industry's work to a range of exhibitions, local, national and later international. Having used newspapers and journals to publicise his work from 1883, Fleming was determined to use every other possible mode of publicity to draw attention to what was happening in Elterwater in the name of Ruskin. One of the earliest exhibitions attended was held at a 'Miss Calder's', address not stated (presumably local), at which exhibits listed in the Industry's papers included '2 squares, 1 yard, 1 Embroidered Tea Cloth' (which confirms that embroidery had been introduced by 1885).[1] In the same year, two squares of linen appeared in an 'Ambleside exhibition'.[2] More significantly, in 1885 the Linen Industry became affiliated to the Home Arts and Industries Association and began to show work on a regular basis at its annual exhibition, begun that year. Founded in about 1884, the association aimed to revive

---

[1] CROK, WDB 73/3, WDB 73/5.
[2] Ibid.

the lost industries and crafts of our villages, and to interest townspeople in the art of making things comely as well as useful. It aspires to restore to the average British workman certain qualities of which the introduction of machinery has almost deprived him; to impart again deftness of touch to awaken his personal interest in fine handicraft; to turn the mere mechanic into an expert artisan, from whose ranks in time new geniuses may be expected to rise.[1]

The association believed that if this was achieved it would make England 'again a nation of skilled craftsmen' and 'effect the artistic regeneration' of the country, which was particularly compatible with Ruskin's beliefs.[2] With its London base, the Home Arts proved to be an excellent national showcase not only for the Langdale Linen Industry, but for the many other village industries operating elsewhere around the country by 1885.

By 1887 Miss Twelves had advanced to sending 'a spinning wheel and an operator' to Arthur W. Simpson's second exhibition, held at his woodcarving workshop in Finkle Street, Kendal.[3] Several items of embroidered linen were also on display on that occasion. Simpson, another Lakeland Ruskin devotee, established his own exhibition of local art and craft work in 1886, which became a particularly important and early local showcase for much of what was produced in Lakeland under Ruskin's direct and indirect influence. In 1891 Langdale linens appeared at the Kendal Arts, Crafts and Loan Exhibition, the most ambitious exhibition held in south Lakeland in the late nineteenth century which, given its scale and significance as a display of local, and in some instances revived, arts and crafts, is treated in detail in Chapter 12. Linens made at St Martin's were known as Langdale linens, but over the years also acquired the general names Lakeland linens and Ruskin linens. However, as Rawnsley noted in 1890, 'Whether the linen is called Ruskin linen or anything else matters little, it will outlast the lives of patrons and promoters'.[4] As with Fleming, the durability and quality of the fabrics took priority. Between 1901 and 1918 linens from St Martin's also appeared at the annual Coniston exhibition. For example, in 1908 some twenty items including pin-cushions, purse-bags, chairbacks and

---

[1] *The Studio*, July 1897, 109. The Home Arts and Industries Association is also referred to hereafter as the Home Arts.

[2] *The Studio*, Aug. 1895, 168.

[3] *Westmorland Gazette*, 28 May 1887.

[4] Sheffield Archives, GSG 21, *The Keswick School of Industrial Arts and Ruskin Linen Industry*, leaflet reprinted from the *Oxford University Extension Gazette*, Aug. 1890.

tray cloths adorned with Ruskin lace were shown by the Langdale Linen Industry.[1] Organised chiefly by Ruskin's secretary, W.G. Collingwood, who had important ties with the revival of Lakeland arts and crafts, the Coniston exhibition was held in the local Institute. Although the first and last were devoted solely to Ruskin, exhibitions held between those years were used to display not only locally made textiles, but all local art and craft work then being produced as a direct and indirect result of Ruskin's presence in Lakeland.

---

[1] Ruskin Museum, Coniston, *Catalogue of the Ninth Annual Exhibition* (1908).

3

ALBERT FLEMING
AND JOHN RUSKIN

Between 1883 and 1889, as Marian Twelves became more committed to her realisation of Ruskin's writings, and spent most of her time at Elterwater teaching new spinsters and embroiderers, preparing for exhibitions, developing Ruskin lace, and holding spinster tea parties, Fleming was increasingly drawn into Ruskin's life at Brantwood. Since he had spent at least ten years communicating with him by letter, and a further number of years consulting him in person on the minute details of the founding and running of the Linen Industry, it was only to be expected that Fleming would become part of what he himself described as an 'inner circle' which represented Ruskin's later years in Lakeland, at the centre of which were Ruskin and Susanna Beever.[1] Indications that Fleming was connected with a privileged circle which surrounded Brantwood also exist in the comment made in 1923 that 'For the last 40 years Neaum Crag has been the home of the late MR. ALBERT FLEMING, the well known litterateur and savant, who was one of the artistic inner circle gathered round the late John Ruskin, with whom he was in intimate relations, both direct and in correspondence'.[2] This aptly expresses the nature of the relationship between Fleming and Ruskin, as one of a rather 'enclosed' or intense sort.

Included in that circle were Edith and Hardwicke Rawnsley, W.G. Collingwood, his wife Dorrie (1851–1928) and their four children, and Joan Severn and her husband, the artist Arthur Severn (1842–1931), who lived at Brantwood with their daughters Lily and Violet. Aside from his work with the Linen Industry, and his role in supporting Rawnsley in his Lakeland preservation campaigns, in 1887 Fleming took on the task of editing Ruskin's letters to the Beever sisters (Mary (1802–83) and Susanna), to whom the writer was devoted. The resulting volume, *Hortus*

---

[1] A. Fleming (ed.), *Hortus Inclusus* (1887), p. xi.

[2] Armitt Library, Ambleside, Sale Catalogue (1923). 'Gathered round' is presumably used in a geographic as well as intellectual sense.

Inclusus (1887), was the product of much correspondence between Fleming and his mentor, and was a revealing study not only of Ruskin's associations with the Beevers, but of the editor's devotion to Ruskin. In February 1887 Fleming made a number of visits to The Thwaite to talk to his 'dear friend Miss Beever' (Susanna) and to examine the two thousand or so letters Ruskin had written to her and her sister. These he described as 'the fruit of the most beautiful friendship', a friendship which was 'so sacred in all' that he could give it only 'the praise of silence'.[1]

The sub-title of Fleming's volume gives enough indication that Ruskin found great solace in corresponding with the Beevers, *Hortus Inclusus* being 'Messages From the Wood to the Garden, Sent in Happy Days to the Sister Ladies of The Thwaite, Coniston, by Their Thankful Friend John Ruskin, LL.D.'.[2] It also indicates the rather 'enclosed' nature of life around Brantwood in the 1880s, and of the close nature of the involvement with Ruskin which marked Fleming's life—and the lives of all those directly involved with the revival of local arts and crafts—in Lakeland. Just as significantly, Ruskin's preface to the volume reveals the high esteem in which he then held Fleming, awarding him the title 'my Master of the Rural Industries', a title awarded to no other.[3] At that time, despite recurring mental illness, he clearly still held a deep respect for the younger man, showing his faith in Fleming as the leader of the revival of rural industries in Lakeland, trusting him enough, as a result, to give him free access to what were some of his most intensely personal letters to two of his closest friends. On the other hand *Hortus Inclusus* attracted criticism from other Ruskinians, including E.T. Cook, who attacked Fleming's editing skills and suggested that the letters should not have been published. In fact *Hortus Inclusus* ran to three editions. That unquestioning trust was a feature of all Fleming's Lakeland Ruskinian activities, and was generally representative of the privileged friendship afforded to Fleming which encouraged him to continue, along with Rawnsley, his caretaking of Lakeland. In *Hortus Inclusus* he returned the compliment to Ruskin:

> Here my pleasant share in this little book would have ended, but Mr Ruskin has desired me to add a few words giving my own

---

[1] *Hortus Inclusus*, p. xii; the HLC has 526 letters from Ruskin to Susanna Beever.

[2] *Hortus Inclusus*, title page.

[3] Ibid., p. ix. Ruskin never awarded Miss Twelves the title 'my Mistress of the Rural Industries'.

description of Susie, and speaking of my relationship to them both. To him I owe the guidance of my life,—all its best impulses, all its worthiest efforts; to her some of its happiest hours, and the blessings alike of incentive and reproof.[1]

Once a doubting solicitor who had experienced a sudden realisation that his lifelong pursuits of 'money-getting and working useless work' were no longer his life's aims, Fleming had finally found through Ruskin personal satisfaction in what he did.[2] In withdrawing to his 'quiet inlet' of Neaum Crag, he had found the contentment and reward of doing something to 'benefit the community', and of leaving something both practical and literary which would be 'memorable and useful to posterity'.[3] That satisfaction and contentment, however, was to be severely tested in 1887, and again in 1889, when two unexpected and significant changes occurred in Fleming's life, both of which were to affect not only his perception of Ruskin, and his work in Lakeland, but the direction of the revival of the local wheels.

The purchase of Brantwood in 1871 had marked something of a turning point in Ruskin's life in a number of ways, not least in that it prompted the sequence of events (beginning with Fleming's arrival at Neaum Crag) which would eventually lead to the revival of Lakeland arts and crafts. One of his prime motivations for buying the property from the poet and wood engraver W.J. Linton (for £1,500) was his conviction that his first serious bout of mental illness would improve if he could only 'lie down' at Coniston. As Collingwood wrote:

> During the illness at Matlock his (Ruskin's) thoughts reverted to the old *Iteriad* times of forty years before, when he had travelled with his parents and cousin Mary from that same New Bath Hotel, where he was now lying, to the Lakes; and again he 'wearied for the heights that look down upon the dale'. 'The crags are lone on Coniston.' If he could only lie down here, he said, he should get well again.[4]

After 1871 Ruskin experienced spasmodic recurring bouts of the illness, which appeared to worsen as he aged. Both before and after his

---

[1] *Hortus Inclusus*, p. xii.

[2] A. Fleming, *In the House of Rimmon* (1873), 20.

[3] Ibid., 16.

[4] W.G. Collingwood, *The Life and Work of John Ruskin* (1893), ii. 112.

death, the nature and origins of that illness provoked much debate, although its exact roots and medical classification are still unclear. In Lakeland, too, debate over Ruskin's exact condition took place. In 1933 R.H. Wilenski suggested that he 'was the lifelong victim of a neurosis which made him oscillate continually and with increasing intensity between moods of elation and self-abasement, and finally overthrew him'.[1] Ruskin himself occasionally attributed his illness to foods he had eaten.[2] Around June 1883, shortly after Fleming arrived at Neaum Crag, Ruskin began to describe his 'broken health' and its effects in letters to the young solicitor.[3] Even during the worst of his illness, however, he was often able to express some sense of gladness in receiving Fleming's replies, and able to indicate his appreciation of the revival of the Lakeland spinning wheels: 'Though my broken health nearly forbids all former correspondence, I am glad to have your letter and to hear what thoroughly good service you have set yourself'.[4]

Possibly as a result of that worsening mental state, in 1887 a serious disagreement occurred between Ruskin and the Severns which resulted in the former temporarily leaving Brantwood. Two schools of thought exist over the 1887 episode, the first suggesting that the anger Ruskin felt towards Joan Severn in particular was the direct result of his mental instability,[5] the second that a complete vindication of the Severns is also not appropriate.[6] When Fleming became embroiled in the disagreement he clearly took the latter view and offered unstinting support to his mentor.

On Whit Monday 1887 Ruskin wrote to Fleming: 'I know you would do all you could for me—but there is nothing whatever to be done—except to get the Severns out of my house—which Joan being ill—of her own rage & shame mostly I believe—I can't yet effect by police force'.[7] As a result of this and subsequent letters, Fleming readily accepted that Ruskin's grievance against the Severns was justified, and with his help Ruskin moved into a local inn before taking rooms at the home of Kate

---

[1] *Westmorland Gazette*, 22 July 1933.

[2] J. Evans and J.H. Whitehouse (ed.), *The Diaries of John Ruskin, 1874–1889* (1959), 872–3.

[3] YUBL, Ruskin to Fleming, 26 June 1883.

[4] Ibid.

[5] J. Hayman, 'John Ruskin's *Hortus Inclusus*: the manuscript sources and publication history', *Huntington Library Quarterly*, lii (1989), 363–87.

[6] B. Maidment, 'Ruskin, *Fors Clavigera* and Ruskinism, 1870–1900', in Robert Hewison (ed.), *New Approaches to Ruskin* (1981), 194–213.

[7] YBUL, Ruskin to Fleming, Whit Monday 1887.

Raven, who had once been housekeeper at Brantwood, on 5 June 1887. On that day he wrote to Fleming: 'I have not a friend left now ... If ever you had a solemn duty laid on you in your life it is to stay by me now, & trust me, and help me'.[1] Fleming evidently never questioned his mentor's behaviour and certainly never contemplated withdrawing his support when it was needed. Whether he was blinded by admiration and failed to see the truth of his condition is not clear. But the solicitor became his closest ally at this time, staying with him on 6 June 1887, after which Ruskin wrote: 'I deeply thank you for staying, I have not often asked a friend for help—though perhaps I might on reflection feel that I had received more than I know. But your support and advice are at present vital to me'.[2] This particular letter marked a significant turning point in their friendship, as Ruskin—for perhaps the first time—began to depend on Fleming. By the close of June 1887 Ruskin was back at Brantwood and all letters to Fleming returned to a discussion of *Hortus Inclusus* which by December 1887 was selling well.

Although Ruskin staged other walk-outs at Brantwood and at times became somewhat aggressive towards the Severns, the 1887 dispute was probably the point at which Fleming's first doubts regarding Ruskin began to surface. Whatever its basis, the incident would have been unpleasant and disturbing for Fleming, and one which perhaps chipped his previously untarnished view of Brantwood as the font of all right knowledge presided over by an impeccable authority who had guided his successful revival of the spinning wheels. On 26 May 1888 he wrote what was probably one of his last letters to Ruskin, adding:

> My thoughts often go back to the troublous times of last May, I have not seen you since then, but if I never saw you again please never doubt but that I hold you in *absolute* faith and love, though all the service I may render you is 'to stand & wait'
> Now and Always
> Your Grateful & Loving
> Albert Fleming[3]

Whether Ruskin replied to the letter is not certain, but correspondence between the two men appears to have ended shortly afterwards, in July that year, and Fleming clearly had not visited Brantwood since the

---

[1] YUBL, Ruskin to Fleming, 5 June 1887.

[2] YUBL, Ruskin to Fleming, 6 June 1887.

[3] HLC, Fleming to Ruskin, 26 May 1888.

previous June. The letter itself suggests a considerable amount of sadness on Fleming's part over previous events, with the seriousness of Ruskin's condition perhaps finally being perceived, along with the realisation that the days of close contact had come to an end.

In choosing to side with Ruskin in 1887 Fleming probably severely strained his relationship with the Severns, which would have made visits to Brantwood difficult. By contrast, Marian Twelves's visits increased in number and frequency, and her friendship with Joan Severn strengthened. Having kept firmly out of the difficulties of 1887 (to which she never alluded), her perception of Ruskin remained wholly unshaken, and she became further committed to the realisation of his theories. Such was her devotion to Ruskin's teachings that, when Fleming questioned her methods in 1889, provoking a dispute, she immediately resigned from St Martin's and headed for Keswick, fully supported by Mrs Severn. There, she offered her services to the Rawnsleys who, by 1889, were running the equally successful Keswick School of Industrial Arts along similarly strict Ruskinian lines. The exact cause of the disagreement with Fleming, and the extent of its severity, were apparently never committed to paper, but some time later Miss Twelves wrote of her departure:

> In 1889, I took my work to Keswick in the hope of obtaining more independence and reliable support in carrying out what I considered (and still consider) to be Mr Ruskin's economic principles, and to obtain a wider influence for the work—*not* to make it a larger industry with an unmanageable number of workers under my own control, but to more firmly establish in the scope within my power of concentration and distribution an example of what may be accomplished by individual effort, *not* how many yards of linen may be made and sold, but how what is done may influence and help the doers within these limits, and be the means of inspiring others to similar effort beyond them.[1]

The difference of opinion was associated with some divergence from Ruskin's teachings. Fleming tried to capitalise on the Linen Industry's success either by taking on more workers or by requesting that more linen be produced, or both. To Marian Twelves, who (unlike Fleming) was still in close contact with Ruskin, the focal point of the Industry was the strict observation of Ruskin's theories. She was concerned solely

---

[1] M. Twelves, *The Ruskin Linen Industry* (*c*.1900), 5 (copy in Sheffield City Archives, GSG 21).

with her workers and what they produced, not with creating a larger commercial enterprise. The pursuit of Mammon and the growth of her industry at the expense of her personal control ran too close to all that Ruskin rejected, and she felt compelled to leave Elterwater. For Fleming commercialism had finally superseded work ethics and he had paid the price.

Miss Twelves's departure must have been another blow to Fleming and a potential disaster for St Martin's, yet for the revival of local arts and crafts the move was ultimately beneficial. In the meantime, St Martin's was taken over by Elizabeth Pepper, one of its longest serving and most accomplished spinsters. Under her guidance the workshop continued successfully, showing linens at various local and national exhibitions (including the Home Arts Exhibition), and also winning international acclaim at the 1893 World's Columbian Exposition in Chicago.[1] Although she lacked some of Marian Twelves's drive and determination, Mrs Pepper was still running St Martin's commercially in the 1920s, having moved it to nearby Tilberthwaite around 1907. While still known as the Langdale Linen Industry and still run according to Ruskin's teachings, by 1910 it consisted mostly of Mrs Pepper, Mrs Nelson and Mrs Fell. As late as 1928 Mrs Pepper was still receiving letters from dedicated customers requesting Langdale linen, which helped to ensure that the revival of the spinning wheels around Elterwater lasted for at least 45 years—considerably longer than at Laxey.[2] Mrs Pepper was also instrumental in ensuring that Ruskin lace making was continued at St Martin's and later Tilberthwaite, with a number of her former workers continuing to make lace in their own homes after the Industry ceased to run commercially. The number of women involved with the Langdale Linen Industry began to decrease around 1905, the result not so much of workers losing interest and leaving Mrs Pepper's employment (which they seemed rarely to do), but of deaths, retirement, or removal from the area when their husbands found work elsewhere. Most of the workforce at Elterwater had consisted of older women, some of whom had by 1905 served the Industry for a considerable number of years. Unable to attract sufficient new recruits after 1900, and having lost its main practical driving force (Marian Twelves) in 1889, the Elterwater Industry began to lose its fight against mechanisation and went into a slow decline. Once again, the traditional skills of hand spinning and

---

[1] Abbot Hall Art Gallery and Museum, Kendal, has a framed certificate awarded to Mrs Pepper for exhibits of Langdale linen shown at the 1893 World's Columbian Exposition held in Chicago.

[2] CROK, WDB 73/19, Letters to Mrs Pepper concerning Langdale linen (1928).

weaving began to die out across Langdale, although the art of making Ruskin lace was never wholly lost and is still practised today on a much smaller scale. In restoring old traditions, Marian Twelves had created new traditions which are still to be found in Lakeland today.

After 1889 Fleming's involvement with the Langdale Linen Industry was minimal and he left Mrs Pepper largely to her own devices. For a short time he evidently felt some resentment towards Miss Twelves, and in at least two accounts of his work written immediately after her departure he stated that he himself had learnt the art of spinning and taught the workers, with the name Marian Twelves ominously omitted.[1] Similarly, in accounts of her work at St Martin's, written immediately after 1889, Miss Twelves omitted Fleming's name. One of the least biased contemporary accounts of the early Langdale Linen Industry was given by Rawnsley—a friend to both parties throughout—in his *Ruskin and the English Lakes* (1901).

After 1889 the Guild of St George also began to play a lesser role at St Martin's, perhaps because Mrs Pepper was not a Companion. How far her personal devotion to Ruskin stretched is open to debate, particularly since there are no accounts of her having any sustained contact with the writer. But her devotion to the continued realisation of his theories was faultless. No attempts were ever made to change the Industry's original format, and her commitment to the arts and crafts of hand spinning, weaving, embroidery and Ruskin lace making was total, postcards of her at work being sold at St Martin's in its later years.

By the time the Industry moved to Tilberthwaite, the Guild was almost certainly no longer offering any financial support, although it did have one important if indirect tie with the Guild during Mrs Pepper's time in the person of Joseph Southall (1861–1944). A member of the equally distinguished Art Workers' Guild and a nephew of George Baker, a member of the Guild of St George, in the early twentieth century Southall became widely known as a designer of Greek (Ruskin) lace. He was also involved with the Birmingham Group of artists and craftsmen and women, as well as being a co-founder of the Society of Painters in Tempera. His designs were worked chiefly by his mother, Eliza Maria Southall, who was probably taught by Mrs Pepper. Their work, seemingly always executed on what is described in exhibition catalogues as Langdale linen (sometimes bought from Harris & Sons Ltd of Cockermouth who dyed linens for the Linen Industry), appeared in a

---

[1] *Ruskin Reading Guild Journal*, no. 2 (Feb. 1889), 37; E.T. Cook, *Studies in Ruskin* (1890).

number of important national exhibitions. From 1900 samples appeared regularly at the Arts and Crafts Exhibitions in London and in 1904 at the Leicester Arts and Crafts Exhibition, as well as being discussed and illustrated a number of times in *The Studio* between 1900 and 1916. For example, in March 1906 a fire screen designed by Joseph Southall and executed by Mrs E.M. Southall, which was exhibited at the 1906 Arts and Crafts Exhibition at the Grafton Gallery, was illustrated.[1] Examples also appeared at the 1911 Second Exhibition of the Arts and Crafts in connection with the Society of Artists, an exhibition arranged to show that good craft work could be done in the city. Whilst the Southalls had no obvious ties with Lakeland, specimens of their work appeared in at least one of the Coniston exhibitions (1906) under the St Martin's name, which indicates some connection with Mrs Pepper and her workshop. There, they showed a chairback entitled 'St Catherine' (price £3 10s.) alongside linen and lace work executed by such local ladies as Kate Stanley, Abigail Pepper, Mrs Pepper, Mrs Fell, Olivia Milward and Christina Ward.[2] Mrs Pepper's work commanded comparatively high prices, which clearly helped to sustain the Industry's image as an art industry, and which saw Mrs Pepper invited to teach other less well known figures—including a small number of admirers from America—the art of Ruskin lace making. Despite the Southalls' involvement in Ruskin lace making, however, it remained strictly a trait of the revival of local arts and crafts in Lakeland, and one of the key features of Lakeland's individuality and separateness. The Southalls chose to use the name Greek lace away from Lakeland rather than Ruskin lace as it is still known locally.

Despite the fact that his regular visits to Brantwood were over by 1887, that his regular sending of letters to Ruskin had finished by 1888, and he had faced Marian Twelves's departure to Keswick in early 1889, Fleming still retained a marked degree of respect for Ruskin in his later years. Many of the letters sent by Ruskin between 1873 and 1888 were kept by Fleming until his death, one of which he fondly marked 'The first letter I ever had from JR'.[3] And he remained a Companion of the Guild of St George for the rest of his life. However, when Ruskin died

---

[1] *The Studio*, March 1904, p. 134.

[2] *Catalogue of the Seventh Annual Exhibition: Coniston Institute, 1906*, 16 (copy at Ruskin Museum, Coniston). There are unidentified pieces of linen and lace work at Abbot Hall Art Gallery and Museum, Kendal, which were probably executed by the Southalls. One piece in particular is strikingly similar to one of the Southalls' textiles which appeared at the Arts and Crafts Exhibition for 1903 (*The Studio* (Feb. 1903), 36).

[3] YUBL, Ruskin to Fleming, 29 Oct. 1873.

in January 1900 Fleming apparently was not among the mourners who attended the funeral at Coniston church, whereas several of his fellow Lakeland Ruskinian devotees, including Canon Rawnsley, W.G. Collingwood and Arthur Simpson, were. Shortly after, on 17 February 1900, Fleming's article 'John Ruskin: Some Personal Recollections' appeared in the *Daily News*. Among other things, he remarked on Ruskin's charm as a letter writer, and described Brantwood as a 'shrine'. Yet he also criticised such things as Ruskin's insistence that he would lunch with nobody but him at Neaum Crag, remarked that the wallpaper at Brantwood would have made William Morris 'turn in his grave', and noted that, whilst he admired the Guild of St George, he had been enrolled by Ruskin almost against his will:

> I admired the scheme as a profoundly interesting experiment, conceived on very noble lines, but I did not care to join formally. However, the Master enrolled me without consulting me, and I believe I am a Companion to this day.[1]

Of the Guild itself he wrote:

> the lawyers worried him (Ruskin) dreadfully even before the thing could be got on to its legs, then the accounts got into a horrible mess, and had to be taken in hand and straightened up by a Companion who happened to be an expert accountant; then some Companions proved to be backsliders, and were ignominiously cast forth; others developed an excess of enthusiasm, and lived on nuts and blackberries, and absolutely refused to use railways, even for correspondence, they wrote their letters, and then walked miles to deliver them; others gave up trades and occupations about which they knew everything, to cultivate and live on bits of land about which they knew nothing. Still the Guild had and has two excellent business men as trustees, and we always point with great pride to the beautiful Museum at Sheffield as a noble result. And whatever the difficulties were we never wavered in loyalty to the Master, nor in kindly fellowship amongst ourselves, and I think we were all of us better men and women for dreaming that beautiful dream, and aiming at the impossible.[2]

---

[1] *Daily News*, 17 Feb. 1900, p. 6.

[2] Ibid.

After 1900 his unquestioning devotion to Ruskin had clearly faded and in its place Fleming experienced an uncertain and changeable attitude towards the man who had once inspired him to make such radical changes in his life. Following a succession of disappointments, a certain sense of resigned maturity crept into his view of the writer, but the realisation that Ruskin was not the infallible being he had once believed him to be came comparatively late to Fleming. By contrast, W.G. Collingwood recognised comparatively early on that Ruskin was by no means 'an infallible authority' but was nevertheless 'a great teacher' because 'he took you by the hand as he went on his voyage of discovery through the world'.[1] To tarnish further Fleming's slightly dulled image of Ruskin, his plans to expand *Hortus Inclusus*—the literary symbol of his years in Lakeland with Ruskin—after his mentor's death were firmly quashed by Ruskin's literary executors, the general view being that the original volume had not only been poorly edited, but had revealed deeply personal aspects of the writer which should have remained undisclosed.[2]

On a more positive note, out of his earlier devotion to Ruskin, Fleming developed a deep and sustained love of the Lake District. Like Ruskin, he revelled in the rural seclusion of his home, and retired permanently to Neaum Crag around 1903 (when he probably bought the property). Indeed, it was his love for the region and for nature which occupied his mind most after 1900, and he spent a total of almost 40 years fighting to protect south Lakeland from railways and other unwelcome invaders. When he died in March 1923 an associate wrote of Fleming and Neaum Crag:

> The beautiful woodland grounds around it [Neaum Crag], carpeted with daffodils, hyacinths and hare-bells in their seasons, teeming with the harmless wild things which he [Fleming] lovingly watched and protected, and presenting in themselves, or in their immediate neighbourhood, every charm of Lakeland scenery, were a constant and ever increasing delight to him and through him to very many others.[3]

Like his mentor, Fleming encouraged others to share what he was fortunate enough to enjoy and entertained many friends and acquaintances at his Lakeland retreat. Among his acquaintances were the Revd

---

[1] W.G. Collingwood, *Ruskin Relics* (1903), 11.

[2] Hayman, 'John Ruskin's *Hortus Inclusus*'.

[3] *Westmorland Gazette*, 31 March 1923.

W. Tuckwell, Dr Martineau and W.E. Gladstone. He also corresponded with, among others, Douglas Cockerell, Walter Crane and T.J. Cobden-Sanderson. But also like Ruskin, Fleming had no direct heirs, and after he died Neaum Crag was auctioned, along with its contents. Fleming was an exceptionally well read man, and he occasionally discussed books with Ruskin. The first day of the sale of the contents of Neaum Crag included 473 volumes. Among them were editions of Matthew Arnold, Walter Raleigh, J.H. Newman, Thomas Carlyle, Mrs Oliphant, George Herbert, Dante, Browning, Tennyson, Disraeli, Spenser, Rossetti, Emily Lawless, Walt Whitman, Tolstoy, George Meredith, Zola, Kipling, Coleridge, Walpole, H.G. Wells, Charles Kingsley, Oliver Lodge, H.D. Rawnsley, W. Tuckwell, Thackeray, W.G. Collingwood, E.T. Cook, Charles Eastlake and Cuthbert Rigby. Of Ruskin's works, he owned not only several editions of *Fors Clavigera* and *Hortus Inclusus*, but also *The Stones of Venice, Aratra Pentilici, The Crown of Wild Olive, Ariadne Florentina, Val d'Arno, The Queen of the Air, The Two Paths, Michael Angelo and Tintoretti, The Bible of Amiens, The Nature of Gothic, Love's Meinie, Arrows of the Chace, On the Old Road, Frondes Agrestes, Notes on Pictures, Praeterita, Proserpina, Studies in Both Arts, St Mark's Rest, Mornings in Florence, The Lord's Prayer, Our Fathers Have Told Us, Modern Painters, The Poetry of Architecture, The Seven Lamps of Architecture, The Elements of Drawing, Sesame and Lilies, A Joy For Ever, Time and Tide* and *The Art of England*. He also had a number of shorter papers by Ruskin and books about him, for example those of Ada Earland and E.T. Cook.[1]

Fleming left some of his books to the Guild of St George. He owned Cook and Wedderburn's *Complete Works* of Ruskin in 39 volumes, numerous individual volumes of Ruskin, parts of the original *Fors Clavigera* issued between 1871 and 1877, the eight early volumes of the complete *Fors* and Faunthorpe's *Index to Fors*, which clearly indicates a deep interest in Ruskin's works, particularly *Fors*. He also had two pages of Letter XCV of *Fors*, in which Ruskin mentioned Fleming and his revival of the Westmorland wheels, framed in oak. Evidently, his experiences with Ruskin and Marian Twelves never jaded Fleming to the extent that he sold or destroyed related material, or failed to recognise the value of the Langdale Linen Industry and what it represented as the years passed. When he died in 1923 the Industry was still running commercially and that would surely have brought him a deal of satisfaction.

Irrespective of his later disappointments regarding Ruskin and the

---

[1] Armitt Library, Ambleside, Sale catalogue.

Linen Industry, Fleming had successfully proved that Ruskin's theories had some practical, economic and ethical value. The indications are, however, that it was Fleming's individual and positive personality, including his unique understanding of Ruskin, which ultimately led to that long-term success. That again sets Lakeland aside from any contemporary handcraft endeavour elsewhere and marks its separateness. Throughout his time in Lakeland, Fleming wrote a number of accounts of his early work with the wheels which appeared in various local and national publications. In not one of those accounts did the Broxbourne bachelor express any concern or doubt about founding and orchestrating a predominantly female industry, or about allowing his housekeeper to run it. Apart from himself and Ruskin, one of the few men involved for any length of time was Robert Thomas Dixon of Kendal who between 1897 and 1927 wove boiled linen for Miss Twelves when she was based at Keswick. Thus only three men were associated with the revival of the wheels at any given time. By contrast, the number of women reached around 120 at its peak, all actively producing high quality textiles. Marian Twelves, of course, would have had most contact with the workers, but at least initially Fleming organised how the realisation of Ruskin's theories would be conducted, including how the women would be trained and paid, and the conditions under which they should work (i.e. without machinery and in the home).

As an educated and forthright man, Fleming questioned Ruskin's attitude towards women, and declared quite openly in *In the House of Rimmon* (1873) that he did not hold with the writer's rather limited view of women generally:

> But, my friend, I do most emphatically and solemnly lay at your door, the distinct charge, that you and your fellow members of our civilized society, have well nigh made any pure and healthy life impossible. You have taken all your women-children, and wrapped them up in cotton wool, and have said to them, 'Dear girls, the objects of life are to look pretty, dress well, get married, and win a position in society; if you manage properly all your life through, you may go delicately as Agag did, and have people to work for you, to dress you, feed you, nurse you, amuse you'. The result of which exactly followed advice is, that you may search England through, and I will give you £5 for every girl under 25, who is at once a lady and a workwoman. But indeed, most emphatically, you must find her somewhere, or you and I must give up all hopes of this better life, and be contented to drop back into the sad old grooves, and wed ourselves to some padded, be-crinolined,

> chignoned, monstrosity scarcely able to put a pin in straight, much
> less add up her butcher's bill properly.[1]

Fleming's interpretation of Ruskin, on which the Linen Industry was founded, included a reconsideration of his view of women. Fleming did not accept Ruskin's inability to recognise a workwoman as a lady, and a lady as one who worked. To him, women had more to offer than merely looking pretty and he was determined to say so. Ruskin's own personal experiences of women appeared to be based largely on his early life as the only child of a domineering and over-zealous mother (from whom he derived little pleasure, according to *Praeterita*),[2] his failed marriage to Euphemia Gray (who subsequently married his close friend John Everett Millais), his friendships with a number of unmarried ladies (including the Beever sisters), and his difficult and dependent (on both sides) later years with Joan Severn.[3] His life was afflicted by a series of fraught relationships with women who were strong, yet dependent on the fortunes of a man, true queens of domesticity who never contemplated working, and who would have regarded work as a source of shame. Ruskin found Susanna Beever to be a woman in the mould of his ideal; for she and her sister Mary

> did not travel; they did not go up to London in its season; they did
> not receive idle visitors to jar or waste their leisure in the waning
> year. The poor and the sick could find them always; or rather, they
> watched for and prevented all poverty and pain that care or
> tenderness could relieve or heal. Loadstones they were, as steadily
> bringing the light of gentle and wise souls about them as the crest
> of their guardian mountain gives pause to the morning clouds: in
> themselves, they were types of perfect womanhood in its constant
> happiness, queens alike of their own hearts and of a Paradise in
> which they knew the names and sympathized with the spirits of
> every living creature that God had made to play therein, or to

---

[1] Fleming, *House of Rimmon*, 30–1.

[2] In Letter LIV of *Fors Clavigera* (*Works*, xxviii. 345) Ruskin noted that his mother's presence was of 'no particular pleasure' to him. But in Letter XLVI (*Works*, xxviii. 170) he noted that she was 'the best sewer in the school' in her youth.

[3] Joan Agnew married the artist Arthur Severn in 1871. Ruskin gave them the lease of 28 Herne Hill which remained their home until 1907 when the lease expired. However, Mrs Severn preferred to live at Brantwood, and they inherited the property on Ruskin's death.

blossom in its sunshine or shade.[1]

Yet when faced with his ideal of womanhood, Ruskin revealed the depth and complexity of his anxieties regarding women, and resorted to treating Susanna Beever as a small child throughout much of their friendship. For example, when she was 68 he described her as a 'naughty little girl'.[2]

With the added complications of a failed love affair with Rose la Touche, the public ridiculing of his exaggerated view of Kate Greenaway's art work (in, for example, *Fairy Land: Mrs Allingham and Kate Greenaway*, a lecture delivered at Oxford in May 1883), and accusations that he was effeminate,[3] Ruskin appeared to suffer extremes of womanhood. The changeable nature of his sometimes confused conception of women and what they represented drew him in Letter XCIV of *Fors Clavigera* (published immediately before the Letter in which he praised Fleming's revival of the wheels) to the rather savage conclusion that a woman was most suitable for:

> scrubbing furniture, dusting walls, sweeping floors, making the beds, washing up the crockery, ditto the children, and wipping them when they want it,—mending their clothes, cooking their dinners,—and when there are cooks more than enough, helping with the farm work, or the garden, or the dairy? Is that plain speaking enough?[4]

In accordance with such views, the women of the Guild of St George were encouraged to make clothes by hand, since it was thought valuable for them to do a 'certain portion of useful work with their hands'.[5] Over Ruskin's lifetime, however, the role of women in society was much discussed, with the plight of the working woman becoming a particularly emotive issue. Bodies such as the Royal School of Art Needlework aimed to offer improved working conditions to one of the most abused groups of nineteenth-century women workers-seamstresses and embroiderers, a considerable number of whom were 'ladies' who had found themselves in altered circumstances and in need of paid employment. To

---

[1] A. Fleming (ed.), *Hortus Inclusus* (1887), pp. vii–viii.

[2] Ibid., 1, Ruskin to Susanna Beever, 14 April 1874.

[3] *Works*, xxxiv. 81.

[4] *Works*, xxix. 491.

[5] Ibid., 17.

Fleming, a generation or so younger than Ruskin, not only had needle-work lost its rightful place in the arts, but those who plied the needle had lost their respected place, their fall to the ranks of sweatshop slaves receiving much attention in *Punch*.[1]

Fleming's personal experience of women may well have fallen into a similar category to his mentor's—a bachelor without children whose house was run by a formidable matriarch (until 1884, Marian Twelves); yet he clearly lacked Ruskin's deep women-related angst. His work as a solicitor must have brought him into contact with women from across the social spectrum, both in the town and the country. Indeed, he was perhaps better able to judge the social situation of women in south Lakeland in the latter part of the nineteenth century, a time when Ruskin's judgement was possibly becoming impaired by ill-health and the almost claustrophobic conditions at Brantwood (where he was particularly exposed to the extremes of womanhood in the form of female servants and Joan Severn and her daughters). It might be said that Fleming had his finger more firmly on the pulse of social change and, as a man of considered opinion, brought his own views on women and the female situation to bear on his organisation of the Langdale Linen Industry. The Industry was most certainly a Ruskinian attempt to bring renewed respect to traditional local crafts, and aimed to bring dignity and self-respect to its workers; but it also allowed them to be called at once workwomen and ladies who were deliberately employed away from the morally corrupt mills and factories. All were considered equal, and each made a valuable contribution to the Industry, irrespective of her social and educational background.

Fleming's comparatively modern attitude towards women as an employable, useful and reliable 'lady' work force appears to have been an important factor in the Langdale Linen Industry's success. He openly encouraged not only his former housekeeper but all his female workers to take part in design as well as production, and awarded them the responsibility for their own work, simultaneously attempting to educate them with readings from Ruskin, Wordsworth and other literary greats. He never expressed the slightest doubt about their creative potential, despite the lack of any formal training at recognised schools of art and design, and never doubted Miss Twelves's ability to create good workers out of relatively poor, older, largely uneducated country women. Ruskin appeared not to believe in female creativity and, in *Sesame and Lilies*

---

[1] See, for example, *Punch*, 16 June 1888, 278, 'The Modern Venus Attired by the Three Dis-graces'.

(1865), summarised the roles of the sexes:

> His intellect is for speculation and invention; his energy for
> adventure, for war, and for conquest, wherever war is just,
> wherever conquest necessary. But the woman's power is for rule,
> not for battle,—and her intellect is not for invention or creation,
> but for sweet ordering, arrangement, and decision.[1]

Yet he did not consider women to be any less valuable than men because
they could not create. Rather, he openly stated that the sexes were equal
because of their differences. Men and women possessed different talents
and abilities, all of which were a necessary part of life:

> We are foolish, and without excuse foolish, in speaking of the
> 'superiority' of one sex to the other, as if they could be compared
> in similar things. Each has what the other has not: each completes
> the other, and is completed by the other.[2]

The domestic queen may well have lacked creative talent, but even
Ruskin recognised that men could not function in isolation.

Given Fleming's support of self-expression in women, the first
indications are that he was attempting to establish a feminist workshop
in the form of the Langdale Linen Industry, with domestic crafts
becoming a potential source of income for the women involved.
However, Fleming was always most specific that, whilst he was happy
for women to earn an income without necessarily losing their right to be
called ladies, it was never intended that the Industry would offer them
a means out of the domestic situation. There he was in total agreement
with Ruskin. The wages paid were never sufficient to allow the women
any semblance of independence; before 1889 even Marian Twelves
rejected any formal payment which would have given her a degree of
financial security. To those who failed (and still fail) to understand the
Industry's fundamental philosophies, that lack of payment would seem
highly irregular and unacceptable. But to Miss Twelves, as a true and
devout Ruskinian, it was a point of great pride. In 1913 she recalled that
her early efforts on behalf of the Langdale Linen Industry were given not
for money, but out of friendship to Fleming and devotion to Ruskin's
teachings. She also quoted from a letter written to her by Fleming:

---

[1] *Works*, xviii. 121–2.

[2] Ibid., 58.

I am exceedingly angry to find that anybody in Langdale or out of it, directly or indirectly, should suggest that you have been paid for your services to my spinning hobby. The help you have ungrudgingly given has been freely rendered, purely out of friendship to me and devotion to Mr Ruskin's teachings, and is wholly different in character and degree to the paid service I have now secured.[1]

Since Mrs Pepper ran the Industry for Fleming after 1889, it may be inferred from this letter that she was paid on a more formal basis for her work. In Miss Twelves's case, as a Companion of the Guild of St George, her independence was further restricted, the Guild overseeing all her movements to a greater extent after 1889. Ultimately, of course, the Industry was run by a man (Fleming) and was based on the teachings of a man (Ruskin), and there was never any attempt to deny that male foundation.

While all this confirms that the Langdale Linen Industry had its own quite definite and individual approach to Ruskin and to the revival of local crafts, the fact that the exercise was specifically aimed at helping the people of Lakeland confirms the Industry's individuality. To Fleming the revival of the wheels was never intended to take hold outside Lakeland and the Industry's spread after 1889 under the direct guidance of Marian Twelves remained principally within the region. Before 1871, Ruskin had developed a strong sense of attachment to the Lake District, partly fuelled by Wordsworth's depictions not only of the majestic landscape but also of the people who lived and worked within that landscape:

> Near the tumultuous brook of Greenhead Ghyll,
> In that deep valley, Michael had designed
> to build a Sheepfold; and, before he heard
> The tidings of his melancholy loss,
> For this same purpose he had gathered up
> A heap of stones, which by the streamlet's edge
> Lay thrown together, ready for the work.[2]

---

[1] *Westmorland Gazette*, 25 Oct. 1913, 'Langdale Linen. The Origin and Principles of the Industry' by Marian Twelves quoting Fleming's letter. The mention of Fleming's name suggests that, whatever her difficulties with him in 1889, by 1913 she had forgiven any earlier dispute.

[2] W.E. Williams (ed.), *Wordsworth* (1988), 86. Extract from 'Michael'. 'Michael of the Greenhead ghyll' was referred to by Ruskin in Letter XII of *Fors*.

By the time he took up residence at Brantwood, Ruskin was more than anxious to help not only the fight against the destruction and alteration of the area, but also to help those whose ways and traditions were under threat. The Lakeland railways he heartily opposed, but on a more personal note he made more direct gestures towards helping the people themselves over a number of years. For example, to the people of Coniston he gave his mineral collection so that they might study more closely their geological heritage; as a means of demonstrating to the children of Coniston how the wheels of heaven went round and how the stars were 'grouped into pictures of the world-old myths of nature', he planned and had made a revolving globe painted with the constellation figures into which they could climb;[1] and for the benefit of local people he spent time experimenting to find which plants and flowers grew best in the region's soil. When Fleming arrived in the area in 1883, already fully conversant with Wordsworth's works (particularly those on the spinning wheel), he followed his mentor's example and immediately joined the local railway defence campaigns. But almost as quickly, he acted upon the vociferous pleas of his 'poor' neighbours who wished to see the return of the Westmorland spinning wheels:

> At last, after long pondering over Wordsworth's sonnets and Mr Ruskin's eloquent appeals in *Fors*, I was lifted into action by the homely speech of one of my poor neighbours. 'When t'ould wheels died out', said she, 'the gude times went too, m'happen they'd coome back if t'wheels did'.[2]

As a result, the Industry became a significant provider of additional income to what was, by that time, one of the most unemployable groups in Lakeland, working-class married or single women who were mostly in their middle or late years, with no education or obvious skills, who were largely tied to a home which, more often than not, was situated in remote countryside. In 1893 the *Westmorland Gazette* reaffirmed that:

> The village industries of flax spinning and weaving by hand were revived in 1883 by Mr Ruskin and Mr Albert Fleming with a two-fold object, to provide employment for the women in the village and to promote and put into practice the principles of pure hand labour, as taught by Mr Ruskin in *Fors Clavigera* and other

---

[1] W.G. Collingwood, *Ruskin Relics* (1903), 10.

[2] H.H. Warner (ed.), *Songs of the Spindle and Legends of the Loom* (1889), 15.

works.[1]

For those women there was now the possibility of earning a regular wage without abandoning the domestic environment or moving away from familiar surroundings, and a chance to do so without jeopardising their self-respect. Whilst the Royal School of Art Needlework and a number of other similar city-based textile endeavours had proved successful employers of poor women by 1883, Fleming was one of the first to show that the need for regular and dignified work relating to needle skills was just as great in the country. It is hardly surprising that, when Marian Twelves moved to Keswick in 1889 to re-establish her spinning and weaving industry, there was a similarly enthusiastic reception, and an equally successful response in the numbers of women wanting to train in comparatively old-fashioned skills.

---

[1] *Westmorland Gazette*, 9 Dec. 1893, article by 'a Correspondent in the *Yorkshire Weekly Post*'.

4

THE CONTINUED REVIVAL
OF HAND SPINNING
IN LAKELAND

For Fleming, living and working in such close proximity to Ruskin had brought both success and difficulties. For Marian Twelves, it appeared to bring only the former, particularly after 1889. When she first arrived in Keswick she clearly believed the Rawnsleys' handcraft school to be closer to her own Ruskinian aims, its classes in metalwork, woodwork and embroidery having already run successfully under Ruskin's direct influence for just over four years. The proposal for starting a linen workshop at the Keswick School was first put forward at a meeting held at Ann Elliot's house in Main Street, Keswick, on 30 April 1889.[1] Miss Elliot was then the School's secretary and saleswoman (and remained so until 1899), and a member of a small local committee who discussed all the developments at the Rawnsleys' arts endeavour. It was finally decided that the idea was viable and that the initial cost of starting the project would be around £50 for looms, bobbins and the like.[2] With the assistance of 'a faithful spinner' from Langdale, for almost a year Miss Twelves set about establishing a new linen workshop in St Kentigern's Parish Room.[3] Based in the centre of Keswick, a far busier and more populous centre than Elterwater, the Parish Room housed the Keswick School from 1884 to 1894. From the outset Miss Twelves was given a greater degree of independence through a nominal fee for her role as

---

[1] The Keswick School of Industrial Arts is hereafter also called the Keswick School.

[2] CROC, DB 111/1, Keswick School of Industrial Arts minutes, 30 April 1889.

[3] H.D. Rawnsley, *Ruskin and the English Lakes* (1901), 143. The Keswick School branch of the Industry was known informally as the Ruskin Linen Industry from 1889. Since the Langdale Linen Industry and associated branches were all linked, the phrase 'Linen Industry' is used here to refer to the Industry generally in all its forms or to a particular branch. Just as Elterwater has been used to refer to St Martin's, the various other branches of the Industry are also referred to by place, for example, the Keswick Industry refers to Miss Twelves's later workshops in Keswick.

teacher and manageress, and was granted a voice at the School's regular meetings. However, she was still teaching what she considered to be a domestic craft, and now worked under the auspices of the Rawnsleys with the continued influence of Ruskin, Joan Severn and the Guild of St George. Creatively, she was given the same freedom afforded at Elterwater, with Ruskin lace and embroidery taking a prominent place in the School's linen production for the next three years. Mrs Rawnsley also continued with her own classes in embroidery, the School successfully running two Ruskinian textile endeavours side by side.

As at St Martin's, the Keswick School's spinning classes were an immediate success, with at least twenty spinsters and a dozen embroiderers employed initially. By 1890 decorated linens were appearing at the Home Arts and Industries Association Exhibition and at the Arts and Crafts Exhibition in London. The Home Arts became a regular venue but, as far as is known, 1890 was the only year in which hand made linens from the Lake District appeared at an Arts and Crafts Exhibition. That was probably the result, in part, of Rawnsley's associations with William Morris who, in the 1880s, had proffered written support for at least one of the cleric's railway defence schemes. Nevertheless, attendance at such a prominent national exhibition (in only its second year of operation) demonstrates the exceptionally high standard attained at Keswick under Miss Twelves's guidance in a short time. At Elterwater she had experimented widely in the production of textiles by hand, and had become extremely proficient in the application of Ruskin's theories. Having laid down very specific and evidently workable guidelines at St Martin's—most particularly the exclusion of all machinery and the encouragement of individual creativity—the formula for Keswick had already been devised. Only the more practical difficulties of obtaining enough spinning wheels and flax, setting up a linen boiler, employing the women and training them had still to be contended with. Theoretically and practically, Keswick ran as the exact mirror of Elterwater and there was never any attempt to create anything other than a sister industry which would benefit Lakeland and help revive its lost traditions.

As with St Martin's, local exhibitions proved to be just as important a showcase for locally produced work and from 1890 hand made linens became a feature of the Keswick School's own annual exhibition. Begun in 1885, the exhibition was an immediate success as a means of promoting and selling the School's wares. So important a part of the School had Miss Twelves's workshop become by 1890 that, at that year's exhibition, Rawnsley read out a poem, specially composed by him (at Miss Twelves's request) for the occasion:

St Kentigern's Spinning Song

Keswick wives and maidens, come!
Bring your flax and bring your wheel—
Spinning makes a cheerful home,
Spinning all your cares can heal.
Whereso'er the wheel goes round
Love and happiness abound.

Hark the music how it hums!
How the light leaps out and glances!
How the flaxen threadlet thrums,
How the treadle dips and dances!
Whereso'er the wheel goes round,
Love and life and joy abound.

Foot the treadle, let the 'fly'
Gather up and fill the bobbins;
Food in plenty, by and bye,
For ourselves and for the robins,
Will in cupboard sure be found
If the merry wheel goes round.

Bring your mind and bring your heart,
Bring your merriest of fingers,
Play again the old-world part:
Still in Cumberland there lingers
Memory of the life that found
Joy the while the wheels went round.

Draw the flax to glossy line,
Keep it long and smooth and even;
Keswick spinners, spin as fine
As the gossamer in heaven;
For true work is only found
Where the wheel with skill goes round.

Spin: odd minutes of the day
Make your spindle bunches fuller,
Spin the weary nights away—
Spinning ne'er made evening duller;
Therefore, let the wheel go round

And more happiness be found.

As you spin your lives are spun,
Keswick wife or Keswick maiden:
Not a day beneath the sun
But with knots and twists is laden.
But the wheel, God's love, spins round,
Makes the rough more smooth be found.

Cheerful trust your own life's wheel
To the hand of your All-Father;
Spin and strive each day to feel
Life's poor threads for good may gather
Only, if, as time goes round, —
Honest spinners you be found.[1]

As a direct result of Ruskin's and Wordsworth's influence, the revival of
the Westmorland wheels successfully established itself in Cumberland,
and Rawnsley's poem was a literary celebration of the event. Over the
years other poems were written about the revival of the local wheels, the
encouragement of individual creativity among the spinsters and
embroiderers, and the Industry's strong literary associations, reflecting a
brief associated literary revival. Once again, ancient ways and traditions
became the subject of local writing, Elizabeth Pepper composing her own
spinning poem immediately prior to Rawnsley's contribution in 1890:

In a little village 'neath the pikes,
There's some industrious people;
Aye! Some that live beneath the shade,
Of Brig Hows' old church steeple.

In passing quietly through the vale,
You hear them gaily singin',
You step aside, and see them spin
Fine thread for Langdale linen.

In days gone by, when t'wheels were mute,
And they were getting rusty,
There were just two who thought about

[1] *Westmorland Gazette*, 12 April 1890.

Reviving this industry.

'Twas work of labour and of love
To set the wheels a spinnin',
But now you'd be surprised to see
The progress in the linen.

One fine old dame peeped o'er her specks:
'Whoa mun we thank for t'spinnin'?
What wod it be if it wasn't for
John Ruskin and Albert Flemin'.

We are grateful to these gentlemen
For helping out our living,
By helping those who'll help themselves-
'Tis better far than giving."

Now, if you want the full address,
And where to buy the linen,
St Martin's, Langdale, Ambleside,
There, too, you'll see the spinnin'.[1]

Although of limited literary merit, such works are important social documents which chart the strength of feeling among the working population of the Lake District not only towards Ruskin and Fleming, but also towards the revival of a culture which had appeared lost. Such poems, not dissimilar to Ruskin's own *Twist Ye, Twine Ye* written a quarter of a century earlier, ensured that Ruskin and Fleming became as important a part of the region's cultural and artistic heritage as Wordsworth.

As if to reaffirm its even more intense Ruskinian nature, the Keswick School's linen workshop became known from the beginning as the Ruskin Linen Industry and its products as Ruskin linens. As a result of that greater devotion to Ruskin, Marian Twelves enjoyed ever-increasing commercial and artistic success, winning the patronage of Princess Louise, marchioness of Lorne (Queen Victoria's fourth daughter), the duchess of Albany (the wife of Prince Leopold, the queen's fourth son) and Lady Muncaster, as well as bringing welcome publicity for the Rawnsleys' School and the revival of the wheels in Lakeland. Towards

---

[1] CROK, WDB 73/22, 'Langdale Linen' by 'Lizzie Pepper', 18 Feb. 1890.

the end of 1890 it was being reported that there were already around a hundred women associated with the Industry in the Keswick district alone, including Mrs Douglas, Miss Gurley, Miss Blunt, Miss Pape, Mrs Scales, Mrs Jamieson, Mrs Thompson, Mrs Youdale, Mrs Brownrigg, Miss Lawson, Mrs Fisher, Mrs Bouch, Mrs Pearson, Mrs Stanley, Mrs Knubley and Christina Swindle.[1] As with their sisters at St Martin's, all were given the opportunity to design and create their own textiles, and to exhibit their work locally and nationally. As with those from Elterwater, all Keswick exhibits were labelled with the maker's name and address, so that 'the actual worker may be communicated with *direct*, should occasion arise when such a course might be expedient', as Marian Twelves expressed it.[2] In 1890 Miss Twelves also ensured that, as well as exhibiting at the Home Arts Exhibition in Birmingham and the Arts and Crafts Exhibition in London, practical demonstrations of spinning were given at the Silverdale village show, repeating the successful idea of 1887 when spinning demonstrations had been given at Arthur Simpson's exhibition. In August the following year, by which time around 50 varieties of linen were being produced at Keswick, Ruskin linens also appeared at the 79th Coniston Horticultural Society Show. After the 1890 Arts and Crafts Exhibition the *Spectator* declared that the Keswick School's linen work was 'beautiful', with a cushion by Mrs Rawnsley, a pupil of Miss Twelves, being particularly admired.[3] In 1891 the *Westmorland Gazette* reported that the School's linen and embroidery work had reached 'a point of perfection hitherto untouched'.[4]

Despite the rapid success of the Keswick School's linen workshop, the School's minute book reveals that Miss Twelves experienced difficulties from the outset and was never wholly satisfied with the conditions under which she had to work. The Parish Room was not ideal for spinning classes, with metalwork and woodwork classes being conducted in the same restricted space, and from the beginning Miss Twelves lodged complaints about inadequate accommodation for her growing enterprise. Other difficulties concerning the weaver employed began to surface in November 1889 and again in April 1890, during which time the weaver originally taken on left and Robert Shearman was taken on as replacement. Shearman proved to be equally unsatisfactory,

---

[1] *Keswick Guardian*, 12 April 1890.

[2] M. Twelves, *The Ruskin Linen Industry* (Keswick, *c*.1900), 4 (copy in Sheffield Archives, GSG 21).

[3] *Keswick Guardian*, 25 Jan. 1890, quoting the *Spectator*.

[4] *Westmorland Gazette*, 23 May 1891.

and a Mr Phillips of Cockermouth was engaged to carry out the weaving on occasional visits.[1] So disillusioned with the lack of accommodation for her spinsters had Miss Twelves become by 1892 that she made the first of what would be a series of threats to resign. She carried on, perhaps persuaded to stay to complete the funeral pall for Rawnsley's friend, Alfred Tennyson. Designed by Edith Rawnsley, the pall was one of the Keswick workshop's most important textiles. Made of hand spun, hand woven linen, it was decorated with 42 wild roses, a laurel wreath of berries representing the poet's 'full fruit of years', the last verse of one of his poems, and the initials 'A.T.'. Church linens and funeral palls had been an important part of the Industry's output from its beginnings in 1883 and Rawnsley's connections with the church brought a greater number of more prestigious commissions for the Keswick branch after 1889, as did his equally strong literary connections. In 1891 commissions included Communion cloths for two churches and the funeral pall for Harvey Goodwin, bishop of Carlisle, a friend of both the Rawnsleys and the Severns.

Although Marian Twelves had little, if any, direct contact with Fleming after 1889, it is clear that his early efforts with the Langdale Linen Industry and his original faith in her practical capabilities played an important part in shaping the revival of the wheels at Keswick after 1889. Whilst she was now more her own boss, she had achieved that position only as a result of Fleming's initial support. The very idea of reviving the wheels had been his; he had made most of the early decisions concerning the theoretical and business sides to the Industry; and had originally encouraged her to learn the art of hand spinning. Thanks largely to him and Ruskin she had left her role as housekeeper behind, and had now become a successful manager of a second thriving textile industry which similarly defied all that the nineteenth century represented. Her visits to Brantwood never ceased and she continued to take advice directly from Ruskin. After the 1890 Silverdale Show the local newspaper reported that 'Miss Twelves showed us a piece of Greek lace—beautiful in design and workmanship—which Mr Ruskin thinks should be employed more than is at present the case'.[2] This indicates that, despite ill-health and a lack of communication with Fleming, Ruskin also continued to advise on design matters after 1889, directly

[1] CROC, DB 111/1, 29 Nov. 1889, 21 April 1890.

[2] *Westmorland Gazette*, 16 Aug. 1890.

shaping the work at Keswick as he had at Elterwater.[1] The Industry continued to benefit from Ruskin's close presence and direct input at a time when he appeared capable of doing little else. Perhaps because of her success, Miss Twelves never had need to make her 'difficulties' with Fleming in 1889 known in detail, and she never publicly betrayed him, possibly because she was aware of the debt she owed him. Through Fleming she had been introduced to one of the most prolific and controversial writers of the time whose teachings dominated her life from 1883 to 1929.

As fellow Ruskinians and Companions, Miss Twelves always expressed a similarly discreet respect for the Rawnsleys, despite leaving their employment in 1894 under circumstances identical to those at Elterwater. Whilst at their School she made a number of gestures of gratitude which marked the beginnings of that respect. At the 1890 Keswick School exhibition she presented Canon Rawnsley (on St Kentigern's day) with a copy of his lecture *St Kentigern of Crosthwaite and St Herbert of Derwentwater* (1888) bound in hand woven linen, and presented to Mrs Rawnsley an old carved oak spinning wheel with an engraved plate. The *Keswick Guardian* reported:

> Mrs Rawnsley said they were all deeply indebted to Miss Twelves, and owed all the success of the Linen Industry to her untiring efforts, and Miss Twelves thoroughly loved her work. She had gathered from the spinners that spinning made the home happier. It was the idea of Mr Rawnsley and herself that the work of the School should be to add happiness to the homes, and if it did not their object was not achieved. But she felt that nobody could take up art without their lives being ennobled and themselves made happier. It was an immense resource to have something in the nature of art to fall back upon. Spinning was an art, and she thought the spinners would agree that it would bring happiness.[2]

Those sentiments reflect the strong sense of mutual support and respect which existed among Lakeland's Ruskinians. That respect became a recognisable trait of the Lakeland revival of arts and crafts, and one which helped the revival spread. Indeed, it was that sense of mutual support, bonded out of a shared respect for Ruskin, which prevented

---

[1] Contemporary newspaper reports do not specify which pattern Ruskin expressed a particular interest in.

[2] *Keswick Guardian*, 12 April 1890.

Fleming from expressing any animosity towards the Rawnsleys for employing Miss Twelves after their disagreement. Rather, he became further involved with Rawnsley's Lakeland defence schemes after 1889, the protection of the region being another strong trait which marked Lakeland's separateness and individuality.

It was also a strong indication of the depth of their mutual respect for Ruskin that the Langdale and Ruskin Linen Industries never worked in competition, but exhibited side by side on several occasions. At the 1891 Kendal Arts, Crafts and Loan Exhibition the Ruskin Linen Industry (under the heading of the Keswick School of Industrial Arts) showed four embroidered teacloths, three decorated cushions, a pinafore, a work bag, a spinster's bag and an ottoman top, along with twelve lengths of Ruskin linens of various qualities and prices.[1] A small branch of the Keswick School then running at Hawkshead sent one specimen of hand woven linen and a workbasket with an embroidered cover, whilst Fleming sent specimens of Langdale linen and a weaver to give demonstrations on a loom. A further twelve spinsters from Elterwater and Langdale sent specimens of hand spun flax yarn. Specimens of needle-work by Mrs Pepper and Mrs Heskett (of St Martin's) also appeared in various other categories. Because of its use of the title 'Keswick School', the Ruskin Linen Industry's exhibits were deliberately collected together under one separate category. But in all other sections spinsters from various sites exhibited their work side by side and whilst an air of friendly competition probably existed between the individual workers, there were never any reports of exhibitions being attended in anything but the best humour. Essentially, the exhibitors were all working for the same industry, all paying homage to Ruskin and to the ancient Westmorland wheels, and were all inextricably bound because of that. Miss Twelves always maintained some contact with Mrs Pepper and other Elterwater spinsters (particularly through local exhibitions), strengthening the bond which existed between the workshops. For many years Miss Twelves also regularly visited Coniston, not only to see Ruskin but also, after 1900, to run her Greek (Ruskin) lace class. A popular local figure, she would have been known to many, respected for her textile work, and an accepted part of local life.

Despite there being two major centres of linen production in south Lakeland by 1890, both running along the same stringent pre-industrial lines, there were plenty of customers for both, which also lessened the

---

[1] See *Catalogue of the Kendal Arts, Crafts and Loan Exhibition* (1891) (copy in Kendal Library).

need for rivalry. At Elterwater by 1884 local customers included Edith Rawnsley (who bought batches of linen of around 14 yards at a time, probably for her embroidery students), Miss Beever (14 yards of linen), and Lady Bective, a keen patron of local arts and crafts (3 yards of linen).[1] Lady Bective later presented a traditional loom to Thomas Dixon, a weaver of Kendal. Dixon wove linen for Miss Twelves for some thirty years using three traditional Westmorland looms. By 1885 Liberty's of London had placed several requests for linen (for example, on one occasion 39½ yards and on another 15 yards), which was presumably sold in their West End shops.[2] In January 1889 the equally well known firm of Morris & Co. ordered 20 yards of linen (10 yards each of No 4 and No 8); and linen was regularly supplied from that year to what is described in order books as the 'Scottish School'.[3] This may have been the Glasgow School of Art which, under the influence from 1885 of Francis H. Newbery (b. 1853), was then in the early stages of establishing a highly respected needlework department which produced linen based embroideries. This is perhaps more likely since Anne Knox Arthur, who worked in the Glasgow School's needlework department for a time, was also a customer. Miss Arthur later also bought copies of *Needleweaving*, a booklet written by Ann Macbeth and published by Arthur Simpson of Kendal in 1922. The Royal School of Art Needlework also bought plain linen on a number of occasions. Widespread public recognition for Lakeland crafts, therefore, was never a problem. St Martin's even sent linens to customers abroad, including the marchesa de Viti de Marco in Rome, as well as numerous other individuals throughout Britain.[4]

Despite running for only five years, the Keswick School linen workshop built up an equally strong patronage, including Princess Louise, the duchess of Albany, Lady Muncaster, Ruskin and Joan Severn, and executed a number of important commissions, such as the church linens and funeral palls already mentioned. Local crafts may have been revived chiefly for the benefit of local people, history and tradition, but they held an appeal which, for a time, won national and international approval.

---

[1] CROK, WDS 0106, WDB 73/1.

[2] Ibid. Liberty's do not have records that would verify the exact nature of the linen sold.

[3] Ibid.

[4] CROK, WDS 0106 and WDB 73/19 include letters from the Marchesa de Viti de Marco of Rome, Alice Waddington of Bolton and an 81-year-old man from Essex who stated his preference for Langdale linen to any other for his towels.

So successful did Miss Twelves and Mrs Pepper become in their task of teaching local women that a number of their pupils began to set up their own smaller workshops and classes, spreading the revival of local arts and crafts still further. A spinning class had already been established in Kirkby Lonsdale in imitation of St Martin's by the mid 1880s, founded by the Harris family.[1] The initial tuition for the class was provided by Miss Twelves and it ran successfully until at least 1900. By about 1890 a Silverdale branch of the Industry had also been established, run by a Mrs Townsend, joined by a branch at Morland (near Appleby), and the Keswick School's small Hawkshead class. That was followed by the Coniston Greek Lace Class which was run by Miss Twelves until around 1910, when it was taken over by Miss Ada Hooper, a later spinster associated with the Keswick branch of the Linen Industry. At Grasmere, the Flaxhome Industry was established and run by Miss Butterwith c.1900, and a few years later the Cottage Linen Industry was founded at Troutbeck Bridge, Windermere, by Miss M.J. Musgrave, which from at least 1908 exhibited at the Coniston Exhibition.[2]

The number of women associated with the Industry by the early 1900s had clearly grown steadily since 1883, with a considerable number of other women choosing to continue with their linen and lace work in their own homes purely for their own pleasure long after ties with any formal class or commercial workshop had ended. Not surprisingly, given their romantic associations, the revived wheels also affected a number of other locals. Among them were Lily Severn (of Brantwood) who used the linen to make aprons and other domestic items (shown at the 1891 Kendal exhibition); Mrs Rawnsley, whose decorated linen cushion owned by Ruskin was also shown at the 1891 exhibition; Miss Le Fleming of Rydal Hall (possibly a distant relation of Fleming), whose carriage rug in Langdale linen was shown at the 1891 exhibition; Jane Simpson (1860–1950), wife of the wood carver Arthur Simpson, a prolific embroideress who used Langdale linen as a base for her work; and Annie Garnett of the Crown Hotel, Windermere, a pupil of Mrs Pepper whose embroidered Langdale linen appeared in the 1891 exhibition.[3]

Despite her rapid and sustained success at the Keswick School, in 1894 Miss Twelves offered her resignation to the Rawnsleys and by April of that year the School's linen production had been wound up. Conditions had evidently proved too trying and, although the Rawnsleys

---

[1] See chapter 10 for the Kirkby Lonsdale class.

[2] Exhibition catalogues, Coniston Institute (1900–19) (at Coniston Musuem).

[3] See chapter 12 for details of exhibitors in 1891.

were in the throes of erecting a new building to house their successful local arts project, Miss Twelves determined to leave. Of the episode she later wrote: 'Again my methods were called into question, and another change to absolute independence became necessary'.[1] Far from being the end of her work with the wheels, however, her departure was again to the benefit of the revival of local arts and crafts, since she immediately established what was arguably the most successful linen workshop in late nineteenth-century Lakeland. On her departure from the Keswick School it was agreed that the School would not sell embroidery for a year and that Miss Twelves would buy the 'plant' (Rawnsley's word) for £100,[2] although the School did continue to run something described as a 'Linen Department' into 1895 and continued with embroidery production, with Edith Rawnsley supervising both. Since there was never any animosity between them, the Keswick School probably bought linens from Miss Twelves's new workshop, since there is no indication that the School bought linens elsewhere or that it attempted to re-establish spinning classes after 1894 in order to produce its own cloth.

Miss Twelves's belief that her methods were again being questioned was the key to her success after 1894. So devout a Ruskinian had she become that she would accept no hindrance to her realisation of Ruskin's theories. She therefore established the Ruskin Linen Industry at St George's Cottage, Keswick, a third major linen workshop which would be the purest yet in its adherence to Ruskin, and arguably the most successful artistically. In making her bid for 'absolute independence' Miss Twelves received more support from Ruskin and more particularly Mrs Severn. As the owner of numerous pieces of linen and lace work, and a friend of Miss Twelves, she was greatly enthusiastic at the prospect of a new workshop being established in Ruskin's name:

> We are so glad to know you have arranged to start the Ruskin Linen Industry on your own account and we wish you every poss- ible success. I enclose the promised help, but you must let me know at any time when you want more, and give yourself no thought or trouble about repaying it.[3]

It is clear that Ruskin's money (and it must surely have been his since he helped to support the Severns) was now being lent to the Keswick

---

[1] Twelves, *Ruskin Linen Industry*, p. 5.

[2] CROC, DB 111/1.

[3] Sheffield Archives, GSG 21, Joan Ruskin Severn to Marian Twelves, 4 Feb. 1894.

spinster, something which had not happened previously. Mrs Severn was also instrumental in collecting a list of signatures of support for Miss Twelves in her bid for independence which included Lord Muncaster, the bishop of Carlisle and the earl of Carlisle, and she helped secure the patronage, once again, of Princess Louise, whose brother, Prince Leopold, was a friend of Ruskin and a visitor to the Guild of St George's museum at Walkley, near Sheffield.

More significantly, in February 1894 Miss Twelves received a letter from Ruskin giving permission for her to use his name in association with her work, and the motto 'To-Day' above the wild rose. Of the letter she wrote:

> On February 8th, 1894 (his birthday), Mr Ruskin signed an authority for me to use his name, and his motto 'TO-DAY' as a Trade Mark, a photographed copy of which I send to be used with this article if desired, and I may here set down once and for all that my Industry is the *only one* of any description having authority from Mr Ruskin to use his name, and that no other Industry in the Lake District or elsewhere, has any connection with it, except a class of Greek Lace Workers in Coniston village, who were taught some five years since under my supervision, expenses over and above a fee of 5s. each paid by the pupils for the course, being defrayed by the St George's Guild.[1]

Miss Twelves was quite specific that her Industry was unique and, to support her belief in its individuality and separateness, it has proved impossible to find any other textile industry (not directly related to those which formed the Lakeland revival of arts and crafts) which was so committed to Ruskin.[2] Because Ruskin's increasing involvement coincided with the growing success of the Linen Industry after 1894, and given that Laxey was then failing, his personal interest must have been essential for a successful Ruskinian industry, but equally Ruskin's teachings had a particular compatibility with Lakeland's history and tradition. Given that Miss Twelves saw Ruskin 'many times' at Brantwood between 1894 and 1899, the last time shortly before his death, there can be no doubt that he continued to contribute directly to

---

[1] Twelves, *Ruskin Linen Industry*, 6–7.

[2] Since Marian Twelves often used the word 'Industry' to describe her work rather than specifying any one branch such as the Ruskin Linen Industry, it has been taken that she considered St Martin's and other related branches of her work to be all part of that 'Industry'.

her work, despite failing health.[1] The result of that contribution was twofold: his influence continued to affect local people long after his death (with the continued use of the spinning wheel), and local people continued to earn additional income long after 1900, carrying out dignified labour connected with the free expression of personal creativity. Or, as Marian Twelves summarised her later work:

> This undertaking has proved entirely successful, and visitors to our dear master's last resting place may find his personal influence still active in the homes surrounding it—at once a practical example of his teaching, and a source of pleasure and helpfulness in the lives of those whose welfare as friends and neighbours was especially dear to him during life.[2]

To Miss Twelves the revival of local crafts revolved entirely around Ruskin and the Lake District and she tolerated no outside influences which might have clouded the true nature of her work, even after Ruskin's death. Similarly, her belief that Ruskin did what he did out of concern for Lakeland and its people never faltered.

Although Fleming's contact with Brantwood had largely (or completely) ended by 1889, Miss Twelves's increased, along with her devotion to her mentor's teachings. Her later meetings with Ruskin she found 'at once sources of new inspiration and heavier responsibility to pass on his message in practical form to all who would hear and heed'.[3] That passing on of his message also involved a more formal contribution from the Guild of St George (after which St George's Cottage was named) which in 1902 officially recognised her Keswick Industry at a Guild meeting. As a devout Ruskinian, Miss Twelves had become an increasingly devout Companion and a guild committee was formed to run the Ruskin Linen Industry. The committee was made up of Marian Twelves and Joan Severn, joined by Mrs Emmeline Stapledon and Miss Jessie Richmond, both of Cheshire, Miss Edith Hope Scott of Liverpool and Miss Frances Adamson of Keswick.[4] Although the Ruskin Linen Industry was officially recognised as affiliated to the Guild of St George only in 1902, from 1885 the Industry generally was mentioned at

---

[1] Twelves, *Ruskin Linen Industry*, 6.

[2] Ibid., 7.

[3] Ibid., 6.

[4] *Ruskin Linen Industry Guild of St George* (c.1918) (copy in the Ruskin Library, Lancaster University).

numerous Guild meetings, including by Ruskin. The Guild became gradually more and more involved with the Industry as time went by. It is probable that the Guild committee, however, with Joan Severn as its leading figure, was a part of the Ruskin Linen Industry from 1894. The nature of the new association with the Guild was later outlined thus:

> The Ruskin Linen Industry was founded by Miss Twelves with the personal help and encouragement of Mr Ruskin until the end of his life. The Industry was designed to carry out that part of the teaching in Fors Clavigera in which Ruskin emphasizes the place of hand-labour as bringing satisfaction and joy to the arts of domestic life; also, to provide a helpful industry for women in their own homes. The work was a great satisfaction to Mr Ruskin, and he expresses this pleasure in the following message to Miss Twelves—that it was 'The best practical outcome of my industrial art teaching'. This industry is now formally affiliated to the Guild of St George, which was founded by Mr Ruskin for the organisation of country life in the best traditions of agriculture, education, and handwork. In the words of Ruskin (spoken of the Guild generally) it is an example 'of reviving the trust of past times in conscience, rather than in competition, for the production of good work; and in common feeling, rather than in common interests, for the preservation of national happiness and the refinement of national manners'.[1]

As a committee member Marian Twelves had a more powerful voice in how her Industry was run and had around her, for the first time, an all-female managerial support team, through which she was given the greatest independence she had yet enjoyed. Through Joan Severn she also had the constant ear and voice of Ruskin.

With the formal support of Ruskin, the Severns and the Guild of St George, the Ruskin Linen Industry developed quickly after 1894. In its first year of independence it gained 21 awards out of a total of 48 exhibits (ten gold stars, ten blue, one red) at the Home Arts and Industries Association Exhibition in London, the highest proportionate number reached by the Industry in any of its forms to date. On that occasion the Princess of Wales (who purchased the Industry's red star exhibit) was presented with a copy of Miss Wakefield's *Ruskin on Music* bound in Ruskin linen. Further awards were gained that year at an

---

[1] Ibid.

Imperial Exhibition in Lancaster (a second prize and two certificates), and nine members of the Industry took awards at the Kirkby Lonsdale exhibition in 1894. Wages for that first year were £217 12s. 10d. This was from capital of £204,[1] which suggests that, with money from sales at exhibitions, the Keswick-based Industry was probably running at a small profit from the start. By the time of the August 1895 Home Arts Exhibition the number of awards gained had risen to 33 (out of 54 exhibits), including two gold crosses for spinning and weaving, and four gold stars for the Greek lace. In June 1896 the Ruskin Linen Industry gained even more awards at the Home Arts Exhibition in London, winning 22 gold stars for linen out of 24 exhibits, a gold cross and 26 gold stars for Greek lace, along with four blue stars and one red for embroidery (a total of 56 exhibits having been submitted).[2] Such consistent success only verifies that the Industry was as much an art industry as ever, and that that reputation was being recognised outside Lakeland for St George's Cottage as well as for St Martin's. Surviving examples of the Ruskin Linen Industry's work show the high standard of production achieved by the Keswick workshop at its peak in the late nineteenth century.

By 1897 the Ruskin Linen Industry had once again attended the Lancaster exhibition and given demonstrations of spinning at the Imperial Victorian Exhibition held at Crystal Palace between May and October. In 1899, after further success at both local and national exhibitions, Miss Twelves publicly attributed that success as:

> due *absolutely* and *entirely* to the inspiration gained, and enthusiasm for better and nobler aims in life contained in Mr Ruskin's writings. From him alone, and through his influence, have I learnt how by endeavouring to put into practice what each of us may feel to be good, and then devoting our energies in earnest self-sacrifice to accomplish our ideal, we have clearer visions of the great possibilities for happy life and work in rural England yet.[3]

As if to illustrate her belief that the realisation of Ruskin's theories took precedence of all else, early in 1900 Miss Twelves collaborated with Mrs Rawnsley and her Keswick School on their mentor's funeral pall. The

[1] Sheffield Archives, GSG 21.

[2] Ibid.

[3] *Woman's Agricultural Times*, Sept. 1899.

School had already lent Miss Twelves money on several occasions to assist in her Ruskinian work (for example, £25 in February 1898),[1] showing that the two never wholly broke contact. So strong was the Ruskin bond in Lakeland that any professional or personal rifts were, if felt, never expressed. The pall was designed by Edith Rawnsley and her associate Harold Stabler (1872–1945) and was made by Miss Twelves and her St George's spinsters, some of whom had worked under Miss Twelves during her time at the Rawnsleys' School. Consisting of plain, unbleached, hand spun, hand woven linen, it was lined with rose-red silk and embroidered with wild roses—the emblem of St George—and rose buds and petals. In the centre was a wreath of wild roses and the words 'Unto This Last', the title of one of Ruskin's more controversial works, published in 1860. Beneath were the initials 'J.R.'. The pall was shown at the 1900 Home Arts Exhibition where it won one of 68 stars awarded to the Industry for its 54 exhibits.

Irrespective of its success and the more formal contribution of the Guild of St George, the Ruskin Linen Industry—like the Langdale Linen Industry—survived commercially only until the 1920s. In October 1902 the Keswick workshop received a visit from Princess Louise who was received at St George's Cottage by the Severns and Miss Twelves. The princess was presented with a dress length of linen (spun by Dorothy Birkett and Agnes Ritson, and woven by Robert Shearman) and a bag worked in Greek lace by Ada Hooper.[2] The local newspaper reported that:

> Mr Severn expressed it as his opinion that this little cottage industry, with no pretensions beyond a determination to do its best in all its undertakings, was a perfect practical example of the teaching of John Ruskin—than which no higher praise can be desired.[3]

Other notable events included an appearance at a specially arranged Ruskin Exhibition at Keswick in 1907 attended by Companions from

---

[1] CROC, DB 111/1, 19 Feb. 1898.

[2] The situation regarding Robert Shearman is not clear. Since he acted as weaver at the Keswick School branch of the Linen Industry, but was recorded in the Keswick School minutes (CROC, DB 1111/), as being unsatisfactory, he may have left. Unless the princess was presented with a piece of linen worked a few years before, Shearman presumably returned to work for Miss Twelves at some point in the early 1900s.

[3] Sheffield Archives, GSG 21, newspaper cutting describing Princess Louise's visit to the Ruskin Linen Industry on the occasion of the opening of Brandlehow Estate, 16 Oct. 1902.

across the country (including Rawnsley and Marian Twelves). Progress continued steadily but in 1905 it was again made clear that no effort was to be made to 'increase the working staff ... but to maintain it in efficiency and so fulfil the Guild motto chosen by its founder—"Yea, the work of our hands establish Thou it".'[1] Exactly how many women worked in association with St George's Cottage is not clear. But the number was substantial enough for the Keswick workshop to run successfully for 35 years. After 1900 Marian Twelves spent more time teaching Ruskin lace to visitors, particularly from America and India, and provided linen for Italy where a similar textile revival among the regional poor took place. With too few new spinsters coming forward after about 1908, as the old workforce died away so too did the small and carefully managed Ruskin Linen Industry.

In about 1913 Miss Twelves moved from St George's Cottage to 2 and 3 High Hill, Keswick, two cottages originally leased by the Guild of St George and bought by them in 1920. These she leased from the Guild for £12 yearly and set up a workroom and showroom. As a result of ill-health and old age, in 1918 she handed over control of the Industry to three sisters from Keswick (one of whom, Frances Adamson, was already on the Industry's Committee):

> After thirty-five years of individual and most successful work and organisation, Miss Twelves has passed the management of the Industry into the hands of the Misses Adamson of Keswick, three sisters, who are carrying it on in the spirit and by the same methods which are the foundation and have always been the inspiration of this unique work.[2]

Its days of intense and creative commercial activity were now drawing to a close. After a brief return, instigated chiefly by loyal customers who wished to see her back at the Industry, in July 1929 Miss Twelves died at High Hill, six years after Fleming, nine years after Canon Rawnsley, thirteen years after Edith Rawnsley and 29 years after Ruskin. Her personal financial situation at the time of her death was less than comfortable and debts she had amassed in connection with the Linen Industry in its later years were written off by the Guild of St George. Ultimately, her determination to work in accordance with Ruskin's teachings above all else had brought her no monetary reward. But in

---

[1] Sheffield Archives, GSG 21, *The Ruskin Linen Industry* (c.1905).

[2] *Ruskin Linen Industry Guild of St George* (c.1918).

other respects she had been richly rewarded. Her efforts resulted in a now incalculable quantity of local art work, some of which has survived as testament to her inspiration and guidance. Most are of an exceptional standard of workmanship and design in relation to the worker, i.e. who not only made the product but designed it too. As Ruskin prophesied, that demonstrated quite clearly that the abandonment of machines in the workplace increased the opportunity for worker creativity, and brought associated artistic and (to a degree) economic success. On her death an inventory was made of Miss Twelves's few possessions. Among them was some broken crockery, a small number of books, two spinning wheels, wooden bobbins, spun flax, photographs of Ruskin and a print of Ruskin in his study.[1] To the end, her devotion to Ruskin was complete, and her work lives on today in the form of Ruskin lace which, still made locally by a small band of dedicated women, continues to proclaim Lakeland's design independence.

---

[1] Sheffield Archives, GSG 21, Inventory, 28 Aug. 1929.

5

HARDWICK D. RAWNSLEY AND THE FOUNDING OF THE KESWICK SCHOOL OF INDUSTRIAL ARTS

The general misconception that the revival of the spinning wheels in Lakeland originated from the broader and slightly later Arts and Crafts movement has, until now, presented two principal difficulties. One is that the work of Fleming and Marian Twelves has remained largely misunderstood and dismissed as a minor, country-based offshoot of what was a larger, city-based arts movement; the other is that the significance of the revival of the wheels as the instigator of a larger and more complex revival of local arts and crafts of definite Ruskinian origin has remained largely unrecognised. The lack of detailed research into Ruskin's associations with the Arts and Crafts (including the Exhibition Society and the movement which followed), the similarity between some of the movement's aims and the aims of Lakeland, and the fact that the two ran side by side for a while appear to be the origin of the use (or misuse) of the Arts and Crafts label to describe the Lakeland revival.

When or how exactly the label came into use is unclear but it appears to have been used first in the 1970s and 1980s by Crawford and Callen. At the same time, a small number of local museums and galleries adopted the phrase but cannot explain its continued use today, except that the name Ruskin was common to both the Arts and Crafts and the Lakeland revival. The fact that neither Fleming nor Miss Twelves ever wrote anything substantial on their Lakeland work has added to the confusion, as have the small number of brief accounts of the revival published to date. Grevel Lindop's short and overly romantic interpretation of the Langdale Linen Industry's beginnings is typical of a number of recent accounts:

> 200 yards further N. is Ruskin Cottage, home of Miss Twelves, an elderly lady from Langdale who was noticed by Ruskin one day

at her spinning wheel. Shocked to learn that she was the last woman in the area who knew how to spin, Ruskin arranged for her to teach others and established a workshop for hand linen production.[1]

In this passage the name of the cottage is incorrect, Miss Twelves was not elderly when she began her spinning enterprise, she was not originally from Lakeland, and Ruskin did not see her spinning, or arrange for her to conduct classes to others. Even Jennie Brunton's more detailed and accurate account, like those of Crawford, Callen, Benjamin and Blake, not only misses the complex origin of the Industry, but also fails to award the Langdale Linen Industry its rightful place as the head of a significant and sizeable Ruskinian revival of local arts and crafts in Lakeland.[2] Given the particularly strong links between the Linen Industry and the Keswick School of Industrial Arts, to give anything less than a full account of both would be to present an incomplete picture of events in Lakeland between 1880 and 1920.

Such was the impact of Ruskin on Lakeland that the region witnessed not only a return to local traditions in cloth production, but a far more complex and diverse revival of local arts and crafts which intensified after 1883. During Ruskin's Brantwood years, Albert Fleming and Marian Twelves were undeniably two of his most loyal Lakeland devotees. But of equal faith and devotion were the Rawnsleys. Like Fleming, Hardwicke Rawnsley's associations with Ruskin began some years before his own move to the Lake District. Originally from Lincolnshire, Rawnsley was introduced to Lakeland and to the writings of Wordsworth and Ruskin in his youth by his teacher, Edward Thring.[3] In 1870 he went to Oxford to study natural science and chemistry at Balliol with a view to practising medicine, and there met Ruskin, then Slade Professor of Fine Art. Immediately struck by him, Rawnsley agreed to take part in Ruskin's Hinksey digging project, a drainage scheme devised by him to help the people of Hinksey and to teach his students respect for manual labour. Working alongside Rawnsley was Lord Milner and also W.G. Collingwood, who would later become

---

[1] G. Lindop, *A Literary Guide to the Lake District* (1993), 177. Ruskin himself was guilty of exploiting the romantic image of the spinning wheel, but as Marian Twelves herself said, it is to that 'which the subject so readily lends itself' (M. Twelves, Leaflet, *The Ruskin Linen Industry* (Keswick, *c.*1900), 1 (copy in Sheffield Archives, GSG 21).

[2] E. Roberts, *A History of Linen in the North West* (Centre for North-West Regional Studies, University of Lancaster, 1998).

[3] Rawnsley later wrote *Edward Thring Teacher and Poet* (1889) in his honour.

Ruskin's secretary at Brantwood and a pivotal figure in the revival of Lakeland arts. After abandoning medicine Rawnsley resolved to join the ministry and went to Bristol. There he began what would be his lengthy career as both cleric and writer, and took part in his first conservation project, helping to save the ancient tower of St Werburgh's church. In 1875 he was seriously ill and went to the Lake District to recuperate, staying with cousins at Wray-on-Windermere and with the Fletchers of Croft, Ambleside. In 1877 he was offered the living at Wray and in January 1878 married the Fletchers' eldest daughter, Edith, at Brathay.

Already a devout Ruskinian by 1877, Rawnsley's decision to accept the post at Wray was surely influenced by his mentor's presence at Coniston. Their acquaintance was speedily renewed and within a short time he was visiting Brantwood. From his home at Wray Rawnsley could easily go 'over the Hawkshead Hill' to talk with Ruskin.[1] Rawnsley spent a good deal of time discussing the Church with his mentor, but he particularly recalled one talk with Ruskin in his Oxford days in which Ruskin had emphasised the need for the clergy 'to make earth heaven by doing certain fair deeds'.[2] Such 'fair deeds' he had described in terms of practical efforts which would ensure a greater degree of happiness and satisfaction in life, most readily translated into parish workshops where village crafts could once more be taught and employed:

> Why don't the bishops admonish their clergy to see to it that side by side with parish church and parish mission room there shall be a parish workshop, where the blacksmith and the village carpenter shall of a winter evening teach all the children who will be diligent and will learn, the nature of iron and wood, and the use of their eyes and hands. 'I would have the decoration of metal and wood brought in later, and these children as they grow shall feel the joy of adding ornament to simple surfaces of metal or wood; but always they shall be taught the use of the pencil, and the delight of close observation of flower in the field and bird in the hedgerow and animal in the wild wood. We must bring joy, the joy of eye and hand-skill to our cottage homes.'[3]

Although the Rawnsleys spent much of 1879 travelling abroad, in 1880 they returned to Wray and settled into the life of the village where their

---

[1] H.D. Rawnsley, *Ruskin and the English Lakes* (Glasgow, 1901), 119.

[2] Ibid., 116.

[3] Ibid., 116–17.

only son, Noel, was born. With Ruskin's words 'not forgotten', immediately on his return Rawnsley set about realising his mentor's vision of 'fair deeds' and the Wray woodcarving class was founded.[1]

As with Ruskin and Fleming, much of what Rawnsley did during his years in Lakeland was born out of a passion for both the region and its heritage (undoubtedly enhanced by both Thring and Ruskin) but also out of concern for its people. As an equally avid student of Wordsworth and later the author of A Reminiscence of Wordsworth Day, Cockermouth (1896) and Wordsworth. Tennyson (1906), by 1880 Rawnsley was already interested in conservation and deeply aware of the unwelcome changes resulting from the introduction of industry in south Lakeland. Imbued with a similarly strong Wordsworthian or Ruskinian notion of what pre-industrial Lakeland represented and an awareness of what had already been lost by way of culture and tradition, Rawnsley decided to establish a woodcarving class for several specific reasons. The village of Wray he noted as having 'no poor among the people', but the villagers themselves as having 'plenty of time' to take up some form of useful pastime.[2] Since traditional song was 'already one of the features of the village life' with the postmaster a musician, and the thought of reviving the 'old spinning-wheel days' spoken of 'tenderly by the village grandmothers' never struck Rawnsley as possible, woodcarving—also a dwindling tradition across Cumberland and Westmorland—was chosen.[3] Such was the initial response that pupils came not only from Wray but from Grasmere and Ambleside—a strong indication in the pre-Langdale Linen Industry days that a revival of local crafts would meet a definite need. Although Edith Rawnsley had some training in the arts, with practical experience of woodcarving and metalwork, a 'lady teacher' from South Kensington was employed to give a course to pupils from Wray, Grasmere and Ambleside, at which point, in Rawnsley's words, the 'home industry' of the Lake District was truly 'set on foot'.[4]

The Rawnsleys' Wray class was the first Ruskinian handcraft venture established in the Lake District, but because it ran for less than three years it did not instigate the wider return to local arts and crafts which occurred in the wake of the much larger and more widely publicised Langdale and Ruskin Linen Industries. It was, however, just as success-

---

[1] Ibid., 117.

[2] Ibid., 118.

[3] Ibid.

[4] Ibid. There are indications that woodcarving classes were run alongside the Royal School of Art Needlework classes in London, teaching women woodcarving as well as needlework. Rawnsley's lady teacher probably came from those classes.

ful in terms of attendance and support, and in the last winter that the Rawnsleys were at Wray (1882–3), Edith began experimenting in repoussé work with a view to introducing it at the class. Early in 1883, before the experiments were completed, Rawnsley accepted the living of St Kentigern's, Crosthwaite, Keswick, and the Wray class was apparently disbanded. Although the class did not set in motion a widespread revival of local arts and crafts, it did form the basis of all the Rawnsleys' art and craft work after 1883 and, just as significantly, it was through the Wray experiment that Rawnsley first coined the phrase 'home art industry' or 'home industry' to describe not only their own class but later the classes and workshops of all those who worked under Ruskin's influence in Lakeland after 1883.[1] When these died away in the 1920s and 1930s, the phrase died out with them and, after a gap of some forty years, the label 'Arts and Crafts' mistakenly began to take its place.

By the time the Rawnsleys moved to Keswick, Fleming had already arrived in the region and, as Rawnsley described it, 'the Langdale spinning-wheels had just begun to hum'.[2] Inspired as much by Fleming's work as by their success at Wray, the Rawnsleys resolved to found another handcraft class. Under the continued influence of Ruskin, and motivated by Fleming's more adventurous aims at Elterwater, they decided to found a larger and more carefully organised class which would become widely known as the Keswick School of Industrial Arts. As at Wray, the emphasis would be on the application of Ruskin's teachings, combined with the revival of local traditions. Although no obvious signs of local traditional crafts existed at Keswick, Rawnsley quickly noted many examples of ancient woodcarving in old farmhouses which hinted that, here too, handcrafts had once thrived:

> but some one had evidently been fond of wood-carving of old, for not a settle nor high 'seat-post' nor meal-ark or kist in the older farms but had careful scroll and vine-roll ornament upon them, dating some of these from King James' time, and the later Restoration down to the middle of last century. There was evidence here that the love of wood-carving detail was cared for

---

[1] In *Ruskin and the English Lakes* (1901), Rawnsley devoted a whole chapter to 'Ruskin and the Home Art Industries in the Lake District', which covered the Langdale Linen Industry, the Keswick School and a number of other local revival classes and workshops, all of which are discussed in this thesis. Rawnsley experienced the revival of 'home industry' at first hand, living through its formative years, taking a direct role in its shaping. His phrase 'Home Art Industries' referred to events which happened at least eighteen months before the Home Arts and Industries Association was founded.

[2] Rawnsley, *Ruskin*, 119.

in Cumberland homes. ... The conventionalised palm-roll on the Cumberland furniture has often set me thinking of the permanency of traditional ornament among a pastoral people.[1]

Thus a woodcarving class was again the obvious choice but, given Edith's skills as both a metalworker and also a needlewoman, accompanied by separate metalwork and needlework classes.

In the winter of 1883–4 the Rawnsleys called together a committee to discuss founding the Keswick School of Industrial Arts. The original committee, very much a local concern, consisted of the Rawnsleys, Dr Knight, John Gardiner, John Birkett, the Revd J. Sharpe Ostle (the school secretary and curate of Crosthwaite), Miss Ann Elliot, and J.W. Oddie, a friend of Ruskin and Rawnsley. They decided on the following objectives:

I   To counteract the pernicious effect of turning men into machines without possibility of love of their work.

II   To make it felt that hand-work did really allow the expression of a man's soul and self, and so was worth doing for its own sake, and worth purchasing even at some cost to the buyer.

III   To try to displace by hand-work the crude metal and wood ornaments that are now produced by steel dies and hydraulic presses.

IV   To show that there was here in England, while we are crying out that German cheap art labour or Japanese cheap art labour is ruining us, an abundance of skill of hand which is wasted, but which, if any education worth its name could be given to the whole working man—to his eye, to his hand, to his heart as well as his head—could and would help England here and now.[2]

Mrs Rawnsley was to supervise the brass repoussé, John Birkett (a local jeweller) was to offer assistance in 'the manipulation of the sheet metal in the matter of beating it up into shape from the flat', advice was to be given by a local artist and designer, and a woman woodcarving teacher from South Kensington—probably the one employed briefly at Wray—

[1] Ibid., 120–1.

[2] E. Rawnsley, *Canon Rawnsley. An Account of his Life* (Glasgow, 1923), 67.

was to be engaged.[1] The classes were to run three nights a week for five months of the year (October to March), and were advertised in the local newspaper at the beginning of each session:

> INDUSTRIAL ART CLASSES.—On Saturday, at the Parish Room, classes will be commenced for the teaching of 'such art industries as can be profitably carried on' in the homes of working men; viz., 'brass and other metal work, carving, embroidery, &c.' The promoters 'hope for assistance from all who are interested in industrial arts, and in the effort to bring the designer into more immediate relation with the workman until they become more or less identified, as was the case at all periods when the arts were truly living.' According to the rules, no persons under 16 years of age will be admitted as members, and the committee reserve to themselves the right to discontinue instruction to any member who does not show sufficient aptitude or carefulness in the work. The instruction will be free to all working men, and tools and materials will be provided. All the work by members will be the property of the committee, who, however, will pay the workers for all articles which have a marketable value. As is but reasonable, no work will be done except from designs approved by the committee. Amateurs will be permitted to join, but they will find their own tools and materials, and pay 2s. 6d. each lesson; but after having received lessons they are at liberty to continue their connection with the class, and may do so by subscribing 10s. 6d. each winter season. While they will have to conform to the rule as to the class of work, they may retain or sell it to the committee, according to arrangement. The amateur classes will meet on Saturday mornings from 10 to 12. The ordinary classes will be held when possible on Tuesday, Thursday, and Saturday evenings, from 7 to 9.30.[2]

To assist the students, drawing classes were also to be held at the School. Miss Elliot of Main Street, Keswick, was to act as secretary and saleswoman, taking orders all the year round for goods which were to be made when the School opened each winter.

Held in the Parish Room in the centre of Keswick, the first session of handcraft classes, staged over the winter of 1884–5, was a success in

---

[1] Rawnsley, *Ruskin*, 121–2.

[2] CROC, DB 111/93, unidentified local newspaper cutting dated Nov. 1884 in Edith Rawnsley's scrapbook.

terms of attendance but financially, with expenses of £181 and sales of only £118, it foundered.[1] Since the Wray class had never run as a commercial venture, the Rawnsleys evidently lacked both experience of running a self-supporting scheme and the astute business sense which Fleming brought to Elterwater from his experience as a solicitor. On the other hand, within a month of beginning the Keswick classes brass and copper finger plates of 'simple' design were being sold.[2] As with Langdale linen there was clearly a market for the goods made, but how that market was approached was where the difficulty lay.

A committee meeting was called early in 1885 and strategies discussed. Given that Rawnsley became acquainted with Fleming immediately on his arrival at Neaum Crag and that the cleric was familiar with developments at St Martin's, it is probable that Fleming offered advice to Rawnsley, particularly since the School's committee immediately elected to follow in St Martin's footsteps by attending exhibitions. The first was that held in Keswick Town Hall at Easter 1885. Until then goods had been displayed only in Birkett's jewellery shop and in Miss Elliot's house. The committee also decided to appoint a Mr R. Little, a 'clever wood-carver' from Carlisle who, such was his enthusiasm for the Rawnsleys' project, asked only for expenses of £9 for the session.[3] A collection was made locally to cover the sum. In October 1885 it was decided that students should sell their work only through the School and that payment to the students would be made only when their work was sold.[4] In the same year, and again following St Martin's example, the Keswick School became affiliated to the Home Arts and Industries Association. After attending the Home Arts Exhibition in London the following year, the School's bank balance grew to just over £60. Expenditure doubled but so also—for the first time—did sales,[5] although it would be June 1888 before the School was satisfactorily paying its way.

Such was the response to the revival of local crafts in Keswick that by the end of 1886 a drawing master had been appointed and a strict condition imposed that students had to show basic drawing ability. Thirty students began that winter's session, with applicants coming from all spheres of life, including the local tanyards and pencil factories, and

[1] CROC, DB 111/100.

[2] Rawnsley, *Ruskin*, 122.

[3] Ibid.

[4] CROC, DB 111/100.

[5] Ibid.

from all age ranges. Keswick, of course, was much larger than Wray and with appropriate advertising in local newspapers the excellent reputation the classes soon acquired ensured that they were always well attended. To assist in the efficient production of metalwork, by 1886 the School had fitted up an 'iron room' next to the (borrowed) Parish Room with 'concrete floor, blow-pipe, anvil, vices and the like', one of the School 'hands' electing to teach himself and then the students.[1] Such was its success that, at the end of the 1886–7 session, the School's assets were £131. Ruskin's and Rawnsley's vision of a parish workshop had been both well and truly realised, and the school was wholly self-supporting. Sales for 1886 were increased by another appearance at the Home Arts Exhibition, and also at Howell & James's art galleries in Regent Street. There, items of metalwork made under the improved conditions were shown, including brass plates, door plates and trays of various designs, all of which were fairly representative of the type of goods made during the school's early years.

Like the Langdale and Ruskin Linen Industries, production in the early years at Keswick concentrated mostly on domestic goods of simple design. Before 1900 smaller items made included boxes, caskets, buttons, finger bowls, inkstands, door handles, door plates, vases, pen trays, napkin rings, tea caddies and watch stands in copper and brass. Similar goods were available in silver plated copper, along with larger items such as entrée dishes, muffin dishes, soup tureens, chargers, teapots and christening mugs. More expensive items, made in silver, included butter knives, bonbon dishes, cream jugs, napkin rings, photograph frames and various small spoons in Celtic, Etruscan and St Kentigern designs, the saint also appearing on trays and ashtrays. This policy, along with the use of Cumberland minerals, gave the School's early products a distinctly local character. Local minerals were also used in jewellery. Items such as brooches, pendant chains and scarf pins were made under Mrs Rawnsley and Birkett, who in 1886 also undertook to instruct pupils in brass work (Birkett was perhaps the 'hand' who, in 1886, mastered the new blow-pipe and vices). Not surprisingly, given Rawnsley's clerical connections, a variety of church items (including textiles) were also available to order, including almsdishes and altar candlesticks, and the woodcarving students produced a wide variety of bowls, boxes, tables, and even spinning stools (a direct result of Wordsworth's and Ruskin's influence). In the mid to late 1880s prices ranged from 7s. 6d. for a silver-lined sugar basin to around 4 guineas for a wood carved gong. The

[1] Rawnsley, *Ruskin*, 123.

spinning stools sold for about 25s. each.

Despite the demands of her role as the wife of an energetic cleric, and her devotion to the Keswick School's metalwork and woodcarving classes, Edith Rawnsley still found time to run needlework classes at the School for almost 25 years. Textiles produced were always of an admirable standard of both quality and design, and some of the embroideries were executed on Langdale and later Ruskin linens. Among the more notable pieces was the Church Congress banner of St Kentigern, the Celtic-influenced design for which, executed by Mrs Rawnsley, was published in *The Studio*.[1] The banner, made by 'various ladies of the diocese and Miss Mitchell of Chester', was also exhibited at the Barrow-in-Furness Ecclesiastical Art Exhibition in 1906.[2] It depicted St Kentigern with his staff, bell and robin, with a border pattern of runic knotwork adapted from an old Cumberland cross. Arguably the most striking embroidery produced during Mrs Rawnsley's time was the white festal altar frontal made for Crosthwaite church around 1900. The striking design at first suggests an Arts and Crafts influence, but it was taken from a tomb at Ravenna which dates back to the time of St Kentigern (AD 553), visited by the Rawnsleys on their travels abroad. Still in use, the frontal includes two facing peacocks made three-dimensional by the addition of actual feathers, surrounded by a vine and tendril pattern on a white and gold background. Accompanying hangings were apparently also made by the School, but those cannot now be traced.[3]

Although Mrs Rawnsley was far from alone in employing the needle, with a number of other classes and workshops across the country producing equally accomplished church textiles (including the Leek Embroidery Society and the Sisters of Bethany), she was abundantly aware that her plying of the feminine plough was a fundamentally important part of Ruskin's 'vision of thread and needlework' outlined in *Fors*.[4] In order to spread that vision further—and Mrs Rawnsley was assuredly aware of that vision as an equally avid Ruskin devotee and

---

[1] *The Studio*, Nov. 1906, 171. The banner has not been traced.

[2] Ibid. Miss Mitchell was probably associated with the Chester Embroidery Society whose embroideries appeared in a number of national exhibitions, including the 1902 Decorative and Applied Art Exhibition held in the Grosvenor Museum.

[3] F.C. Eeles *The Parish Church of St Kentigern, Crosthwaite* (Kendal, 1953), gives details of the frontal and hangings.

[4] Leek Embroidery Society was founded in 1879 by Mrs Elizabeth Wardle and produced many ecclesiastical embroideries. The School of Embroidery of the Sisters of Bethany was based in Lloyd Street, London, and produced church embroideries of all kinds, some under the direct supervision of architect John Ninian Comper (1864–1960).

reader of *Fors*—sewing parties were held at Crosthwaite Vicarage from at least 1886.[1] Children's sewing parties were also held, designed to pass on handcraft skills to the next generation, the same reason that the children of Coniston were taught to make Ruskin lace. Mission sewing parties were also held at the Vicarage (once the home of the novelist Eliza Lynn Linton), presumably to raise funds. In 1887 the *Manchester Guardian* wrote of the Keswick School:

> If the dropped thread of English design, which was once as naturally sound and fanciful and good as till late years it was the contrary of those things, can thus be picked up, and if the carpenter or brass worker can once more become an artist as was his ancestor two centuries ago, a great and salutary work will have been done in England, and such pioneers as those of Keswick will not miss their due meed of grateful recollection.[2]

This was a most appropriate analogy to describe what the School was trying to achieve. When Miss Twelves joined the Rawnsleys' project in 1889, that reputation grew and for just over four years two successful Ruskinian textile ventures thrived at Keswick.

Such was the success of the Keswick School that in 1885 it established its own annual Whit week exhibition where anything up to seven hundred items were shown. By 1886 Howell & James of London were acting as official agents. With repeated prize winning appearances at the Home Arts Exhibition, by 1889 some £500 worth of goods were sold in the year, which rose to £700 in 1891. By then the committee was able to consider building a new school, a testament to the successful realisation of Ruskin's theories which still stands today. In late 1891 an application was made for the purchase of a field close to Greta Bridge in Keswick (opposite Southey's former home) as the site for a new School of Industrial Arts. By March 1893 plans had been drawn up by Paley, Austin & Paley of Lancaster. The estimated cost was £1,300, to which the School contributed £300 and the county council £200, with the balance covered by donations, including one from Ruskin's friend Mrs Talbot. The building consisted of a workshop, showroom, office and designer's room. In 1893 Mrs Rawnsley was authorised to buy books and other necessary items for the new school.[3]

---

[1] Crosthwaite parish magazine, 1886.

[2] *Manchester Guardian*, 19 Nov. 1887.

[3] CROC, DB 111/1.

Following Ruskin's praise of traditional Lakeland architecture in *The Poetry of Architecture*, the new building incorporated local stone and slate and a spinning gallery. Like round chimneys, spinning galleries are unique to Lakeland (except for a few just over the Yorkshire border), and around 40 survive today as a reminder of the days of the spinning wheels in Cumberland and Westmorland. Spinning galleries can still be found in Troutbeck and Hawkshead, and one at Hartsop was photographed several times at the turn of the twentieth century by the Lakeland photographer Herbert Bell. Debate over their actual purpose has raged for many years, some believing that they were never used as places for spinning. Rawnsley, however, was in no doubt that the galleries were used by local spinsters:

> But it was not only to the content and comfort of the households that the spinning-wheel till the end of the last century contributed, it added to the picturesqueness of the estateman's home also. Anyone who remembers the picturesque gallery and overhanging eaves of the farm at Monk Coniston, of the well-roofed entrances and stairway landings or balconies of the houses at Hawkshead, of the farmhouse at Smethwaite Bridge near Great Howe, and one or two of the more ancient houses on the Borrodale road and at the entrance of the courts at Keswick, will understand how the need of sitting out of doors in our long twilight evenings of April and May, or in rainy weather throughout the year to go on with the business of the spinning-wheel made these balconies or galleries an imperative and natural addition to house architecture in the Lake District.[1]

With Southey's clock placed in the hall, the new School was as much a tribute to Lakeland and its heritage as to Ruskin's theories, the two aptly combined to produce a purpose-built centre for teaching revived local crafts on a scale never before seen in Keswick. The opening ceremony took place on 4 April 1894, when letters of congratulation were sent by, among others, G.F. Watts, Mrs Holman Hunt, Walter Crane and Mrs Severn who, on behalf of Ruskin, wrote 'You have Mr Ruskin's best wishes always in all your good works'.[2] Gifts were also sent, including specimen sheets from the Kelmscott Press donated by William Morris. Sales for 1894 totalled £816, the highest yet achieved,

---

[1] Rawnsley, *Ruskin*, 132–3.
[2] *Carlisle Patriot*, 6 April 1894.

despite Miss Twelves's departure early that year. With its new premises the School enjoyed increasing success, with the numbers of pupils reaching 80 (60 metal workers and 20 wood carvers) by the time it had run its first complete year.

In many respects the Keswick School of Industrial Arts is the most complex and difficult of all the Lakeland or Ruskinian endeavours to discuss, not only because it survived for almost a hundred years, but because it was inextricably interwoven with Rawnsley's other Ruskin-driven efforts in the Lake District. Because of his work in London and Broxbourne, until 1903 Fleming was limited in his application of Ruskin's theories by lack of time, relying on Marian Twelves to carry out his wishes during his winter absences from Neaum Crag. For Rawnsley, no greater or lesser a Ruskinian than Fleming, the particularly early introduction to Ruskin's work (through Thring) and his more permanent presence in the Lake District from 1877 (six years prior to Fleming's arrival) gave him greater opportunity to live and work according to Ruskin's teachings. At the same time as swelling the congregations at both Wray and Keswick with his ebullient, thought-provoking sermons, he not only put into practice Ruskin's teachings on handcrafts and parish workshops, but followed Wordsworth's and Ruskin's example by campaigning against local railways. As an undergraduate Rawnsley had read *A Protest Against the Extension of Railways in the Lake District* (1876) by Robert Somervell (1851–1933), a Westmorland man, in which it was noted:

> The author of *Modern Painters* earnestly requests all persons who may have taken interest in his writings, or who have any personal regard for him, to assist him now in the circulation of the enclosed paper, drawn up by his friend Mr Somervell, for the defence of the Lake District of England, and to press the appeal, so justly and temperately made in it, on the attention of their personal friends, —Ed.[1]

In a preface to the pamphlet Ruskin added a commendation of Somervell's 'temperate mastery' in putting forward his objections to the Lakeland railways, their beliefs, he added, 'tending in the same direction'.[2] Ruskin's support of the opposition campaign, he declared, was based not on selfishness, but on a greater desire to preserve all those

---

[1] J. Ruskin, *On the Old Road* (1899 edn), ii. 312.

[2] Ibid.

'sweet landscapes of England' from which he had learnt so much,[1] and because:

> I passionately wish to improve the minds of the populace, and because I am spending my own mind, strength, and fortune, wholly on that object, that I don't want to let them see Helvellyn while they are drunk. I suppose few men now living have so earnestly felt—none certainly have so earnestly declared—that the beauty of nature is the blessedest and most necessary of lessons for men; and that all other efforts in education are futile till you have taught your people to love fields, birds, and flowers. Come then, my benevolent friends, join with me in that teaching.[2]

When the Buttermere to Braithwaite railway scheme was put forward early in 1883 while he was still at Wray, Rawnsley followed the tradition of Lakeland defence (set by Wordsworth and followed by Ruskin) and immediately proposed an opposition strategy.

The Buttermere scheme was Rawnsley's first major attempt to defend the Lakeland landscape from industrialisation and was successful. In letters to local and national newspapers Rawnsley and his fellow campaigners (including Fleming) aroused widespread antagonism towards the spread of the railways in Lakeland, backed by Ruskin who wrote, albeit despairingly: 'It's all of no use—You will soon have a Cook's tourist railway up Scawfell, and another up Helvellyn, and another up Skiddaw, and then a connecting line all round'.[3] Ably assisted by W.H. Hills of Ambleside and Gordon Somervell (Robert's brother), Rawnsley adopted Ruskin's stance that the natural beauty of the Lake District was essential to the nation's health, an argument which he would repeat many times in the future. As a result of the success of the Buttermere defence scheme, the more permanent Lake District Defence Society was founded with the aim of preventing any other unwelcome changes to the region. Rawnsley and Albert Fleming were joint secretaries and distinguished members included Ruskin, Tennyson, Browning, Frederick Leighton, Alfred Waterhouse, Edward Thring, the 9th earl of Carlisle, William Morris, and Ruskin's friends Charles Eliot Norton and Octavia Hill.

The initial idea for a more structured Lakeland defence organisation, first proposed at the April 1883 meeting of the local Wordsworth

---

[1] Ibid., 314.

[2] Ibid., 318–19.

[3] E. Rawnsley, *Canon Rawnsley*, 51.

Society, was principally Rawnsley's. Almost immediately, the Lake District Defence Society was called into action to oppose the Ennerdale railway scheme which was put before Parliament, with Rawnsley appearing before the Commons committee to put the case for the defence. With the support of a recognised society, Rawnsley was again successful, winning both national attention for his work and the first of many appearances in *Punch*.[1]

After its further success when the Windermere to Ambleside railway proposal was quashed in 1886, the Defence Society was to play a major role in maintaining the Lake District as Wordsworth had known it and as Ruskin desired to keep it. Although the defence of a rural landscape might appear to have little to do with the revival of local arts and crafts, both were a fundamental part of Ruskin's vision of a Lakeland exalted in Wordsworth's poetry, a vision which equally drove the Lakeland handcraft revival. As with Fleming and Marian Twelves, Wordsworth and Ruskin inspired Rawnsley's every move and he expressed the same desire to keep Lakeland unchanged, whether it be by preventing the desecration of a green valley by a railway line or the demise of the spinning wheels. To the cleric, both Wordsworth and Ruskin had:

> the same thoughts about the need of keeping inviolate the sanctuary for thought and health and national happiness which the English Lake District, still undestroyed and unvulgarised, truly is. Read Wordsworth's protest against the projected railway from Kendal to Windermere, and set side by side with it Ruskin's preface to the pamphlet titled *A Protest Against the Extension of Railways in the Lake District*. The feeling and the spirit of both writers are the same. They had the same reverential regard for the life of the simple dalesmen amongst whom they dwelt.[2]

To Ruskin and his Lakeland followers, the curative powers of the wheels were only slightly less potent than the curative powers of the Lakeland landscape. Like the revival of the wheels, the revival of domestic crafts at Keswick and the protection of Lakeland were all part of a concentrated effort to protect not only the landscape but also the people who lived and worked in it, and the traditional regional culture which had developed from a particular way of life. Were the landscape to alter in any way, significant changes would ensue, not least of which would be

---

[1] *Punch*, 5 Feb. 1876, cartoon 'Lady of the Lake Loquitor'.

[2] Rawnsley, *Ruskin*, 168–9.

the loss of the artist's and writer's (and now also craftsman's and craftswoman's) muse-nature. It was no coincidence, therefore, that Rawnsley's Lakeland defence work ran parallel to his arts endeavours, the students at Wray and then Keswick being taught to study their natural surroundings for inspiration.

From 1883 until his death in 1920, Rawnsley worked ceaselessly on his Lakeland defence campaigns as well as on the Keswick School's committee, challenging not only the railways, but such equally controversial issues as Manchester's use of Thirlmere for its water supply, the erection of overhead power lines and telephone posts, bridge preservation, unsightly sewerage systems, the right to use footpaths, and the protection of wild flowers. Whenever necessary, an official body was formed, taking on a title appropriate to its cause. For example, in 1885 Rawnsley revived the Keswick and District Footpaths Association and kept the original name. Just prior to his death, in 1919, he also founded the Society for Safeguarding the Natural Beauty of the Lake District. Arguably the most successful and enduring of those was (and is) the National Trust to which Ruskin again made a direct contribution. At Ruskin's suggestion, in 1893 Rawnsley put his idea for the purchase of land for public use to Octavia Hill and by November of that year the National Trust for Places of Historic Interest and Natural Beauty had been founded by Rawnsley, Octavia Hill and Sir Robert Hunter, with Rawnsley as honorary secretary.

Although the Trust was from the start a national body, by 1947 it had acquired a considerable estate in the Lake District, including some 7,563 acres in Westmorland, 9,744 acres in Cumberland, and 6,650 acres in Lancashire. Along with the Lakeland land, the Trust took charge of 35 farms, eleven houses, 78 cottages, and five ancient buildings. Those included the lease of Wray Castle, the freeholds of Seathwaite Farm (614 acres), Penny Hill Farm, Eskdale (156 acres), Lingy Bank, Rosthwaite (21 acres), Green End Estate, Hawkshead (200 acres), Sawrey and Hawkshead (575 acres), land and houses at Coniston and Skelwith, farms and cottages at Medlock Vale, Daisy Nook (1,036 acres), Harry Place and Millbeck Farms, Langdale (289 acres), Little Langdale, farms (341 acres), and Troutbeck Park Farm (1,941 acres).[1] One of the largest single donations to the Trust was made by Beatrix Potter who, on her death, left them her 4,050 acre Sawrey and Hawkshead estates.[2] The

[1] *Westmorland Gazette*, 30 Sept. 1944; see G. Murphy, *Founders of the National Trust* (1987); M. Waterson, *The National Trust: The First Hundred Years* (1994) for Hill and Rawnsley.

[2] *Westmorland Gazette*, 30 Sept. 1944.

Potters were long-standing friends of the Rawnsleys but, although she lived in the Lake District from 1905 until 1943, Beatrix was not a fellow-admirer of Ruskin. As she wrote in her diary:

> Soon after we came back to town papa bought a curious book at the second-hand booksellers, Ruskin's *Modern Painters*. It had Mr Ruskin's autograph on the title page, stating he gave the book to D.G. Rossetti. Interesting copy, not that I think much of either chappy.[1]

An accomplished artist, she is another important figure in Lakeland's history and her work on fungi is still underrated. Her paper 'On the Germination of the Spores of the Agaricineae' (written in 1896) was eventually read to the Linnean Society in London, delivered by a man since women were excluded. On her death, some of her drawings of fungi were given to the Armitt Library, Ambleside.

[1] L. Linder (ed.), *The Journal of Beatrix Potter* (1966), 54.

6

RAWNSLEY, RUSKIN AND THE DEVELOPMENT OF THE KESWICK SCHOOL OF INDUSTRIAL ARTS

Although the Rawnsleys encountered only success during their time in the Lake District, like Fleming and Marian Twelves, as Lakeland Ruskinians they had to contend with the daunting prospect of Ruskin's increasing deteriorating health. To live and work in such close proximity to their mentor whilst successfully realising his teachings, and for him to be afflicted by both old age and ill-health, must have proved at times frustrating. Nonetheless, the intensity of their devotion never lessened, and there was never any diminution in their commitment to the realisation of his teachings. Nor were any outside influences allowed to affect that realisation. Rather, the opposite applied, and—like Marian Twelves—their determination to live and work according to Ruskin's personal as well as written direction only grew. Although, like Fleming, Rawnsley has left little indication as to which of Ruskin's works he favoured, his own extensive writings (including some 43 separately published volumes as well as newspaper and magazine articles) reveals a familiarity with all the fundamental aspects of those teachings which influenced Fleming, with specific reference to his readings of *Fors Clavigera* in *Ruskin and the English Lakes*. He notes, for example, that

> Ruskin heard that Brantwood was for sale; £1,500 was the price that Linton asked him for the house and its fellside ground, and the Professor bought it without sight of it. He tells us in his seventh volume of *Fors Clavigera* that it was 'a mere shed of rotten timber and loose stone', and that it had to be furnished and repaired.[1]

---

[1] H.D. Rawnsley, *Ruskin and the English Lakes* (Glasgow, 1901), 33.

102

Rawnsley also acknowledged the influence of Fleming as 'the hand of Fors' in his own arts and crafts work after 1883, *Fors* in its practical as well as written form influencing him in his founding of the Keswick School.[1] Like the Langdale Linen Industry and its founder (Fleming), there was a clear association between the founder of the Keswick School and Ruskin, and also Ruskin's *Fors Clavigera*.

Although Rawnsley and Fleming did not meet until 1883, their like-mindedness towards Ruskin, *Fors Clavigera* and Lakeland immediately drew them together when Fleming arrived at Neaum Crag, and they remained close friends and admiring colleagues for the next 37 years until Rawnsley's death in 1920. Mutually supportive in all they did, but particularly in their restoration of local crafts and the defence of the region, the work of both was the successful embodiment of all that Ruskin represented. As strong-minded individuals, they each put their own personal experience and perception of Ruskin into practice in the revival of Lakeland crafts. Rawnsley's experience of Ruskin as a writer stretched back to his childhood under the influence of Thring (himself an admirer of Ruskin), laying foundations at an early age which would steer his adult life. His personal experience of the writer began shortly after his arrival at Oxford, their separation (when Rawnsley went briefly to Bristol) being only temporary. But it was only on arriving in the Lake District and as a result of more sustained contact with Ruskin, that Rawnsley too set about realising the writer's theories. Yet again, for those in late nineteenth-century Lakeland, that personal as well as theoretical element proved fundamentally important in the realisation of Ruskin's theories. For Rawnsley, there was an additional bond with Ruskin in the form of an earlier and equally intense love of the Lakes, a bond which he believed gave them a particular closeness marked further by their shared interest in God and the Church.

As a young man Rawnsley visited the Lake District a number of times in the company of Thring (who was also an admirer of Wordsworth) and fell under the spell of the region and its literary culture, just as Ruskin had during his childhood. By the time Ruskin arrived at Brantwood in 1872, Rawnsley was familiar not only with Wordsworth's works, but with Ruskin's continuation of Wordsworth's opposition to any changes as a result of industrialisation. Given Ruskin's associations with Wordsworth and the Lake District, Rawnsley perceived Brantwood to be the only 'fit place' for him to come in ill-health, an appropriate centre from which to champion Wordsworth's cause, as well as a healing

---

[1] Ibid., 136.

landscape in which to live and work.[1] To Rawnsley, Ruskin and
Wordsworth were two lone voices expressing equal concern for the Lake
District, not merely conveying 'the same thoughts' about preventing the
spread of railways, but 'the same reverential regard for the life of the
simple dalesmen amongst whom they dwelt'.[2] The more pressing issue
might have been to air widespread dismay over the ruination of the
landscape. But underneath in both men ran a deeper compassion for the
people of the region and what they stood to lose from the introduction
of machinery, the same compassion subsequently expressed by Fleming,
Marian Twelves and the Rawnsleys.

As with Marian Twelves, Ruskin's compassionate concern for the
poor, and his desire to be 'made by his tender approachableness one of
the family', particularly appealed to Rawnsley.[3] The 'peasant's lot',
written about so lyrically by Wordsworth, was also Ruskin's concern,
both resolving (in Rawnsley's mind) that:

> In order to teach men how to be satisfied it is necessary fully to
> understand the art and joy of humble life ... the life of domestic
> affection and domestic peace, and full of sensitiveness to all
> elements of costless and kind pleasure, therefore chiefly to the
> loveliness of the natural world.[4]

With an equal concern (as Rawnsley perceived it) for the children of the
peasants, the revival of local crafts under Ruskin's direct influence had
an additional potency, offering to future generations the 'domestic
affection and domestic peace' which had been destroyed by machinery.
To Wordsworth and Ruskin, wealth had become the 'only means of
pleasure'[5] when a nation's true wealth 'was not mammon but men',
something which Fleming echoed in *In the House of Rimmon*.[6]

So engrossed in Ruskin's life did Rawnsley become that in 1901 he
was moved to write *Ruskin and the English Lakes*, a detailed study of his
mentor's associations with the region where he chose to live his later
years. He did not write any similarly detailed account of Ruskin's life
away from the Lake District. His interest in the writer concentrated

---

[1] Ibid., 31.
[2] Ibid., 169.
[3] Ibid., 169–70.
[4] Ibid., 170.
[5] Ibid.
[6] Ibid., 171; above, p. 14 for Fleming on money and worth.

almost exclusively upon his years in Lakeland after 1872, with earlier references mostly concerning Ruskin's visits to Lakeland before 1871. Like Fleming, he left a literary as well as artistic testament to the writer's experiences in south Lakeland, quoting Ruskin's first memory of the region formed on a childhood visit:

> There was one district however—that of the Cumberland lakes, which needed no charm of association to deepen the appeal to realities. I have said somewhere that my first memory in life was Friar's Crag on Derwentwater: meaning I suppose my first memory of things afterwards chiefly precious to me:[1]

He described how, for a period of seven years in Ruskin's youth, Lakeland 'haunted him like a passion'.[2] Rawnsley recounted every detail of Ruskin's attachment to the region: the continued visits into adulthood, the poetry written in imitation of Wordsworth, the special bond with Wordsworth (which filled two chapters), and the longing for a particular way of rural life. The purchase of Brantwood was described, followed by a chapter on 'Ruskin and the Home Art Industries in the Lake District', in which he gave his own interpretation of the Langdale Linen Industry, the early years of the Keswick School, and the founding of other local classes and workshops, including Annie Garnett's (1864–1942) The Spinnery and Arthur W. Simpson's The Handicrafts, which ran directly under Ruskin's influence and in accordance with local history and tradition. Rawnsley closed the chapter with a description of Ruskin as 'the guardian and inspirer of village handicraft', noting how 'there came to him cheer from loyal followers in the lakeland vales', summarising their work thus:

> Insignificant as these experiments in Home Art Industry were, the Master's desire for a happier England for the working man, seemed at last to find some promise of fulfilment. The Home Art Industries at the Lakes gave him true joy, and were welcomed by him with sincerest thankfulness and constant approval.[3]

No outside influences were acknowledged as diluting or polluting that pure adherence to Ruskin and to Lakeland tradition. The 'constant

[1] Rawnsley, *Ruskin*, 3.
[2] Ibid., 8.
[3] Ibid., 148.

approval' of Ruskin as an ever-present force during the initial years of the Lakeland revival was exceptionally important to Rawnsley, as it was to Fleming and Marian Twelves.

Again like Fleming, during his early years in Lakeland (from 1877), Rawnsley was able to seek Ruskin's advice in person on a more regular and consistent basis than ever before. It was that personal element which also shaped much of what Rawnsley did after he arrived at Wray, not only prompting the founding of the Wray and Keswick classes, but heightening his awareness of his additional power as a clergyman to effect change. Fleming's work always had a fundamental Christian basis. *In the House of Rimmon* suggested the new importance of God and the Church in his life and work after 1873, by which point he had rejected Mammon, and begun to study nature as well as to associate dignified labour with working hand-in-hand with God. The book indicates most strongly that, on reading Ruskin's works, he not only rejected the pursuit of money, but experienced a simultaneous developing love of nature:

> Only the other day, I was walking in the fields with a friend, and we picked up two wild flowers: not all the art of the finest Parisian manufacturer could have equalled the setting of the tiny buds on the stem, nor the pale pure tints, mellowing from grey to violet and so on to stormful purple: for your town-made flowers I must have given perhaps ten shillings, but these Heaven-made ones were flung at my feet as lavish and as free as Heaven's gifts only are. Having been all my life thinking of money-getting and working useless work, I knew not even the name of His gift, nor any one thing about it, so little, you see, that I have to speak of bud and stem, when, if I knew rightly, I should say calyx, petal, and stamen, and indeed, be tangibly better for knowing it.[1]

Although Marian Twelves was less specific about the role of religion in her life and work, as a Companion of Ruskin's Guild of St George she had agreed in 1883 to love God and to live by his laws, and always advocated hand labour as contributory to a godly life. Elizabeth Pepper attended church and studied the Bible.[2] And the Linen Industry in all its forms always produced some church textiles. For Rawnsley, however, the Church obviously played a greater role in all that he did (as it did for

---

[1] A. Fleming, *In the House of Rimmon* (1873), 19–20.

[2] CROK, WDS 0106 and WDB 73 (the Langdale Linen Industry papers) contain several small Bibles belonging to Mrs Pepper and her husband. Some contain notes presumably written by the owners.

Plate 1. John Ruskin at Brantwood, *c.*1885.

Plate 2. *Left:* Albert Fleming. *Centre:* Hardwicke D. Rawnsley, 1911. *Right:* W.G. Collingwood, a self-portrait of 1893.

Plate 3. *Above:* Neaum Crag, Skelwith Bridge, Ambleside, the home of Albert Fleming. *Below:* Brantwood, Coniston, the home of John Ruskin; a view from the garden.

Plate 4. *Left:* Elterwater with St Martin's Cottage in the background (centre left), c.1890. *Right:* A spinster, probably Marian Twelves, at the doorway of St George's Cottage, Keswick.

Plate 5. Sheep shearing beneath a spinning gallery, Hartsop, *c.*1890. A photograph taken by Herbert Bell of Ambleside, who also provided pictures for H.D. Rawnsley's *Ruskin and the English Lakes* (1891). Bell's photographs provide an important record of a way of life in Lakeland which has almost vanished.

Plate 6. *Above:* The Spinnery, Bowness-on-Windermere, 1905. *Left:* Spinning stool made by Maggie Tyson of the Coniston carving class, dated 1896. Similar stools were used at The Spinnery and were also made by the Keswick School of Industrial Arts. It is believed that the stools were supplied in kit form and could be put together and carved by the students.

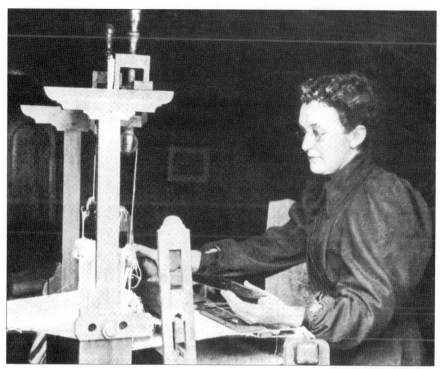

Plate 7. *Above:* Mrs Pepper, one of the Langdale Linen Industry's most loyal workers, photographed in 1900 at St Martin's, Elterwater. *Below left:* A photograph of *c.*1895, thought to be of Annie Garnett at her spinning wheel. *Below right:* Mrs Heskett spinning outside St Martin's, Elterwater, in 1900.

Plate 8. *Above:* The showroom of the Keswick School of Industrial Arts in the late nineteenth century. *Below:* A workroom at The Spinnery, Bowness, *c.*1905, showing embroideries and textiles. The wheels on display were probably made by Arthur W. Simpson.

Plate 9. Copperwork by the Keswick School of Industrial Arts. *Above left:* Copper vase, *c*.1890. *Above right:* Copper lamp, post-1900, designed by Robert Hilton and made by Matthew Armstrong. *Below left:* Copper bowls, *c*.1910, attributed to G.M. Collinson, typical of the school's work shown at the Kendal Exhibition of 1891 and the annual Coniston exhibition. *Below right:* Copper plaque, *c*.1899, sold for £4 5s. Design attributed to Harold Stabler.

Plate 10. *Above:* White festal altar frontal designed and made by the Keswick School of Industrial Arts for St Kentigern's, Crosthwaite, Keswick. The peacocks represent the Resurrection. *Below:* A detail of the central panel of the altar piece at St Kentigern's.

Plate 11. The reredos for St Oswald's. Burneside, *c.*1887, executed by Alfred Willink's wood carving class under the supervision of Arthur W. Simpson. Those who worked on the nature-inspired project, including some of the local women carvers, were: A. Bigland, W. Case, S.L. Clarke, T. Davis, R. Davis, T. Jones, W.P. Line, E.M. Love, J.C. Pittaway, W. Roper, J. Todd, A.H. Willink and H.A. Willink.

Plate 12. Littleholme, Kendal (*c.*1910), designed by C.F.A. Voysey for the Simpsons. The house had just been completed when the photographs were taken. Over the fireplace is Mrs Collingwood's painting *Gentians* (Plate 21). On the oak beam hangs one of Simpson's own carved panels. On the windowsill in the centre is a pen tray designed by Voysey. Various pieces of pottery painted by Ann Macbeth and furniture designed by Simpson can also be seen. In the bottom right-hand corner is a spinning stool, one of the key symbols of the Lakeland revival.

Plate 13. Blackwell, Windermere (*c*.1900), designed by M.H. Baillie Scott, with details of a stained glass window and a peacock frieze.

Plate 14. *Left:* Sundial designed by Dan Gibson, *c.*1890, for Graythwaite Hall gardens, Far Sawrey. Situated in the Dutch garden, the sundial bears the words 'Beware for thy last hour'. Along with Richard Knill Freeman, Gibson assisted Mawson on the Graythwaite commission, for which he also designed a garden gate. *Below:* The gardens at Wood Hall, Cockermouth, designed by Thomas H. Mawson for Edward Tygarly, *c.*1900.

Plate 15. *Above:* Arthur W. Simpson in his Kendal workshop, from a drawing by Cuthbert Rigby (1893) that was later used by Simpson in promotional material. *Below:* Simpson's staff, including Thomas Dixon, outside the Queen Katherine Buildings workshop, *c.*1899. *Left to right:* William Philipson (foreman until 1922), Alfred Bowers (carver), Jack E. Robinson, J. Shearer, N. Farrer. Thomas Dixon, Leonard Lancaster (apprentice carver), William Newby, Arthur Dixon (Tom's son, foreman 1922–1950), T. Graham, Tom Philipson (foreman's son) and James E. Cookson (known as Jim Carver). The carvers wear smocks and the cabinet-makers aprons.

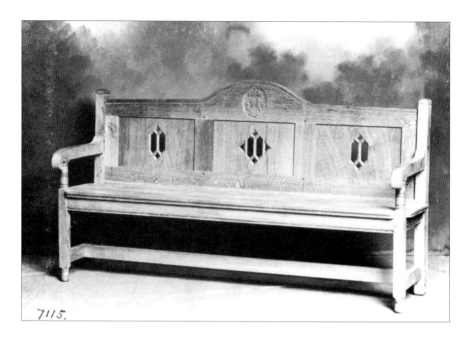

Plate 16. Two pieces of furniture made at The Handicrafts, Kendal, *c.*1900.

Plate 17. *Above:* The new Keswick School of Industrial Arts, opened in April 1894. Built of local slate and stone, the school incorporated a traditional Lakeland spinning gallery. *Below:* The Handicrafts, Queen Katherine's Buildings, Kendal, *c.*1906, occupied by Simpson's workshop from 1896 to 1922. Previously it had been in Berry's Yard and was originally in Finkle Street, elsewhere in Kendal.

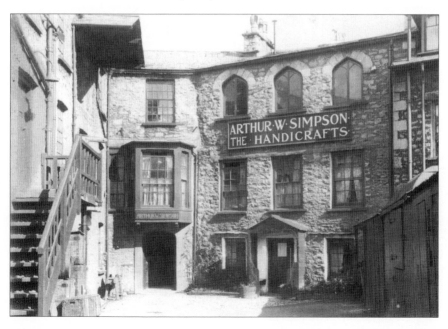

Plate 18. *Above left:* Dog Rose Panel by Arthur W. Simpson, 1889, believed to be Simpson's first carved nature panel. *Above right:* 'Iris' panel, designed and executed by Simpson *c.*1913, which won a gold medal at the 1913 Paris Exhibition. *Below:* Simpson's carver's models executed for Grizedale Hall, *c.*1906.

Plate 19. *Above:* Carvings by Alec Miller and the Guild of Handicrafts, executed for St Mary's church, Urswick, 1909–12. *Below:* Ruskin's memorial cross in Coniston churchyard, designed by W.G. Collingwood, with a detail of the central panel on the west side, representing *Fors Clavigera,* Albert Fleming's inspiration in founding the Langdale Linen Industry.

Plate 20. *Above left:* Pin-cushion made of hand spun, hand woven linen decorated with Ruskin lace, *c.*1906, attributed to the Coniston lace class originally run by Marian Twelves. *Above right:* Lavender bag made of Langdale linen, decorated with Ruskin lace, *c.*1900. *Below:* Two pairs of cuffs, worked in Ruskin lace, *c.*1905, attributed to a St Martin's outworker. The cuffs show how the threads are removed from the hand woven linen to form a 'spider's web', on which the lace is then worked.

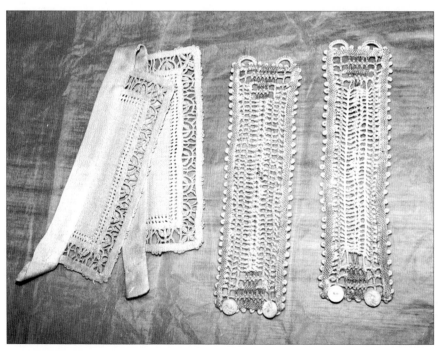

Plate 21. *Above: Gentians* by Mrs Collingwood, May 1907. The painting hung in Littleholme (Plate 12), the Simpson family home designed by Voysey, and is still owned by the family. *Below left:* Trays made by the Heversham metalwork class, *c.*1915, with a tooler's hammer used to beat the metal. *Below right:* Matchbox holder, also made by the Heversham metalwork class, *c.*1915.

Plate 22. *Above: Mill Dam Cottages, Coniston* by Alfred Heaton Cooper (1900). *Below: Landscape with Cottages* by Cuthbert Rigby (1917). The painting typifies Rigby's work during his Lakeland years.

Plate 23. *Above left:* Child's gown, made of hand spun, hand woven linen, *c.*1900, attributed to the Ruskin Linen Industry, Keswick. *Above right:* Book cover, *c.*1898, made of hand spun, hand woven linen decorated with silk embroidery, made by the Ruskin Linen Industry for Joan Severn. This was probably the item lent by Mrs Severn for the 1899 Kendal Exhibition. *Below left:* Dandelion, *c.*1900, worked on Langdale linen, hand dyed and embroidered with silks, now in the Elizabeth Pepper Collection at the Ruskin Museum, Coniston. *Below right:* Embroidered slippers, date unknown, attributed to the Langdale Linen Industry.

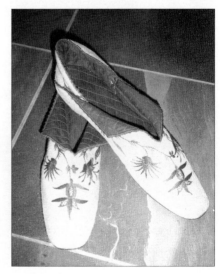

Plate 24. Lakeland work by Ann Macbeth. *Above left:* Detail of a textile, attributed to Ann Macbeth made for Patterdale church, *c.*1935. *Above right:* Lakeland fireplace decorated with tiles hand painted by Ann Macbeth, *c.*1935. *Below:* Detail from *The Good Shepherd, c.*1938. The complete hanging shows Christ the shepherd standing against a background of Hartsop, Deepdale, Caudale Moor and Kirkstone, with notes from *Jerusalem* running across the bottom.

Edith), and both the Wray and Keswick enterprises were closely linked with (and situated near to) his churches. He also believed Ruskin to be 'a messenger from God' or a holy prophet whose teachings demanded reverence for God, but more specifically nature, God's creation.[1] As a clergyman, Rawnsley saw himself occupying a privileged position from which he could spread Ruskin's Christian doctrine, believing that he too might 'brighten the life and bring happiness to the lot of the labourer'.[2] In his capacity as God's (and Ruskin's) worker, he was also able to recognise that God was in everything—hence his devotion to the Lakeland landscape (God's creation) and its defence—and that, ultimately, art was 'the expression of man's delight in the work of God'.[3] In her biography Eleanor, Rawnsley's second wife, acknowledges that that particular line her husband took directly from Ruskin's writings.[4] As a cleric, Rawnsley was also in the privileged position of being one of a small number of clergy to receive letters from Ruskin on the Lord's Prayer, intensifying their discussions concerning the Church.

As Companions of Ruskin's Guild from about 1884, both Edith and Hardwicke Rawnsley reaffirmed their resolve to live by the same fundamentally Christian laws as Fleming and Miss Twelves, including those which advocated a daily love of God and respect for his teachings.[5] However, whilst their Wray and Keswick endeavours certainly had a solid Christian foundation (teaching, among other things, a love of nature, that hand labour was God's work, and concern for others), the Rawnsleys never attempted to sell religion to their students. As Rawnsley's second wife concluded in 1923, he 'made as much way with the Keswick folk in the chair as in the pulpit, and a large amount of his best spiritual work was done by his life of genuine feeling towards theirs'.[6]

Whether the students were made up of regular attenders at St Kentigern's, or came from other parishes, or were atheists with nothing more than an interest in craft work, was never recorded. But the general intention to 'brighten the life' of and 'bring happiness' to the students was certainly of religious as well as Ruskinian origin, as was the desire to teach respect for nature through drawing and design work. Despite

[1] *Westmorland Gazette*, 24 Feb. 1900.

[2] E. Rawnsley, *Canon Rawnsley. An Account of his Life* (Glasgow, 1923), 66.

[3] Ibid.

[4] Ibid.

[5] Rawnsley, *Ruskin*, 181 for the Guild of St George and its laws.

[6] E. Rawnsley, *Canon Rawnsley*, 63.

Rawnsley's religious intensity, there is no indication that the students at either Wray or Keswick had to profess a constant daily belief in God, and no indication that they were purposely excluded from the classes if found to be lacking in religious conviction.

In one respect, however, the Keswick School loudly proclaimed its associations with the Church—in its production of church wares, and in its more specialised church commissions. From the outset Rawnsley established the School's reputation for producing competent church work (something which was not done at Wray to any noticeable degree), a reputation which was successfully sustained throughout much of its hundred-year existence, with wood-carvers, metalworkers and embroiderers all encouraged to take part. Although such work was carried out for churches across the country, a particularly high concentration can still be found in the churches of Cumbria. Among other things, the School produced font covers, candlesticks, altar vases, altar crosses and almsdishes, as well as a variety of textiles (such as the Church Congress banner mentioned earlier) for a number of local churches. More artistically demanding were the one-off commissions which included the Bernard Gilpin memorial made for St Cuthbert's church, Kentmere, around 1901, and the silver bronze enamel processional cross made for Carlisle cathedral around 1928. When Marian Twelves arrived in 1889, the number of church textiles produced rose temporarily, including such prestigious commissions as the funeral palls for Tennyson and Harvey Goodwin, as well as Communion cloths made of the School's hand spun and hand woven linen. However, the Keswick School's main output always consisted chiefly of domestic goods made for the open market, church work being mostly specially ordered.

St Kentigern's church, where Rawnsley remained until his retirement in 1917, bears witness to every period in the Keswick School's hundred-year existence, particularly the early years. Between 1883 and 1917 Rawnsley was responsible for a considerable amount of repair and alteration to St Kentigern's, and in the same period Edith Rawnsley, who was largely responsible for the practical application of Ruskin's theories at the Keswick School, designed and made some of the church's more decorative features. Among other things, with Mr Ferguson, Rawnsley instigated alterations and additions to St Kentigern's which included repairs to the east end and a new east window which was made in the Kempe studios. The window is a crucifixion scene enclosed by St Herbert and St Kentigern—figures which are repeated in the reredos which was also largely Rawnsley's idea. Under his guidance, structural work including pointing, underpinning and the rebuilding of buttresses was also carried out. While Rawnsley took Fleming's role as the 'ideas' man or the more heuristic influence, Edith took Marian Twelves's role as the one who carried out much of the actual design and production—the more physical representation of Ruskin's theories. The churchyard at Crosthwaite contains some of the runic crosses and recumbent stones she designed. The church gates, bearing the four emblems of St Kentigern—the tree, the fish, the bird and the bell—were also her work and would have been made at the Keswick School. The emblems are repeated inside the church, most noticeably in its mosaic pavement prepared by Burke & Sons of London (installed in Rawnsley's time) and in its present-day kneelers.

Inside the church are a number of copper light fittings or 'lamps' (*c*.1888) executed to Mrs Rawnsley's design and paid for by subscription. The ironwork was made by the village blacksmith and similar fittings were made by the School for the Keswick Museum and Art Gallery, founded in 1882. Arguably the most striking works executed by the early Keswick School (alongside the festal altar frontal) are three impressive altar panels for St Kentigern's in gilded metal. The panels, worked by Mrs Rawnsley, John Birkett, Robert Temple and a Mr G. Jackson to their joint design in about 1893, are pictorial representations of the birth, death and resurrection of Christ. Set into an oak reredos designed by an architect identified only as Mr Ferguson, and executed by a Carlisle wood-carver (probably Mr Little), the panels also represent the artistic peak of the Keswick School during the period 1883–1900 when it was under Mrs Rawnsley's direct care. Minor traces of the Keswick School in St Kentigern's include a small number of plaques. The memorial plaque in the vestry dates from *c*.1890.

Although Fleming and Rawnsley were independent Ruskinians, in that they had their own personal experiences of Ruskin and their individual understanding of his teachings in accordance with that experience, when it came to Lakeland and the revival of local arts and crafts they were exactly in accord. Indeed, after 1883 their lives took a strikingly similar direction, despite their different professions, as reviver of the local spinning wheels and reviver of local woodcarving. The Wray class was a comparatively brief experience for the Rawnsleys and, whilst it gave them some idea of the difficulties of reviving local crafts on a small scale (and the idea to introduce metalwork), it was never as ambitious as the Langdale Linen Industry. In its three years it never took on a commercial edge, remained chiefly a Ruskinian exercise in reviving woodcarving as a pleasant pastime for the less-than-poor, and had no committee structure or rules. After they moved to Keswick, where the local newspapers regularly reported public house brawls, where as many men as women were unemployed, and where industrialisation (in the form of mills and factories) was greatly more evident, the Rawnsleys looked to Fleming's example (as the hand of *Fors*) for inspiration. From the outset, therefore, the Keswick School echoed the Langdale Linen Industry and had strong associations with Ruskin's *Fors Clavigera*. So compatible were the two that in 1889 Marian Twelves saw the Rawnsleys' project as the only fit place to continue with her realisation of Ruskin's theories.

Like the Linen Industry, the Keswick School has never previously been investigated with a view to establishing its place as part of a broader Ruskinian revival of Lakeland arts and crafts. Indeed, the Keswick School itself has until now lacked any detailed account of its life or achievements in relation to Ruskin.[1] Even the occasional appearance of the names of Walter Crane and William Morris as authors of letters of support sent to Rawnsley has failed to excite widespread interest. In practical terms, the Keswick School was straightforward to organise and run, despite the larger number of pupils than at Wray. But in concept, it too was greatly more ambitious and complex than anything seen in south Lakeland before. As with St Martin's, it benefitted from Ruskin's direct and personal input in its first sixteen years, which built an all-important solid association with the writer which continued throughout the School's existence, and helped to create organisation and teaching methods which remained largely unchanged for a hundred years.

Like Fleming, in his pre-Lakeland years Rawnsley developed a particularly strong admiration for Ruskin's writings which, after his arrival in the Lake District, was followed by an increased intensity in admiration for the man also. Not only did their talks speedily give Rawnsley the same idea as Fleming (to revive local crafts), but encouraged him to seek the writer's approval of the initial idea through to its realisation—twice on Rawnsley's part (at Wray and then Keswick). Before the Keswick classes began in the winter of 1884, the Rawnsleys took their first experiments in brass repoussé over to Ruskin at Brantwood, Rawnsley later recalling:

How pleased he was to hear about it all. How grieved he was to think that we should allow our workers to work in a mixed metal. Copper yes, gold yes, silver yes, but this brass was neither fish, flesh, nor good fresh herring. It was a base alloy. And yet though he clapped his hands over it, and vowed it was shockingly

---

[1] I. Bruce, *The Loving Eye and Skilful Hand* (2001) contains an outline of the Keswick School.

immoral, he admitted the work was careful and true, and was forced to allow that much of the sunshine that dazzled the eyes of the heroes of Homer's song, was just this brass, this base alloy on shining threshold and on glittering helm.[1]

Despite being further away at Keswick than when they lived at Wray, the Rawnsleys were able to visit Brantwood regularly until about 1890, after which, as a result of Ruskin's deteriorating health, they visited less frequently, finding the writer 'a saddened memory of the old teacher quietly waiting for the end'.[2] Of Rawnsley's later visits to Ruskin at Brantwood Eleanor wrote:

> at one time depressed almost to agony by the thought that his [Ruskin's] life had been wasted, and his work, as he spoke of it to Hardwicke, 'one long darkness of the light of God,' at another 'entirely calm and peaceful, sitting with folded hands at his study window, looking no longer on the lake and mountain side, but gazing intently and with love on a bunch of flowers which had lately been brought into his room.'[3]

Ruskin was able to send what Rawnsley described as 'tender messages' to the School until shortly before his death, but whether he ever visited is uncertain.[4] As at St Martin's, it is probable that he did see the realisation of his theories at Keswick for himself, and was certainly sent gifts of metalwork and woodwork as well as a linen cushion made by Mrs Rawnsley under Miss Twelves's direction. As if to clarify any possible doubt about its central focus, when the new Keswick School opened in 1894, a testament to the successful realisation of Ruskin's teachings, a photograph of the writer set in a wooden frame carved by Mrs Rawnsley was hung on the wall. Of the new building Rawnsley wrote: 'But the spirit that had made the whole venture possible, was the spirit of him whose face hangs now upon its walls, the spirit of John Ruskin'.[5] As if further confirmation were needed, even the motto over the new door, 'The loving eye and patient hand shall work with joy and bless the land', was chosen for its Ruskinian appropriateness.

---

[1] Rawnsley, *Ruskin*, 129.

[2] E. Rawnsley, *Canon Rawnsley*, 146.

[3] Ibid.

[4] Rawnsley, *Ruskin*, 129.

[5] Ibid., 124.

As with the Langdale spinsters, for those who attended the Keswick School there was never any compulsion to follow the Rawnsleys' devotion to Ruskin. Neither were there any attempts to force Ruskin's doctrine on them, or to coerce them into joining either St Kentigern's or the Guild of St George. In 1884 Keswick was fast developing into an industrial town, yet the Rawnsleys' School was always well attended with demand soon exceeding the number of places. In the face of expectation, the people of Keswick demonstrated a similarly enthusiastic willingness towards, and interest in, learning lost handcraft traditions, and the abandonment of machinery was embraced wholeheartedly. The rejection of machines in the workplace had already been tried and tested at Wray, and so could not be attributed solely to the example set by Fleming. But the scale on which it was undertaken at Keswick was on a par with Elterwater and Fleming's experiment with its similar numbers of students would have guided the Rawnsleys to some degree. The similarly strong receptiveness to Ruskin's teachings in Keswick was again due to the writer's earlier presence in the Lake District (in 1872–83), and was also affected by the Langdale Linen Industry. But it was also due to the ties between Ruskin and Keswick which Rawnsley believed existed, often noting that Ruskin 'must always have had a weak spot in his heart for Keswick'.[1] Turner's painting of Derwentwater had always hung in his London home at Denmark Hill, and the writer's vision of heaven had always been a cottage in 'the dells of Matlock or the Vale of Keswick'.[2] If the people of Keswick were not already aware of Ruskin's connections with the town through widespread publicity surrounding Ruskin and his Lakeland railway opposition work, Rawnsley would certainly have made them aware. Rawnsley had a strong reputation for expressing his views and beliefs by whatever means necessary — sermons, lectures, or writings.

Although, in contrast to Elterwater, the majority of the Keswick students were initially men, with women attached mainly to the needlework classes and a small number who took separate woodcarving classes from the men, the emphasis again was on reviving and teaching domestic crafts, the intention being to offer an additional rather than independent income. The emphasis always remained on making and selling domestic goods, and full-time commitment was generally discouraged.

Along with the study of nature, the abandonment of machines was a

---

[1] Ibid., 29.

[2] Ibid.

fundamental part of the Keswick School's Ruskinian creed which indicated an overriding dual objective of rejecting the pursuit of Mammon and of questioning nineteenth-century methods. To Rawnsley too, the 'curse of the age' was to 'get rich by fair or foul means',[1] the School being an exercise which would show that 'man's labour of hand and brain shall not be taken for nought' and that 'as consumers and purchasers, the responsibility for the lives of the makers of the article rests upon our shoulders'.[2] In the same vein, the Langdale Linen Industry proclaimed that:

> The buyer of a thing may seldom think of the workers' sacrifice in producing it, yet the sacrifice of unremitting and often ill-rewarded toil should be thankfully acknowledged. And as sacrifice demands sacrifice, it is well to remember what John Ruskin has written, that the toiler can be best helped 'by a right understanding on the part of all classes of what kinds of labour are good for men, raising them, and making them happy, by a determined sacrifice of such cheapness, convenience, and beauty, as is only to be got by the degradation of the workman, and by the equally determined demand for the products of healthy and ennobling labour.'[3]

Not only what was made, but how it was made, mattered. Hand labour was valued over machine labour at Keswick as well as Elterwater, and a love of nature in its undisturbed, pre-industrial state encouraged. In the case of the latter, both Hardwicke and Edith Rawnsley set the example, as did Fleming to a lesser degree. Over a number of years Rawnsley (joined by Fleming) actively defended the Lake District from change, and wrote various volumes of poetry and prose, such as *Life and Nature at the English Lakes* (1899), which glorified the region. As a competent artist, Edith produced numerous watercolour studies of the Lakes, some of which were exhibited nationally as well as locally. In 1882, as Edith Fletcher, she showed *A bit of Helvellyn, Wythburn* at the Royal Academy. Edith also exhibited several works at the New Watercolour Society and provided the drawings for her husband's *Flower-Time in the Oberland* (1904). In 1894 it was noted that, in an attempt to bring the students even closer to nature, the School windows were filled with vases of 'pale iris, wreathing sprays of woodbine, and tall glasses filled with

---

[1] H.D. Rawnsley, *The Spirit of Honesty* (Keswick, 1897), 8.

[2] Ibid., 14, 15.

[3] H.H. Warner (ed.), *Songs of the Spindle & Legends of the Loom* (1889), 8–9.

foam of cherry-bloom';[1] out of their observations the Rawnsleys developed designs for trays and other household items with names like 'Hydrangea', 'Blue-bell' and 'Skiddaw', which were sold alongside such things as 'Ruskin' vases (what exactly a 'Ruskin' vase was is not clear since none have been located, nor any photographs). None of this, however, affected Rawnsley's drive for commercial success, and like Fleming he unashamedly exploited every available means of publicity to promote and sell the work of the School, bringing not only a commercial edge not usually associated with local handcrafts, but also the same respected title of 'art industry'.

[1] CROC, DB 111, article from the *British Workman*, *c*.1894, on 'The Craftsmen of Keswick. How Working-men may Turn their Leisure to Good Account' by Alice Wayte.

7

FURTHER DEVELOPMENT OF THE RAWNSLEYS' HANDCRAFTS SCHOOL

The long-term success of the Keswick School was clearly attributable not only to the satisfactory application of Ruskin's teachings in a particularly receptive climate, and to the role of Ruskin as a near presence, but to the concentrated early groundwork laid down by both Edith and Hardwicke Rawnsley. Together, they played a fundamental role in ensuring that the application of Ruskin's teachings was carried out to his personal instruction, and both shared responsibility for the School's direction and development, supported by its specially formed committee. Although described as essentially a 'ploughing' (rather than a loitering) ecclesiastic,[1] whilst Rawnsley is attributed with both learning and teaching at Wray, there are no indications that he actually taught at the Keswick School, or took any active part in designing or producing. Eleanor Rawnsley noted that 'it was owing to his [Ruskin's] influence and teaching that woodcarving classes were held in Wray at which Edith and Hardwicke themselves both learnt and taught'.[2] However, like Fleming he went to extensive lengths to ensure that there was national awareness of his revival of local crafts, deliberately cultivating the same broader image of his project from the outset, and determined to create an art industry with wider appeal.

For the first 25 years of its existence, the Keswick School made a concentrated effort to produce its own publicity material, written chiefly by Rawnsley or by Edith, repeating the aims and intentions of the School for the benefit of those unfamiliar with it or with Ruskin. A leaflet of 1887 stated that

The aim of the promoters of the School is to bring the designer

---

[1] *Westmorland Gazette*, 6 Dec. 1890.

[2] E. Rawnsley, *Canon Rawnsley. An Account of his Life* (Glasgow, 1923), 47.

and workman into such relation that they become identified as was the case when the arts were truly living. At present the boys are put through a course of drawing before they begin the brasswork or wood carving. All the Articles Exhibited by the Keswick School of Industrial Arts are HANDWORK from the first to last—no part, even the finishing, is done by machinery.[1]

This in itself is highly suggestive of Ruskin. Other leaflets made more direct use of Ruskin's works, one published in 1904 suggesting that

> For the continual education of the whole people, and for their future happiness, they must have such consistent employment as shall develope all the powers of the fingers and the limbs and the brain; and that development is only to be obtained by hand-labour, of which you have these four great divisions—hand-labour on the earth, hand-labour on the sea, hand-labour in art, hand-labour in war.[2]

In other material, some of which was written several years after Ruskin's death, quotations from his works such as 'All art is praise' appeared at the beginning or end of certain sections to illustrate a particular point. A leaflet of 1904 referred to 'a dazzling array of brass, "the base alloy" as Ruskin called it, shining as bright & golden as ever it did in the eyes of the heroes of Homer's tale' and noted that

> Ruskin says:– 'Let a man once learn to take a straight shaving off a plank or draw a fine curve without faltering or lay a brick level in its mortar, and he has learned a multitude of other matters which no lips of man could ever teach him.' It is these 'other matters' which have been the real aim of the promoters of the School & which are the real value of it to its members.[3]

Rawnsley probably had an underlying belief that links with the writer's name would stimulate wider commercial interest in the Keswick School in the same way that Fleming saw the advantage of associating his linen industry with Ruskin and Wordsworth. How much this actually affected

---

[1] CROC, DB 111/100, Leaflet dated April 1887 by Mrs Hardwicke D. Rawnsley, Crosthwaite Vicarage, Keswick.

[2] CROC, DB 111/100, Leaflet on *The Keswick School of Industrial Arts* (1904).

[3] CROC, DB 111/100, Various early leaflets produced by the Keswick School.

sales is difficult to assess. But as devout Ruskinians, neither Fleming nor Rawnsley would have passed up an opportunity to spread Ruskin's doctrines, and neither would they have neglected an opportunity to sell what was made in the name of Ruskin. In some respects, both pre-empted those such as William Howson Taylor (1876–1935) who, with his Ruskin pottery, demonstrated a slightly later exploitation of the writer's name, Ruskin being synonymous with certain standards in the arts.

To increase public awareness, in 1885 the Keswick School took the unprecedented step of establishing its own annual exhibition, and of holding other one-off events which were regularly reviewed in the local newspapers. In 1897 W.G. Collingwood repeated a lecture to the Keswick School students on the life and art teaching of Ruskin, after which it was reported that

> Canon Rawnsley, in thanking the lecturer, sent to his old friend, Mr Ruskin, congratulations from the art school upon his having attained to his 79th year. He urged the people to believe that but for Mr Ruskin there would not have been this School in Keswick.[1]

Like the Langdale spinsters, the students at the School clearly had some exposure to Ruskin other than in working to his theories, although a concerted effort was made never to force Ruskin's doctrine on them. In setting up its own exhibition the Keswick School gained a slight edge over the Linen Industry (in all its forms) since neither Fleming nor Miss Twelves ever attempted to hold similar exhibitions at either St Martin's or St George's Cottages. Yet when she joined the School in 1889 Miss Twelves clearly benefitted from Rawnsley's more vigorous publicity efforts, establishing a second successful linen workshop which saw her exhibiting not only at the Home Arts, but in 1890 at the more prestigious Arts and Crafts Exhibition in London, the only time (as far as can be ascertained) that the Linen Industry did so. The Industry never attempted to build its own premises as the Keswick School did, and so lacked accommodation in which to hold special events. But Fleming and Miss Twelves also lacked the sort of contacts which Rawnsley made through his other work, particularly his Lakeland railway opposition campaigns which saw him communicating with, among others, William Morris and Walter Crane (the probable reason for the appearance at the Arts and

---

[1] CROC, DB 111/93 Cutting, probably from the *Keswick Guardian*, 9 Feb. 1897.

Crafts Exhibition in 1890). Crane visited the Keswick School in 1897 on a brief visit to Brantwood, meeting the Rawnsleys and the Severns on his travels.

Whilst Rawnsley's persistence in all areas of his life and work brought him national attention, where the Keswick School was concerned his clerical connections gave him another edge over Fleming. The generally more amenable attitude towards the promotion of handcrafts in the late nineteenth century, starting in the 1870s with favourable reviews of the work of, for example, the Royal School of Art Needlework, was particularly reflected in the leading journals of the day, including the *Art Journal* (1839–1911). *The Studio*, founded in 1893, followed their example, as did the *Art Workers' Quarterly* (1902–6), both of which reported on handcraft developments across the country. Those who led the Lakeland revival naturally featured, winning numerous mentions in exhibition reviews. But in the case of the Keswick School useful additional support came from the clerical newspapers. To Ruskin the notion of a clergyman running a rural parish workshop was a most fitting example of his rightful role, but to the Church Rawnsley was evidently an exception—as well as something of a novelty—and won the praise of a number of clerical publications. In 1894 the *Sunday Chronicle* reported the opening of the new Keswick School, noting with enthusiasm how the Rawnsleys' project was a 'fertilising light' which was being 'poured into the dim corners of many minds', the result of which was 'Beautiful work' done by 'skilful hands'. It added that Ruskin's photograph hung on the School wall, above which were his words 'Art is the expression of man's delight in the works of God'.[1] In 1901 the *Sunday Companion* published a more detailed illustrated article on the Rawnsleys' project entitled 'Clergyman's Remarkable Experiment', which reported the School's latest commissions: a silver service book made for Kasagana, King of Toro, and a large rosewater dish, presented by the workers to the mayor and corporation of Winchester on the occasion of the Millenary of King Alfred. The article commented that 'Canon Rawnsley has certainly worked wonders for his village, and other clergymen and ministers might follow his example with advantage'.[2]

Despite such publicity, Rawnsley appeared to have had no imitators outside Lakeland, and there was nothing to compare nationally with the Keswick School between 1884 and 1984. Its strict Lakeland Ruskinian origins ensured that it was part of a unique local exercise which could

---

[1] *Sunday Chronicle*, 29 July 1894.

[2] *Sunday Companion*, 14 Dec. 1901, 393.

not be repeated in quite the same way anywhere else. This helps to reaffirm the uniqueness of his approach to the Church and the place of handcrafts in the teachings of the Church, a uniqueness resulting from two very particular and powerful forces—Ruskin and Lakeland. Locally, a small number of craft classes ran in imitation of the Keswick School, some under the guidance of the clergy. But they were much smaller projects and did not survive for long. In the late 1890s a Mr Saunders ran a repoussé class at Braithwaite near Keswick and in 1900 asked the Keswick School to take over its supervision. The request was declined and the School committee recommended that the students be sent to the Keswick School.[1] For a short time prior to 1897 the Revd R. Shearman Hulbert ran a technical education class where subjects such as cookery were taught along with drawing and carving. That too survived only a few years.[2] Neither of these could be considered as having any direct associations with the local revival.

Although national exhibitions were one of the best forms of publicity and an excellent method of increasing sales, the Keswick School's Lakeland Ruskinian origins were often lost amidst the wealth of other handcraft work displayed and there was little opportunity for the products to be judged on anything but their standard of design and execution. Like the Linen Industry, the School attended the Home Arts Exhibition on an almost annual basis, but saw it chiefly as a selling opportunity rather than a means of publicising any theoretical origins, however important. With the exhibition's emphasis on the handcrafts and the insistence that every piece of work be labelled with its maker's name, certain individuals came to the forefront of the national arts world in a way which never occurred in the old days of Lakeland crafts. As a result, those involved with the Lakeland revival gained a wider reputation as excellent and practised craftsmen and craftswomen, the latter term in particular never having been used before 1883 in relation to Lakeland spinsters. In the early years, up to 1920, at national exhibitions, Henry Towers, William Robinson, Jeremiah Richardson, John Sparks (one of the School's earliest brass workers who died in 1892), Thomas Sparks (Richardson's apprentice in 1890), John Gardiner and John Peill won a variety of awards and certificates for the Keswick School, including a certificate of merit from the Armourers and Brasiers' Company in 1891. Other national exhibitions where the same names appeared included the Manchester Arts and Crafts Exhibition (in 1895), the Leeds exhibition

[1] CROC, DB 111/1, 1 Nov. 1900.
[2] CROC, DB 111/93.

(on several occasions), the London Arts and Crafts Exhibition (in 1890 and 1903), the Dublin exhibition (on several occasions) and the 1904 Port Sunlight exhibition. In the late 1890s *The Studio* not only reviewed the School's exhibition work, but began to illustrate examples by its leading craftsmen, and to include occasional short articles on selected pieces written by Rawnsley.[1] Like their fellow craft workers at St Martin's and St George's Cottages, the Keswick School students were given a portion of all prize money won at exhibitions, enhancing the Ruskinian importance of individual as well as collective effort. They were not, however, given the same share of the end-of-year profits.

Like the Langdale and Ruskin Linen Industries, with its equally high standard of craftsmanship, the encouragement of design and production among its students, the winning of a number of important commissions, and appearances at reputable national exhibitions, the Keswick School soon won the same acclaimed title 'art industry' without ever losing its true domestic nature. Given its association with the Home Arts and Industries Association from 1885, the Keswick School was considered nationally to be practising the 'Home Arts', but when exactly it was first described as an 'art industry' is not clear. Like Fleming, Rawnsley always considered his Lakeland project to be an art as much as a craft endeavour.

The adoption of a strict Ruskinian basis brought both individual and collective success, as Ruskin predicted. All this played an important part in securing the School's reputation and contributed to its consistent growth and long-term survival. But to Rawnsley, as to Miss Twelves and Fleming, local exhibitions had an equally significant (if not greater) contribution to make to that success and longevity. They were not only an excellent showcase for what was being made in Lakeland between 1880 and 1920 in the name of Ruskin, but also an opportunity to publicise more effectively the Ruskinian origin of the revival of Lakeland arts and crafts. The latter was understandably of greater value to those who lived and worked in close proximity to Ruskin, and to those who valued their local heritage, of which Ruskin had become an integral part at least by the 1870s. Like Fleming, Rawnsley never suggested that the revival of local crafts should ever spread outside Lakeland, or be conducted out of reach of Ruskin, either before or after his death (to his Lakeland devotees, Ruskin's burial at Coniston meant that he was an ever-present local figure). Whilst he happily endorsed

---

[1] An illustration of a jug designed and executed by Thomas Sparks appeared in *The Studio*, July 1896, 96.

national exhibitions, he was much more closely involved in local exhibitions, always anxious to promote the display of local work.

Although the various village shows such as Silverdale and Coniston proved an appropriate annual window in which to display a small amount of work produced by the various branches of the Linen Industry and the Keswick School, the 1891 Arts, Crafts and Loan Exhibition held in Kendal was the first opportunity for Lakeland's Ruskinians to make a collective statement. Because of its significance as the largest display of local arts and crafts ever held in south Lakeland, the 1891 exhibition is discussed in Chapter 12, but it is important to note here that Rawnsley played a leading role in realising the initial idea for the event, helping to create a very public confirmation of Lakeland's perception of itself as separate and individual. Although the idea was not his, so enthusiastic was Rawnsley that he attended all the original meetings in Kendal Town Hall and wrote letters to other local supporters suggesting that the exhibition be made 'open to the whole of the Diocese of Carlisle' and be held 'yearly at different centres'.[1] Mrs Rawnsley was nominated one of the judges and the Keswick School submitted an assortment of linens, embroideries, woodcarvings and metalwork. Included among them were a variety of copper bowls, an assortment of candlesticks, a silver-plated writing set, a carved oak cradle, a box seat, and a 'Music Canterbury'.[2] Virtually every other class and workshop associated with the revival also submitted work for display.

When the similar but less adventurous Kendal Exhibition of Pictures and Decorative Art was held in 1899, the Rawnsleys jointly acted as honorary district secretary for Keswick and as members of the general committee. On that occasion Rawnsley was invited to give the opening address, and took full opportunity to publicise the Ruskinian nature of what was happening in Lakeland, directly attributing the success of the Keswick School (again one of the exhibitors) and its regional contemporaries to 'living within touch of that great prophet and artist of our time—John Ruskin—and that, animated by his spirit, much was possible'.[3]

Having already publicly stated in 1897 that 'but for Mr Ruskin' there would have been no Keswick School, Rawnsley now made it equally and publicly clear that the success of the School and its Lakeland contempor-

[1] *Westmorland Gazette*, 29 March 1890.

[2] *Catalogue of the Kendal Arts, Crafts and Loan Exhibition* (Kendal, 1891) (copy in Kendal Library).

[3] *Woman's Agricultural Times*, Sept. 1899.

aries hinged on Ruskin's near presence as well as theoretical influence.[1] When the 1907 Ruskin Exhibition was held in Keswick as a tribute to the writer and his Guild of St George, Rawnsley delivered a public vote of thanks to Marian Twelves for her dedication to realising Ruskin's teachings. He also took the opportunity to mention again the writer's particularly strong links with Keswick, showing that his place in the Lake District and its regional heritage was still important locally some seven years after his death, with Rawnsley clearly helping to keep alive and intensify that local interest.

As a thriving, successful art industry, the Keswick School clearly owed much to Rawnsley's tireless work in bringing his project to national as well as local attention; and during its first 25 years it was he who became the public face of the School. Yet in terms of dedication, Edith Rawnsley was his equal. Whilst Marian Twelves was probably introduced to Ruskin's writings through Fleming in the early 1880s, Mrs Rawnsley was a devotee of the writer's works long before she met her husband in 1875 and it may have been that shared interest which drew them together. Like her local female colleague, Mrs Rawnsley spent the majority of her time dedicated to the practicalities of reviving local crafts under Ruskin's influence. She rarely spoke publicly about her work at the School or gave interviews, and appears not to have left any writings about her time at Keswick. Much of her artwork, including a study of Helvellyn shown at the Royal Academy in 1882, also remains untraced. She is thus a much more elusive figure than her husband. In many respects, like Miss Twelves, she was the more artistic and creative force, overseeing the practical realisation of Ruskin's teachings on a day-to-day basis, establishing boundaries in terms of transferring the written word into physical objects. In her later years, as the chief orchestrator of the Ruskin Linen Industry, Miss Twelves received some recognition, with St George's Cottage the subject of a small number of articles in such journals as the *Woman's Agricultural Times* which stressed that the Industry's success was largely due to her hard work and natural talents as a needlewoman. However, she was never the central subject of interest in such major journals as *The Studio* or the *Art Workers' Quarterly*. For Mrs Rawnsley too, there was no deliberate cultivation of a public profile, and no play on her high artistic and design achievements as a woman, her success similarly hidden behind the much larger endeavour which her arts project quickly became under Ruskin's influence. She clearly had personal reasons for remaining discreet, although she collected a

---

[1] CROC, DB 111/93, Cutting, probably from the *Keswick Guardian*, 9 Feb. 1897.

considerable number of cuttings from local and national publications covering the period 1884 to 1910 in which the Keswick School was praised, revealing a vivid sense of pride in what her project achieved.[1] That elusiveness, however, was as much the result of working to Ruskin's teachings as natural reticence, and was a reflection of the extent of her devotion to her mentor.

As a native of Westmorland, Edith Rawnsley naturally shared Ruskin's compassion for the people of Lakeland, as well as his concern for the changes taking place in the late nineteenth century, and so had a particularly potent desire to see the Keswick School succeed artistically and commercially. Like Marian Twelves, she has left little indication of her preferences where Ruskin's writings were concerned, but was certainly influenced by Rawnsley's own readings of Ruskin, and by his experiences of the writer prior to 1877. But she was influenced to a greater extent by her visits to Brantwood in the company of her husband. The result of that new, more personal relationship with the writer was the joint realisation of his teachings, that realisation, for Edith as well as Rawnsley, beginning only after direct contact had begun. Her knowledge of Ruskin's works prior to 1877 would have given her an advantage, but, as the recipient of more formal training in the arts, she also brought her skills in drawing and woodcarving to the Keswick School. Irrespective of that training, as a devout Ruskinian Mrs Rawnsley took no payment for her work. She believed that, as the embodiment of Ruskin's teachings, her local arts project should be neither a profit seeking exercise nor an opportunity for self-promotion. The welfare of the students took priority and, whilst she was responsible for some design work at the School, the majority of the designs in the first 25 years were either directly attributable to those who actually made the products, or were the work of one student and made by another. Because of the lack of payment, she too fell into the category of voluntary teacher. The Ruskinian nature of that voluntary role, and her similar reluctance to develop a large or unmanageable project (demonstrated in 1894 by the restricting of the size of the new Keswick School building), remained largely misunderstood outside Lakeland.

On a more general level, its domestic nature also affected the national view of the Keswick School, and, while it was regarded as an art industry, it was also labelled a domestic industry, the students intended to carry out much of their work in the home. Like the Linen Industry,

---

[1] CROC, DB 111/93, Edith Rawnsley's scrapbook, containing an extensive collection of cuttings from local and national newspapers and journals.

only a small number of workers remained permanently at the school. Yet under Mrs Rawnsley's guidance, and the influence of Ruskin, the School did verge on becoming a more professional arts school, creating a number of exceptionally skilled craftsmen as well as proposing that a separate Keswick School of Design be established in 1891.[1] The first more definite signs of a move away from this domestic organisation appeared in 1894 when the Keswick School opened its new building, one of only two purposely designed to house a local revival workshop (the other being Annie Garnett's addition to The Spinnery some years later). It was at that point that the School, then producing over eight hundred items a year for sale and exhibition, began to succeed the Linen Industry as the leading project in the revival of local arts and crafts.[2] Not only did it own its own premises, but it was producing more goods each year, was teaching more students, and was exhibiting on a wider scale as well as holding its own annual exhibition.

The second indication of such a move occurred four years later. In 1898, when she was 52, Mrs Rawnsley decided not only to take a less active role in running the Keswick School, but to take on its first permanent director, Harold Stabler. Prior to that, at both Wray and Keswick the Rawnsleys had employed a wood carver from Carlisle and a qualified designer from South Kensington on a temporary basis (something which the Linen Industry never did), and so had some experience of dealing with professionally qualified staff. But Stabler was the first permanent arts figure to be employed at the School. His arrival marked another step away from its domestic roots but was a reaffirmation of the appropriateness of the label 'art industry' to describe it, and of the success attained under Mrs Rawnsley.

In many respects Stabler was the most fitting choice for a Lakeland revival industry. Although neither a strict devout Ruskinian nor a Companion of the Guild of St George, he was a native of Levens (close to Heversham, the site of another handcraft class) and the product of the local Kendal School of Art. Having trained and worked under Arthur Simpson of Kendal between 1886 and 1898, he was also the product of Ruskin's teachings if not a devotee himself, and as a result always retained some Ruskinian basis in his approach to the arts. As a wood carver he was competent enough to supervise Simpson's summer school at Gill Head, Windermere, and it was probably Simpson who recommended his pupil, the Rawnsleys being close friends with all those who

[1] CROC, DB 111/1, Keswick School minutes, 1891.
[2] *Sunday Chronicle*, 29 July 1894.

led the local revival. Indeed, it was a strong trait of the revival that, from the outset, all those involved offered each other unstinting support, both professional and personal, their shared devotion to Ruskin and to the reintroduction of local arts and crafts overriding any personal differences. To demonstrate the complexity of the revival, Simpson had already taught at the Keswick School in 1887, from which date the School had begun to exhibit at his annual exhibition. Because of the close links between the School and St Kentigern's, Stabler's appointment was reported in Crosthwaite parish magazine and noted as beginning on 1 November 1898. As 'permanent instructor', his role was to take a class in modelling in clay (which would enable 'workers in wood and metal to see shadow and light, and give their work life and reality'), and to give lessons in woodcarving, metalwork and drawing out of School hours 'to any in the neighbourhood who desire it'.[1]

Stabler remained at the Keswick School for less than two years, leaving to join the metalwork department at the prestigious Liverpool School of Art in 1900, and later the Sir John Cass Evening Art School in London. He continued to raise the public and artistic profile of the Rawnsleys' School; *The Studio* in particular praised pieces of his work shown at the 1899 Home Arts Exhibition, illustrating three jugs designed by him and executed by Thomas Sparks.[2] A review of the 1900 Home Arts Exhibition described Stabler as an 'excellent artist' responsible for 'some of the most satisfying decorative inventions' which the Keswick School was then carrying out 'with sincere enthusiasm and rare technical ability'.[3] Although he had left Keswick by March 1900, *The Studio* continued to discuss his influence on the School and as late as 1905 Stabler jugs and Stabler Bird Screens were still being made and sold at Keswick, the latter for a respectable 7 guineas.

Disillusioned with the Arts and Crafts approach he encountered on his move from the Lake District, around 1912 Stabler founded the Design and Industries Association with Hamilton Smith, Ernest Jackson and others. Despite achieving national and international success as a designer in his later years, Stabler never abandoned his Lakeland roots and remained in contact with Simpson. Over the years a number of gifts were sent to the Simpson family, including a figurine designed by Stabler's wife Phoebe in 1908. In April 1909 he and his wife loaned a carved panel, several small statuettes, and a portrait bust of his father George

---

[1] Crosthwaite parish magazine, Nov. 1898 (at St Kentigern's Church, Crosthwaite).

[2] *The Studio*, July 1899, 104.

[3] Ibid., July 1900, 85.

Stabler, the former schoolmaster at Levens, for an exhibition in Levens School. The exhibition was yet another local event organised as a tribute to local talent. As a Lakeland designer, a more permanent reminder of Stabler exists in Levens churchyard in the form of his parents' gravestones which he is believed to have designed and carved.

After leaving Keswick Stabler became the first craftsman to be admitted to the Goldsmiths' Company. He also designed posters, including some for the London Underground, taught at the Royal College of Art (1912–26), and was a partner in the successful ceramics firm of Carter, Stabler & Adams. In 1903 he became a member of the Art Workers' Guild and in 1936 was appointed by the Royal Society of Arts one of the first Designers for Industry. His greatest advances were made in enamels, examples of which appeared regularly at the Arts and Crafts Exhibitions held between 1906 and 1912. In 1915 *The Studio* devoted an entire article with illustrations to Stabler and his enamels.[1]

Such was the success of Stabler's (albeit brief) appointment that the Keswick School's committee—still very much a local concern in 1900, and still very much headed by the Rawnsleys—agreed to take on Herbert Maryon as a replacement. At that time the School was in its strongest ever position both financially and artistically, and Maryon—a former pupil of Lethaby at the London County Council School of Arts and Crafts—was employed as head of the Keswick School in 1900 at a salary of £110 a year. Like Stabler, he was an experienced and qualified designer, and his work under the Rawnsleys brought a deal of useful publicity for almost eight years, winning the comparatively small arts school an even greater reputation as a centre of artistic excellence. As a proficient wood carver, leather worker, modeller, jewellery designer and author, Maryon undoubtedly exerted a strong and positive influence over the students. Under his influence, the committee decided in 1901 to offer a scholarship for children of those already at the School (Lizzie Stanley was the first pupil, taken on in February 1901), and in 1903 decided to attend the Arts and Crafts Exhibition in London. But it was his own work which attracted the greatest attention: his designs at the Keswick School included a silver enamel casket which was presented to Princess Louise on her visit to the Lake District in 1902. In the same year he designed a challenge cup for the local elementary school which was shown in *The Studio*,[2] and in 1905 designed a cup for HMS *Cumberland*

[1] *The Studio*, Feb. 1915, 34–31.

[2] Ibid., Dec. 1902, 211.

and a silver challenge shield which were also illustrated in *The Studio*.[1]

Maryon had a wider experience of design than Stabler and was affected to a greater extent by what was happening in London just before 1900, particularly in relation to the Arts and Crafts. In that respect he was an interesting challenge for the Keswick School, and was the only artistic figure employed during the Rawnsleys' time to attempt to turn the School away from its local, Ruskinian roots in the name of progress. As the first director to have no immediate experience of Ruskin in Lakeland, or comprehensive knowledge of Lakeland's unique history and tradition, Maryon came to Keswick armed with quite definite ideas, and was determined to introduce changes which would see, among other things, the establishment of a full-time craft course. The committee treated the proposal with concern, since the School's chief purpose was still to teach local domestic crafts rather than to produce professional craftsmen or designers. Between 1900 and 1908 Maryon made repeated requests or complaints to the School committee[2] and was clearly frustrated by the committee's refusal to turn the School into a full-time arts school, although he had many positive effects there. His encouragement to students to devote more time to the School and to their craft work brought further success at national exhibitions, and raised the standard of work. To Rawnsley, the School was already fulfilling its original aims of reviving local crafts under Ruskin's influence and improving the lives of the students, and in 1901 he wrote:

> Go to the homes of any of the workers. Ask their wives or their brothers and you shall learn. Go to any of the workers themselves and you shall learn that the good of the School to them has been that they now have always something to turn to on a dull evening and something that has opened their eyes to see what they used to pass by without notice in flower life and bird life, and beauty of light and shade, of cloud and sunshine, upon the fellside of their native vale.[3]

Any attempt to alter the status quo rather than enhance it would potentially threaten all that the Ruskinian project represented.

Perhaps because of its domestic nature, Maryon was never wholly satisfied with conditions at the Keswick School, registering a number of

---

[1] Ibid., Dec. 1905, 263–4.

[2] CROC, DB 111/1, Keswick School committee minutes.

[3] H.D. Rawnsley, *Ruskin and the English Lakes* (Glasgow, 1901), 127–8.

complaints throughout his eight-year stay before he resigned in 1908. The difficulties included the resignation of Dorothea Carpenter (with whom Maryon disagreed professionally), unfulfilled orders, the discontinuation of enamelling due to unspecified problems and numerous demands for an increase in salary.[1] To an outsider, the School's reluctance to change its methods and work practices evidently proved frustrating, but to those such as Rawnsley who understood its true nature those methods, far from being restrictive, brought success of all kinds—individual, collective, financial, artistic and commercial. Among other things, the personal development of those who attended the School proved, as in the case of the Linen Industry, that, in the face of mass industrialisation, the individual still mattered, and that the old ways still had some fundamental value. From that Ruskinian basis, by the time Stabler left Keswick in March 1900 the School was making goods worth around £1,700 a year, and the figure rose further under Maryon's influence.[2] A bronze relief of Rawnsley, executed by another member of the Maryon family, Edith, was shown at the Royal Academy in 1903,[3] suggesting that there was little personal animosity between Maryon and the School during his stay.

By late 1908 Maryon had taken over craft classes at University College, Reading (a position probably secured by W.G. Collingwood), having failed to steer the Keswick School along previously unexplored avenues and away from its origins as a local handcraft school or rural parish workshop. After some 24 years, the School (like the Linen Industry) still declined to attempt to effect change on the national stage, and remained a healthy, thriving anomaly perched on the edge of mainstream design, its strong regional character (embodied permanently in its exterior Lakeland domestic architectural traits) ensuring that it remained largely unchanged when challenged by outside, non-Ruskinian, non-Lakeland influences.

In employing Maryon, the Rawnsleys clearly believed him to be the most suitable replacement for Stabler, although he perhaps proved not to be. Like Stabler, however, he too left his mark, contributing to the School's already somewhat eclectic design personality, as well as to the annual Coniston exhibition of local art and craft work. Like the Linen Industry, the School always encouraged its students to seek design inspiration chiefly from their natural surroundings, but also encouraged

---

[1] CROC, DB 111/1, Keswick School committee minutes.

[2] Rawnsley, *Ruskin*, 127.

[3] A. Graves (ed.), *The Royal Academy Exhibitors* (1905), p. 208.

the use of local minerals in metalwork, giving a generally local feel to much of their work. In answer to Ruskin lace, the School also developed its Ruskin vases, probably using the writer's name and image for other items such as trays and ashtrays in the same way that St Kentigern's image was used. But from the outset, under Mrs Rawnsley's guidance, the School developed a library (enlarged in 1894) where pattern books (including *Die Zimmergotik in Deutsch Tirol* (1893)) and books on Greek, Egyptian and Roman design in architecture and sculpture, as well as actual specimens and photographs of design, were stored, collected by the Rawnsleys on their travels abroad.[1] Although the Linen Industry took inspiration for its lace patterns from European examples, design played a much more prominent role at the School, not least because it was running three different classes at once (metalwork, woodwork and embroidery), and was producing many more items per year. Edith's professional training in the arts and her reading of Ruskin gave her a distinct appreciation of the value of the study of international as well as national and regional design, and she clearly set a trend for diversity which the School followed throughout its hundred-year existence. When Marian Twelves joined the School in 1889, she widened its scope further with her embroidery and lace designs and techniques, introducing her Keswick spinsters and embroiderers to the many diverse and ancient patterns which became absorbed into the town's design history along with those which were newly created by the women. The strict geographical and theoretical boundaries within which the revival operated in no way hindered design, with individual preferences particularly encouraged.

   Although the majority of Edith Rawnsley's students were male, she was evidently a strong female (but never feminist) design force in south Lakeland between 1880 and 1920 and for a time, like Marian Twelves, she almost defied her unpaid, domestic, Ruskinian status to become a successful design figure in her own right. Because of their devotion to Ruskin and to the revival of local domestic crafts, however, self-promotion was cast aside, and both slipped into relative obscurity after their deaths. As a result, both have remained unappraised not only as successful realisers of Ruskin's teachings (a fate not shared by their male Pre-Raphaelite predecessors), but also as individual female design figures, and—just as significantly—as the leaders of a new, collective and considerable female design force which began to emerge in south

---

[1] A small number of books belonging to the Keswick School have survived and are kept at Keswick Museum and Art Gallery.

Lakeland under their influence in the 1880s and lasted for over 25 years.

Before 1883 the potential for local women to become creative figures in the home had always been there, with textiles produced by hand in a domestic setting. But it was initially Marian Twelves, joined shortly after by Edith Rawnsley who, as Ruskinians, reintroduced home textile production with a view to developing it into a newly respected and creative activity. Together, they not only offered paid employment to a considerable number of poor women (as well as men), but returned to them their regional heritage, simultaneously offering them traditional dignified labour combined with a new creative freedom. When Miss Twelves and Mrs Rawnsley began their respective Ruskinian projects, they could have had little concept of how successfully local arts and crafts would be reintegrated into Lakeland life, and certainly could not have realised how many women as well as men would come forward to train in apparently outmoded crafts.

The emancipation of women was no more in their minds than in Ruskin's in the early 1880s, but by 1889, when Marian Twelves (openly supported by Mrs Severn) joined Mrs Rawnsley, there were more positive signs that local women in particular were being given more opportunity to design and create than ever before, to show their creations nationally as well as locally, and to win awards for their work for the first time. The money earned gave them little opportunity for financial independence, but given the numbers who willingly joined the Linen Industry and the Keswick School (male and female), money was never the main concern. Although apparently never described as such at the time, the women were clearly 'craftswomen', just as their male contemporaries were 'craftsmen'. However, the Ruskinian nature of the local revival rewarded them with other titles such as the virtually obsolete 'spinster' or 'embroideress' which, whilst equally respectful and denoting gender, lacked an expression of the new high standards reached by the Lakeland women in their chosen artistic field.

Edith Rawnsley's talents in particular were both exceptional and diverse. She designed in and practised woodcarving and metalwork, designed and made jewellery, executed designs for textiles (including Ruskin's funeral pall with Stabler), carried out embroidery, and learnt to make Ruskin lace. An exhibitor at the Royal Academy and the New Watercolour Society, she was also one of the first women members of the Lake Artists' Society, along with Dorrie Collingwood, another influential force at work in south Lakeland in the late nineteenth century. Her drawings were used in Rawnsley's *Flower Time in the Oberland* published in 1904, and in 1913 she designed the catalogue cover for the Lake Artists' Society's Coniston exhibition. Probably under her influence, as one of only two female committee members (Ann Elliot being the other), the Keswick School always employed some female staff (but not in the post of director), giving employment to women craft workers from outside Lakeland and the opportunity for other women to influence the School's direction.

One of the most notable earlier figures was Isabel McBean of New Cross who later became a prominent designer, and whose work was illustrated in *The Studio*. Although employed for only a short time (1901–2), Miss McBean's influence contributed to the increasingly high standards of design practised by the School, and her part in its success at the 1902 Home Arts Exhibition was particularly noted.[1] Miss McBean's work at the Keswick School was a conglomeration of typically diverse styles reflecting Arts and Crafts, Art Nouveau, medieval and Dresser-like qualities. What Ruskin made of the collective success of the revival's women is not recorded, but given his encouragement of Marian Twelves, his meetings with both Hardwicke and Edith Rawnsley, and his earlier encouragement of Susanna Beever and her *Frondes Agrestes* (1875, her selections from *Modern Painters*), he clearly had no qualms about women taking an equally prominent role in local arts and crafts. At the core, of course, remained a conscious devotion to Ruskin as well as to Lakeland and, like Marian Twelves, Mrs Rawnsley never lost that devotion. She probably attended Ruskin's funeral, at which the pall she and Miss Twelves worked on was displayed, and at which her husband's specially composed hymn was sung, both indications of their unfailing loyalty. When she died in 1916, Edith Rawnsley followed Ruskin's example and chose to be buried where she felt most at home — Crosthwaite churchyard. Her husband followed in 1920, a permanent reminder that both also considered Lakeland to be their own. Until shortly before their deaths, both remained on the Keswick School committee.

After her husband's death, Rawnsley's second wife Eleanor remained active in the School and continued some work with the National Trust, the Keswick and District Footpath Preservation Association and the Lake District Safeguarding Society. She was also concerned to preserve traditional Lakeland life. In 1944 she lectured on 'Village Plays', tracing their origin back to the fifteenth century, and gave short recitals to the Lakeland Dialect Society in dialect from well-known Grasmere plays.[2] In 1921 she acted as honorary secretary for the Grasmere exhibition

---

[1] CROC, DB 111/1, Keswick School committee minutes.

[2] *Westmorland Gazette*, 26 Feb. 1944.

where items made by the Keswick School were shown alongside, among other things, Wordsworth memorabilia.[1] Her work doubtless helped to keep alive all that Ruskin and the Rawnsleys believed in, long after their deaths. Eleanor died in 1959 and was buried in Crosthwaite churchyard.[2]

---

[1] Ibid., 23 July 1921.

[2] Where there is a memorial over her grave.

8

ARTHUR W. SIMPSON
AND THE HANDICRAFTS

Such was south Lakeland's receptiveness to Ruskin's teachings in the late nineteenth century that, far from functioning in isolation, the Linen Industry and the Keswick School instigated a wider return to local arts and crafts which, by 1900, had created a concentration of handcraft workers probably larger than in any other region of England. Local awareness of Ruskin was never a problem in south Lakeland, and judging by the considerable numbers who came forward to take part in the revival, there was an equally vivid awareness of the Ruskin-based Keswick School and Linen Industry. With anything up to a hundred women working for the leading branches of the Linen Industry, and up to 80 craftsmen a year working with the Keswick School, by the mid 1890s few from any level of Lakeland society could have been unaware of the revival, or remained unaffected by it. With their regular reports on Ruskin and those at the heart of the revival, the local newspapers did much to aid local awareness, as did the numerous, well-attended local exhibitions. The *Westmorland Gazette* in particular continued to report on Ruskin long after his death, helping to keep the writer at the forefront of local attention. In 1933 it gave a detailed account of a tour of Brantwood and its grounds organised by J. Howard Whitehouse (then president of the Ruskin Society) for a group of visiting Canadian writers, announcing that a permanent host and hostess were to be installed at the house to receive other Ruskin devotees now that the Ruskin Society owned the property.[1] A similarly detailed article on Ruskin and the plight of Brantwood appeared in 1944.[2]

On the other hand, since the Lakeland revival was a comparatively late realisation of Ruskin's teaching (coming like Laxey, some thirty years later than the Pre-Raphaelite Brotherhood, for example), and because Ruskin was an elderly and sick man by the 1890s, the spread of

---

[1] *Westmorland Gazette*, 22 July 1933.
[2] Ibid., 30 Sept. 1944.

the revival gradually came to depend to a much greater degree on the example set by its two leading industries. The sight of Ruskin's theories in action, rather than any sustained, direct communication with the writer, became the wider driving force as the revival spread. Whilst the pioneers were moulded by Ruskin's direct contribution as well as theoretical influence, those who came immediately afterwards could be best defined as the followers of Ruskin's Lakeland devotees. Although equally avid readers of his texts, because of their lesser degree of direct contact with Ruskin, they became distinguishable in two principal ways: they were not inspired to join the Guild of St George, and they were already living in Lakeland before Ruskin arrived in 1872. As a result, they were secondary Lakeland Ruskinians, or the wider ripples emanating from the central core of Ruskin in Lakeland.

Although the roots of the revival of Lakeland handcrafts could never be attributed to anything but Ruskin's direct and indirect influence over Fleming and Rawnsley, in the long term the revival itself succeeded and thrived chiefly as a result of the dedication of those involved, not only to the realisation of Ruskin's teachings in Lakeland, but also to their chosen craft. Of no less dedication to both were Arthur Simpson of Kendal and Annie Garnett of Bowness-on-Windermere whose respective woodcarving and spinning workshops deliberately functioned in imitation of the Keswick School and the Linen Industry. Like the Hawkshead branch of the Keswick School and the smaller branches of the Linen Industry based at Troutbeck, Grasmere, Silverdale, Morland and Coniston, they represented the first signs of a definite outward spread of the revival, or secondary signs of Ruskin's influence in Lakeland, coming just after the revival began. Both were avid readers of Ruskin and shared the same enthusiasm exhibited by Fleming, Miss Twelves and the Rawnsleys, but neither had any personal experience of Ruskin prior to his arrival at Brantwood, having neither met him nor written to him before 1872. After 1872 some direct contact was established in both cases, although it was always limited. Simpson is believed to have visited Brantwood at least once when he first returned to Kendal in 1885 after working in London;[1] and Miss Garnett's diary confirms that she too visited the house, but not regularly.[2] Both had begun to read Ruskin several years before contributing to the Lakeland revival, probably encouraged by Ruskin's presence in the region, and both had that same period of literary ingestion as those at the heart of the revival, accepting

[1] Information from the Simpson family archive.
[2] AHM, Annie Garnett's diary.

the writer as an active part of Lakeland's history and tradition. They also benefitted from the example set by the already well-established revival, becoming involved at the earliest opportunity. In geographic terms, Simpson and Miss Garnett were particularly important because they established the Ruskinian revival in Kendal and Bowness, two previously unaffected centres, but they also made their own particular contributions to the promotion of local crafts which helped not only to win national interest for Lakeland, but also to raise its design profile further.

Whilst Annie Garnett was a pupil of Mrs Pepper at Elterwater and so was a direct product of the revival, Simpson began his career as a wood carver under a local cabinet-maker in 1871, just before Ruskin's arrival at Brantwood. After moving to Gillows of Lancaster and then to Samuel Barfield of Leicester, in 1881 he returned to Kendal and attempted unsuccessfully to establish himself as an independent craftsman under the title 'Architectural & General Wood Carver'.[1] Although the Rawnsleys' Wray class was then up and running, the revival of local crafts, particularly woodcarving, had yet to take a firm hold in south Lakeland, and Simpson moved to London to work for William Aumonier. By early 1885 he had returned to Kendal, finding a quite different scene artistically to four years previously, and was confronted by the sight of two major handcraft workshops running in the name of Ruskin. He immediately set about attempting to establish himself again as an independent craftsman, and this time succeeded, creating a handcraft workshop which survived for more than sixty years. Given his earlier failure in 1881, the indications are that, by the time Simpson returned some time in late 1884 or early 1885, south Lakeland, under the influence of the Linen Industry and the Keswick School, had become particularly receptive to Ruskin's teachings, especially the idea of a return to local crafts, and this contributed to his success. The revival probably also played some part in influencing how Simpson went about establishing his workshop, with Fleming and Rawnsley providing successful examples of the realisation of Ruskin's teachings. Since no evidence survives to show exactly why Simpson failed in his first attempt but succeeded in his second, or on what basis he attempted to run the first, that success cannot be attributed only to the influence of the Keswick School and the Linen Industry. But in terms of how he orchestrated his second attempt, surviving papers and photographs of work show a definite correlation with both industries which was neither accidental nor coincidental. In relation to work ethics, Simpson applied the same fundamentally Ruskinian principles which

---

[1] E. Davidson, *The Simpsons of Kendal* (1978).

affected not only what was produced but how it was produced.

Simpson amassed a collection of books which was no less than Fleming's. Many were gifts from fellow artists and craftsmen, but others he bought, including a selection of Ruskin's texts. A complete catalogue was never made, and most were sold immediately after his death in 1922, but he certainly owned *Giotto and his Works in Padua* and *Sesame and Lilies*, and his descendants maintain that he owned other texts which he read as he embarked on his training. Ruskin was by no means the only writer familiar to the Kendal carver (he also read A.H. Mackmurdo, William Morris and Wordsworth among others) and, as far as can be ascertained, did not make up the larger part of his collection, but he was clearly exposed to, and familiar with, Ruskin some years before establishing himself in Kendal. In 1885, in addition to a theoretical basis, Simpson was presented with two examples of practical Ruskin, as well as the opportunity to talk to the writer.

Just as significantly, around the time of his first (and possibly only) visit to Brantwood, Simpson met W.G. Collingwood, Ruskin's secretary. The two men began to correspond and between 1885 and 1900, through Collingwood, Simpson had the constant ear of Ruskin. Samples of Simpson's carvings were even shown to the writer, with Collingwood relaying any advice or comment given. For example, on 27 August 1887 Collingwood wrote to Simpson: 'Mr Ruskin has gone away—last heard of at Folkestone—and I am afraid, not so very well as was hoped: so your carving will have to wait a bit … '. As a result, Collingwood and Simpson became close friends and continued to write until Simpson's death in 1922. Simpson was thus in the particularly privileged position of not only corresponding with a likeminded Lakeland Ruskinian, but also receiving regular information on Ruskin's state of health, his and Collingwood's respective work, life at Brantwood, and Ruskin's art theory, and in that respect had some form of constant contact with Ruskin.[1]

As a Lakeland artist and the author of *The Art Teaching of John Ruskin* (1891), Collingwood also played an important role in shaping Simpson's approach to design after 1885, helping to mould him into what Rawnsley fittingly described in 1901 as 'a true follower of Ruskin's teachings'.[2] As a Westmerian, Simpson would have been fully aware of his regional artistic heritage from a young age, and his choice of woodcarving as a career probably stemmed partly from that knowledge

---

[1] AHM, Letters from Collingwood to Simpson.

[2] H.D. Rawnsley, *Ruskin and the English Lakes* (Glasgow, 1901), 146.

rather than from the theoretical influence of Ruskin. In his work ethics, however, he was patently influenced almost exclusively by the examples set by the growing revival in which Ruskinian principles dominated. For Simpson too there was to be a clear alignment with past local tradition, for which he needed no tuition, but there was also to be a new awareness of modern needs which he similarly felt were not being met by machine production. Although such potent hostility to mechanisation might suggest the founding of another Lakeland domestic handcraft industry, Simpson was clear from the outset that he was forging a career rather than taking up a domestic pastime, and purposely devised a financially viable, efficient workshop which would employ more than twenty full-time staff and which would compete at the highest levels in national and international exhibitions. His pursuit of profit (or Mammon), however, would never override the welfare of his workers, or affect the high standards of work produced, and in one of his publicity leaflets he outlined his money-making philosophy:

> Don't think you will succeed if your chief aim is to make money. Decorate things for the pleasure of it. Thus, you store up your pleasure to be partaken of by all in sympathy with your aims. Without this love your efforts are likely to be futile.[1]

With the founding of The Handicrafts (as his workshop became known from 1906),[2] Simpson represented a new aspect of the revival of local crafts—the professional craftsman now elevating local domestic handcrafts to the position of a full-time occupation by which national commissions were still won (as with the Keswick School and the Linen Industry), but financial independence could also be achieved.

In local terms Simpson's underlying and constant support of domestic crafts was never undermined by his intent on earning a wage, and he went to considerable lengths to continue the promotion of woodcarving as a home pastime revived by the Rawnsleys. The very fact that he had a colourful and varied career elsewhere but made the decision to return to Lakeland in 1885 suggests not only that Simpson came back because he had heard about the revival and Ruskin's role in it, but that he came back determined to become involved in the reintroduction of regional handcrafts. That determination resulted not only in Simpson founding

---

[1] A.W. Simpson, *Observations on Woodcarving by a Craftsman* (1910), 7 (copy in Simpson family archive).

[2] Simpson's workshop was initially known simply as Arthur W. Simpson of Kendal but is referred to here throughout as The Handicrafts.

The Handicrafts in July 1885, but in his volunteering to teach at the nearby Burneside woodcarving class, a small evening class run strictly as an amateur exercise by a local man, Alfred Willink.

The founding of the Burneside class in the summer of 1885 was almost certainly the result of the example set by the Keswick School, as was the establishment of two other amateur woodcarving classes at that time at Gatebeck and Milnthorpe which also represented the further spread of the Lakeland revival. Shortly after Burneside started, Simpson began teaching at Gatebeck and Milnthorpe where leather work was also taught. Given the proximity of all three classes, the close dates of their founding, and Simpson's position as their chief tutor, he may well have been instrumental in their conception. Run on the same strict Ruskinian principles as their larger, more adventurous contemporaries, Burneside, Gatebeck and Milnthorpe produced a similarly high standard of craft work, some of which appeared in local exhibitions in south Lakeland. Burneside has left perhaps the most permanent reminder of the resurgence in village woodcarving in late nineteenth-century Lakeland in the form of a reredos in the church there. The ambitious nature of the reredos illustrates not only the high artistic standard reached by the local people and what could be achieved by the successful application of Ruskin's teachings, but also Simpson's excellence as a tutor and craftsman. Although its design has been attributed to a local lady, Mrs Crewdson, Simpson supervised the project throughout (starting in 1886) and, given its reliance on nature, evidently influenced the finished design.

How long Simpson's smaller woodcarving classes ran is unclear, but in 1927, forty years after the initial conception of the Burneside reredos, Willink attended the Hawkshead exhibition of local arts and crafts as chairman of the Westmorland Education Committee. There he delivered a Ruskinian speech on the merits of woodcarving, the benefits of learning hand-eye coordination and the role of nature in good design, and referred to the Lakeland revival in the 1880s and 1890s: 'To people who followed monotonous vocations, such as at factories, arts and crafts in their spare time brought them back to nature'.[1] As long ago as 1859 Ruskin had written that 'To men surrounded by the depressing and monotonous circumstances of English manufacturing life, depend upon it, design is simply impossible'.[2] Such was the extent of the permeation of his teachings in south Lakeland that they were still the subject of addresses at local exhibitions in the late 1920s, and the revival still

---

[1] *Westmorland Gazette*, 6 Aug. 1927.

[2] J. Ruskin, *The Two Paths* (1859), 125–6.

coloured local life, thanks to the survival of the Keswick School, various branches of the Linen Industry, Simpson's The Handicrafts, and Annie Garnett's The Spinnery, nearly 27 years after Ruskin's death.

Today it is particularly difficult to establish the true extent of the spread of the Lakeland revival. Such was the amateur, domestic status of the smaller classes that their histories are known largely through word of mouth. Although the number of students may be uncertain, their general place in the revival can be ascertained from surviving papers of Fleming, Rawnsley and Simpson, and specimens of work which reflect clearly the application of Ruskin's teachings. In the case of Burneside, in 1901 Rawnsley offered one of the clearest indications of its links with the wider revival, noting of it and The Handicrafts that 'how truly Ruskin's mind was over all', and also that 'Anyone who has ever visited Burneside church and delighted their eyes with the carving of the reredos there would feel that there too Ruskin's spirit had been at work, the guardian and inspirer of village handcraft'.[1]

The association can be confirmed by Simpson's regular appearances at local exhibitions. From 1885 he also gave lectures on Ruskin's teachings around south Lakeland and at such local establishments as Bowness Art School, aiding the revival by spoken word as well as practical example.[2] He was particularly clear on the Ruskinian issue of the value and pleasure of the home arts. In November 1886 he spoke on 'Art at Home' (his first lecture) in Endmoor schoolroom:

> Mr Simpson said he intended to speak of art as applied to home surroundings, and emphasized the fact that art was for the poor as well as for the rich, and added that everyone was capable, with a little training, of producing some art work more or less valuable, for the beautifying of the home.[3]

On a more practical level, Simpson established his own annual exhibition in which he displayed and promoted the work of the revival at all levels—whether domestic, as at Burneside, or more professional, as at Keswick, making yet another vivid statement of Lakeland's independence and unity.

[1] Rawnsley, *Ruskin*, 146.

[2] Although contemporary references to these lectures have not been found, they are known to the family. Given that he gave other lectures locally on aspects of art and design which clearly echoed Ruskin's teachings, it seems safe to accept that he also lectured on Ruskin.

[3] *Westmorland Gazette*, 20 Nov. 1886.

Simpson's first exhibition was held at his Finkle Street workshop in Kendal in June 1886 to mark his first successful year as an individual Lakeland craftsman and his association with the local revival. Like the Keswick School's annual exhibition established the previous year, which probably provided the model, it was first and foremost an opportunity for Simpson to exhibit and sell his own work. But from the beginning he resolved to exhibit the work of other artists, most of whom were directly associated with the revival of local arts and crafts. As a result of his friendship with Collingwood, the first exhibition combined some 40 exhibits of woodcarving by Simpson and his Burneside, Gatebeck and Milnthorpe classes, with paintings of Lakeland executed by W.G. and Dorrie Collingwood, one of the earliest public statements of unity among the revival's artists, craftsmen and craftswomen.

So successful was the exhibition (with the popularity of the revival still on the increase at that time), that it was repeated in May 1887 but on a noticeably more ambitious scale. Invitations were sent out for a 'private view' before the two-week event opened, and two rooms were used to house the greater number of exhibits. Paintings and drawings by some 23 Lakeland artists, including not only the Collingwoods but also Reginald Aspinwall, John Crane, Hubert Coutts, Arthur Severn and Miss Mabel Nash, were hung in an upstairs room at Finkle Street, while brass work from the Keswick School, leather work from Gatebeck, linen and embroideries from the Langdale Linen Industry, and finished panels of the Burneside church reredos were displayed downstairs. The Linen Industry also gave demonstrations of hand spinning. With the textile work of the Linen Industry, the leather work from Gatebeck and the paintings of Mabel Nash and others, Lakeland's female artists and craft workers in particular were given a regular opportunity to display their talents in Kendal. Given that his wife also exhibited leather work and embroideries at these exhibitions (which ran for at least seventeen years), Simpson was actively involved in promoting the work of local women as well as men, and helped to set a positive example to Lakeland women.

Simpson's Burneside, Gatebeck and Milnthorpe classes were the epitome of the vision of a parish workshop envisaged by Ruskin (and Rawnsley), with the spiritual needs of the students met by the local church (for whom the students would make carvings such as the Burneside reredos), and their creative and practical needs met by the local handcraft class. Respect for nature, God's creation, was encouraged, as was respect for regional crafts and local heritage, and individual as well as collective effort. There was never any intention that the classes would effect any kind of wider change, and so never spread beyond

Lakeland's boundaries; work was rarely (if ever) submitted for national exhibition (as with the Keswick School's Hawkshead class and the smaller branches of the Linen Industry). Although always heartily involved with his well-attended classes, and an active supporter of the local revival of arts and crafts (he founded a summer school at Gill Head, Windermere, in the early 1890s to promote and teach wood carving, assisted for a while by Harold Stabler of the Keswick School), Simpson went to considerable lengths to ensure that his own workshop attracted widespread attention and gained the reputation of being an 'art' (as well as a craft) industry. Like Fleming and Rawnsley, he managed not only to win national and international acclaim, and to succeed commercially, but to do so without compromising his fundamental Ruskinian beliefs.

From the outset Simpson adopted a similar business strategy to Fleming and Rawnsley, producing a number of publicity leaflets between 1885 and 1922 in which he outlined his approach to woodcarving and the role of Ruskin in his life and work, particularly in relation to design. In 1910 Simpson argued that, aside from the absolute rejection of machines in the workplace, all articles made in his workshop should 'give pleasure to the worker and user alike', and that they should be simple in design, the 'trade mark of true greatness'.[1] He also upheld the Ruskinian belief that all truly great design originated from nature as God's creation:

> Ruskin said 'All noble ornamentation is the expression of man's delight in God's work,' thus indicating that the best designs are founded on some adaptation of nature. Working in this spirit you show your delight in God's work. The suggestion of nature gives pleasure, because it carries the mind back to the beautiful things out of doors.[2]

His own particular expression of 'delight in God's work' most often took the form of highly distinctive decorative carved panels whose designs were based upon such things as daffodils, acanthus, hawthorn and ivy. Like the Keswick School's Ruskin vases and Skiddaw trays and the Linen Industry's Ruskin lace, they are quite unlike anything produced outside Lakeland at the turn of the century and certainly helped to create a strong design identity unique to the region. One particular panel, based

---

[1] Simpson, *Observations on Woodcarving*, 8.

[2] Ibid., 7.

on thistles, was presented to Princess Louise when she opened the 1891 Kendal exhibition and another, entitled 'Iris', won a gold medal at the Paris Exhibition for 1913, the year in which he joined the Art Workers' Guild. Although on occasions Simpson incorporated references to nature into his furniture (a cabinet with doors inlaid with a small flower design being one example), on the whole, chairs, tables, cabinets and other items made at The Handicrafts were always decorated economically. Arguably the most satisfying of his nature pieces was the tiny ivy brooch carved by Simpson on his engagement to Jane Davidson of Kendal in 1887. Made of fruit tree wood (probably pear), the brooch is barely larger than a coin and has survived intact, a testament to Simpson's exceptional ability as a designer and craftsman able to work on the smallest as well as the largest scale.

Simpson also expressed his attitude towards the encouragement of individual creativity and self-expression in others:

The end of all study and work in art is to express the individuality of the worker. Without that individuality there can be no art worthy of the name. Do not trouble about what others are doing. The artist and craftsman should learn the principles of design and of the craft, then go his own way; otherwise he can never experience the full gratification from the work he does.[1]

Like his Burneside, Gatebeck and Milnthorpe students, the carvers at The Handicrafts took an active part in design and production, and, in equal defiance of modern methods of mass production, Simpson always maintained that, when used once, a design should be thrown into the fire.[2]

Strict adherence to such principles might at first suggest limitations in design, since the lack of repetition would demand ever-increasing numbers of new and different designs, yet, like the Linen Industry and the Keswick School, The Handicrafts produced an extensive range of goods, chiefly influenced by the needs of the average Westmorland cottager. On sale from 1885 were an assortment of settles, stools, cupboards, bookshelves, lamp stands, tables, chairs, racks, wall brackets, beds, wardrobes, sideboards and gun cabinets, and every conceivable smaller household item, from teapot stands, pipe racks and coat rails to bread platters, coal boxes and sewing cabinets. Diversity was increased

---

[1] Ibid., 5–6.
[2] *The Friend*, Nov. 1922, 803.

by Simpson's use of a wide variety of woods, including yew, walnut, oak, mahogany and padouk. Locally, Simpson advertised the entire fitting out of houses, and at his 1887 exhibition set up a model room of cottage furniture adapted specifically to the needs of the traditional Westmorland cottage, including four rush-seated chairs, a couch and a bookcase.

As a lifelong socialist, Simpson showed a compassion for the working-class man in Lakeland not dissimilar to Ruskin's (according to Rawnsley, Ruskin made many an effort to stop and talk to his poor neighbours on his walks around Brantwood), and brought the first hints of a possible political dimension to the local revival. Yet his similarly ardent religious stance as a Quaker also coloured his career and his contribution to the revival. Whilst the Lakeland revival remained almost wholly apolitical (never expressing, for example, the socialist basis which fed the Arts and Crafts movement), and took no definite political influence from Ruskin (who never declared an allegiance to any one political party),[1] its religious undertones were always present, particularly locally, with the Keswick School producing church art work until 1984. Like Fleming and Rawnsley, Simpson took a keen interest in Ruskin as a religious prophet and kept a comprehensive list of passages the writer learnt from the Bible as a child, similarly acknowledging that art was the expression of man's delight in God's work, and that art and religion were inseparable.[2] As a result Simpson became closely associated with the Church Crafts League, a London organisation founded in 1899 with the object of halting falling standards in church arts. Along with G.F. Watts, Ruskin was the League's foundation patron, and probably influenced Simpson's initial involvement, as did Francis C. Eeles, a committee member and close friend of the Rawnsleys. Out of that association, Simpson won a number of local and national church commissions which enhanced his reputation as a designer.

Locally, Simpson not only actively encouraged his woodcarving classes to contribute to beautifying the region's churches, but produced his own specially commissioned work which, over a period of 37 years, affected almost every church in south Lakeland. For smaller churches such as Cartmel Fell, The Handicrafts replaced interior woodwork which was damaged or decaying, while for other churches more artistic carving

---

[1] In *Time and Tide* (1867) (*Works*, xvii. 402) Ruskin described himself as a 'thoroughbred Tory and Conservative' and in Letter I of *Fors Clavigera* (Jan. 1871) (*Works*, xxvii. 13) he called himself a 'violent Illiberal' as opposed to a Conservative who wished to keep things as they were. But by July 1871 in Letter VII of *Fors* (*Works*, xxvii. 116) he was describing himself as 'a Communist of the old school—reddest also of the red'.

[2] The list survives in the Simpson family archive.

work was executed. For Old Hutton church he designed a lectern
(pre-1920), for Christ Church, Whitehaven, a carved reredos (*c.*1905), for
St Martin's, Kensal Rise, a carved reredos and screen, for St George's,
Kendal, an altar and flower table, and for Staveley the choir stalls.
Nationally, one of his largest commissions was for St Margaret's,
Prestwich, which included reredos, choir stalls, pulpit, altar rail and
panelling. Executed over more than twenty years from 1899 this work
was carried out in association with his Lakeland friend, the architect Dan
Gibson (1865–1907), and with its designs based on poppy heads,
pomegranates, iris, thistle, vine, hawthorn and honesty is a tribute to
Simpson's (and Gibson's) fundamental advocacy of nature as God's
creation and the role of art (particularly church art) in praising that
creation. Other important commissions included woodcarvings for Bury
Infirmary, interior fittings for the Tudor Café, Leamington Spa (possibly
Simpson's (and England's), answer to Miss Cranston's Glasgow tea-
rooms), the pulpit for Salen church on the Isle of Mull, and a processional cross for All Saints', Windsor. Such commissions proved an
ideal additional means of publicising Simpson's skills and his Ruskinian
ideas to a wider audience.

As for Fleming and Rawnsley, exhibitions proved one of the most
regular means of publicity for Simpson, and he too deliberately sought
attention by submitting work to a range of events. Nationally, Simpson
(rather than The Handicrafts) exhibited on numerous occasions in Leeds
and London, and had his first piece accepted for an Arts and Crafts
Exhibition in 1889. He secured publicity in, among other journals, the
Building News, The Studio, and the *Art Workers' Quarterly.*[1] His own
articles on aspects of the arts appeared in a number of national journals,
one of the last, written in support of Stabler on 'D.I.A. Principles
Applied to Furniture Design', appearing in 1918.[2] This particular article
was taken from a lecture delivered by Simpson to the Manchester branch
of the Design and Industries Association.[3]

National exhibitions offered more than merely an opportunity to
increase public awareness and sales, and through the London Arts and
Crafts Exhibition Simpson became acquainted with one of the leading
architects of the day, C.F.A. Voysey. Although his wide circle of friends
eventually included the architect C.E. Mallows, the designer Walter

---

[1] e.g. *Art Workers' Quarterly* (1906), 47.

[2] *The Cabinet Maker and Complete House Furnisher*, 2 March 1918.

[3] Letters from Ambrose Heal to Simpson regarding his membership of the association
survive in the family archive.

Crane, the designer Nelson Dawson, the artist Harold Nelson (like Simpson, a member of the Art Workers' Guild) and Ann Macbeth (who later moved to Patterdale), Simpson developed a strong and mutually beneficial relationship with Voysey, encouraging him to visit south Lakeland, to attend his local carving classes and to visit The Spinnery and other local workshops. In return Voysey exhibited a 'Looking Glass' at the 1899 Arts and Crafts Exhibition in London, made by Simpson to Voysey's design. He also designed Littleholme for the Simpsons, a small detached house on the edge of Kendal, a permanent reminder of the artistic presence of both men in Lakeland.

The site for Littleholme was surveyed in June 1909 during one of Voysey's visits to Kendal, and the design was begun at once. The house was built entirely of local materials and the architect came frequently to view progress, inspecting the finished building in February 1910.[1] Externally Littleholme is little more than an unadorned oblong with a pitched roof. The interior has characteristic features such as polished wood floors and staircase, latched doors, heart-shaped window catches, green Pilkington half-tiles and an inglenook fireplace, but also what the family found to be ill-proportioned kitchen fitments and low windows. Against the architect's advice, curtain fabrics designed by Morton's of Carlisle (who for a time also printed Voysey's designs) were used, possibly because Simpson was an agent for the firm, which employed his son, Ronald (b. 1890), for many years as a designer. Although the house itself lacked any strong regional traits, and made no obvious contribution to the revival (other than to reaffirm Simpson's artistic status), its contents told a different story. Simpson's furniture and woodcarvings were set alongside Keswick School metalwork, Cuthbert Rigby drawings and paintings, Langdale linen, Dorrie and W.G. Collingwood paintings, and Ann Macbeth hand painted pottery, all of which pronounced his place first and foremost as a Lakeland craftsman.[2] Extensions to Littleholme were proposed by Voysey in 1923 but not executed.[3]

The garden at Littleholme was entirely Jane Simpson's work, coordinated to be used as design inspiration for her floral embroideries, and the house serves as a constant reminder that the Lakeland revival was never a closed, introverted movement, but an outward looking attempt to create a wider association for the local arts, and to enhance

---

[1] CROK, WDX 515.

[2] Since the categorisation of Voysey as an Arts and Crafts architect has been challenged by David Gebhard (*Charles F.A. Voysey, Architect* (Los Angeles, 1975), 5, he is not discussed here as an Arts and Crafts influence upon either Simpson or Lakeland.

[3] *Catalogue of the Drawings of the Royal Institute of British Architects* (1989), 28.

the arts in Lakeland. Littleholme even inspired something of a minor artistic reaction of its own. Silverdale poet Gordon Bottomley wrote *Littleholme*, published in 1925, which included these lines:

> A carver at his bench in a high gable
> Hears the sharp stream close under, far below,
> Tinkle and chatter, and no other sound
> Arises there to him to change his thoughts
> Of the changed, silent town and the dead hands
> That made it and maintained it, and the need
> For handiwork and happy work and work
> To use and ease the mind if such sweet towns
> Are to be built again or live again.

> The long town ends at Littleholme, where the road
> Creeps up to hills of ancient-looking stone.
> Under the hanging eaves at Littleholme
> A latticed casement peeps above still gardens
> Into a Crown of druid-solemn trees
> Upon a knoll as high as a small house,
> A shapely mound made so by nameless men
> Whose smoothing touch yet shows through the green hide.[1]

Ronald Simpson, a gifted draughtsman, designed a Littleholme notepaper which, with its tell-tale Voysey heart shape design, was used by the family during their 42 years living in the house.

Despite the status he achieved, crowned by his acceptance into the Art Workers' Guild in 1913, and his association with those who moved in artistic circles outside Lakeland, Simpson never attempted to move away from Lakeland, or to set up an additional workshop elsewhere. His return to Kendal around 1885 was assuredly deliberate, as was his decision to remain in Lakeland. Whilst his work was praised both in London and abroad (for example, at the 1913 Paris Exhibition), his overriding commitment was to Lakeland and to the spread of local handcrafts; his connection with both was never broken after 1885. The clearest sign of that commitment, apart from his long-term involvement with the local woodcarving classes, was his support for local exhibitions which he attended throughout his career as an independent craftsman (1885–1922).

His earliest appearance was at the Kendal Conversazione held at the

---

[1] G. Bottomley, *Poems of Thirty Years* (1925), 20–1.

Kendal Literary and Scientific Institute in March 1886, when Simpson gave practical demonstrations of woodcarving and exhibited examples of work by his Burneside and Gatebeck pupils. The Conversazione, however, with its emphasis on municipal regalia, clearly left the Kendal wood carver pondering the function of local exhibitions, and shortly afterwards he followed the Keswick School's example by founding his own, establishing an annual showcase more suited to local arts. With four years experience of running his own exhibition, when the Kendal Arts, Crafts and Loan Exhibition was proposed in 1890, Simpson was able to make a strong contribution, attending all the early meetings with Rawnsley and others, and helping to devise a plan. He volunteered to act as district secretary for Kendal and as a guarantor, as well as exhibiting work by himself and his chief carvers. Like the Linen Industry and the Keswick School, Simpson always maintained that all work made at The Handicrafts should be credited to its maker and all exhibits at the 1891 Kendal exhibition were labelled accordingly. One of his leading craftsmen, Thomas Dixon, showed his own designs for a carved panel (influenced by his employer's teachings), along with various other items of carving, some made to Simpson's design (for example, '326. Peartree Panel (Design by A.W. Simpson), Thomas Dixon, Kendal'). Members of his local carving classes also exhibited work and Simpson showed 'Various Pieces of Artistic Woodwork'.[1]

When the Kendal Exhibition of Pictures and Decorative Art was proposed in 1899, Simpson took a similarly active role alongside his regional revival colleagues, acting as a member of the general committee, a guarantor, joint honorary secretary (with his friend and colleague Cuthbert Rigby (1850–1935)), and an exhibitor of, among other things, an 'Iris' panel.[2] Other carvings by Simpson appeared at local shows at Silverdale and Ambleside, and between 1900 and 1919 at the annual Coniston exhibition, another concentrated local exercise which helped to promote Ruskin and his Lakeland followers. In 1906 Simpson showed three items including a carved panel which belonged to Mrs Colling-wood, and in 1907 showed eleven items including a copper-lined tray and an oak inlaid stationery cupboard, alongside leather work by Jane Simpson. Although a self-taught embroideress, Jane was taught the art of leather work by Alfred Bowers, another of Simpson's leading craftsmen, who taught at the Gatebeck and Milnthorpe classes. In 1910

---

[1] *Catalogue of the Kendal Arts, Crafts and Loan Exhibition* (1891) (copy in Kendal Library).

[2] *Catalogue of the Exhibition of Pictures and Decorative Art, Kendal, 1899* (copy in Kendal Library).

Simpson showed his largest number of exhibits at Coniston (19), the number dropping to around 11 by 1912. His last appearance locally was at the Grasmere exhibition held in July 1921, not long before his death. There, he showed specimens of furniture, and also a small collection of wooden fowls made as children's toys.[1] As a guide to the level of independence achieved by women in local arts by 1921, at least half of Grasmere's organising committee were women (including Eleanor, Rawnsley's second wife), and at least half the exhibitors were women. Wordsworth and Ruskin, however, were still just as prominent, and were referred to both directly and indirectly in Lady Chance's opening address.

Given his national success, the best explanation for Simpson's almost continuous support for local exhibitions was his firm belief that what was happening in Lakeland was just as important as what was happening elsewhere, that local exhibitions could make a valid statement about local arts, and that the revival of local arts and crafts was significant enough to require the establishment of local exhibitions. Simpson evidently experienced the same duality as Fleming and Rawnsley, able to cultivate national appreciation for his work, with commissions coming from far and wide, and yet at the same time able to see himself as a devout Lakeland Ruskinian who always worked to a specific set of beliefs (which apparently contradicted the times). His work became a regular and well-respected sight locally, and he always upheld a belief in the value of regional handcrafts. Although his love of Lakeland did not result in any active part in Rawnsley's preservation campaigns, Simpson did form a local walking group and in January 1900 walked the considerable distance from Kendal to Coniston to attend Ruskin's funeral.

Perhaps because of this duality, Simpson's work endured, and after his death in 1922 his son Hubert (b. 1889) took over The Handicrafts, seeing it survive until 1951. Out of his father's teaching, Hubert Simpson was inspired to co-found the Red Rose Guild of Designer Craftsmen. Based in Manchester, the guild was formed with the deliberate objective of promoting the work of northern craftsmen and craftswomen. Despite his presence at the Arts and Crafts Exhibition in London, and occasionally exhibiting some of his carvings at the Cumberland and Westmorland Society of Arts and Crafts Exhibition, held annually in Carlisle from 1897, which probably had more definite ties with the Arts and Crafts movement, Simpson has yet to earn an 'Arts and Crafts' label. To

---

[1] *Westmorland Gazette*, 23 July 1921.

Rawnsley, however, he was always quite firmly placed under the title 'Home Art Industries' which, given that Simpson apparently never attended the Home Arts and Industries Association Exhibition, referred specifically to the Lakeland revival. He not only describes him as a follower of Ruskin's teachings, but discusses his work solely in relation to that of the Keswick School, the Langdale Linen Industry, and Annie Garnett's The Spinnery.[1] This confirms that Simpson was a valid part of a regional domestic arts movement, which was driven principally by internal influences.

---

[1] Rawnsley, *Ruskin*, 115–48.

9

ANNIE GARNETT
AND THE SPINNERY

Although Lakeland had to wait for the local revival to take full effect before local women artists came to the fore, led chiefly by Dorrie Collingwood and Edith Rawnsley after 1885, throughout the period 1883 to 1920 the number of craftswomen remained generally equal to the number of craftsmen. One of the primary reasons for the early proliferation of craftswomen in Lakeland was, of course, that the revival began with the re-establishment of a female-friendly industry involving hand spinning and needlework. But it was also the case that, because of the early and positive example set in local crafts, in which women received both paid employment and full training as well as the opportunity to develop personal creativity, women who had no previous arts education were encouraged to come forward and take part at an earlier stage. With the considerable numbers actively involved in the Langdale Linen Industry and later the Ruskin Linen Industry, it was always more likely that the women at the forefront of the revival would be crafts oriented rather than artists. For them, the domestic nature of the Lakeland revival, where practical skills would earn regular money, held far more appeal than the financial uncertainty of the individual wielding of the artist's brush. Yet they were no less artistically motivated in their work, and the particularly strong example set by Marian Twelves and Elizabeth Pepper, neither of whom had any formal arts training, was evidently enough to inspire a new generation of successful Lakeland craftswomen. By far the most active of that second generation, which also included spinsters and embroiderers connected with the Grasmere, Coniston, Hawkshead, Troutbeck, Silverdale and Morland branches of the Linen Industry, was Annie Garnett of Bowness-on-Windermere. Like Simpson, she had solid and direct ties with the Lakeland revival throughout her career and represented its outward spread, geographically, theoretically and practically.

Like many of her colleagues, Annie Garnett had little education and no formal training in the arts, and her experience of arts developments outside Lakeland in the 1880s was limited. Born in 1864 at Fairfield, the dower house to the Crown Hotel in Bowness, Annie Garnett was the second of six children. Her three brothers went away to university, and eventually established careers in medicine and the law, but she and her two sisters, Wilhelmina (Winnie) and Frances, stayed at home. Like Simpson she had an enquiring mind, and was an early reader of Ruskin, her studies of his works assuredly influenced by his actual presence in Lakeland from 1872. Given his practical impact on south Lakeland and local curiosity surrounding Brantwood, Ruskin would certainly have made a considerable impression on the region in a literary sense, inspiring those in Lakeland who might not normally have done so to read his works. With a similar interest in drawing and painting her natural surroundings, Miss Garnett began to develop her artistic talents. Aware that Ruskin was living close by, she and her father made several visits to Brantwood in the 1880s, chiefly to ask for artistic advice. A direct link with the writer was, therefore, established at around the time that Simpson returned to Kendal and made his first visit to the house. Some of those visits were recorded in a diary. She recalled one occasion when Ruskin talked to her about 'the beautiful country life at Coniston' and of the necessity for the artist to go to nature, advice which she followed for the remainder of her life.[1] Another time her father called at Brantwood alone, taking some of his daughter's paintings. Those Ruskin criticised, being 'very pleased' with a study of roses and a small landscape, and that gave her 'great encouragement' to continue with her art work.[2] Although Miss Garnett never became an independent artist, and never exhibited her paintings locally or nationally, her art work was to be the basis on which her lengthy career in textiles would be founded, out of which her reputation as an excellent craftswoman and the producer of textiles no less important than those produced by, for example, Morris & Co. (whose highly reputable textile department included a needlework section which, from 1885, ran under the guidance of May Morris) and the Haslemere Weaving Industry, would grow.[3]

Not content merely with accepting Ruskin's personal advice, in 1889, shortly after Mrs Pepper had taken over at Elterwater, Miss Garnett visited St Martin's. By that time the revival was well established, and she was presented with a flawless example of Ruskin's theories working

---

[1] AHM, Miss Garnett's diary, 22 Jan. 1900. The diary is by no means a complete record of Miss Garnett's life and in parts is in the form of a memoir.

[2] Ibid.

[3] See A. Callen, *Angel in the Studio. Women in the Arts and Crafts Movement 1870–1914* (1914) for May Morris, the Morris & Co. needlework department and Haslemere.

in practice in relation to local handcrafts. The impact of that first visit was tremendous, and for the remainder of her life she was to refer back time and again to the moment when, aged 25, she entered St Martin's:

> I was literally set down again in the old world never to be again far from it and I found myself longing to be surrounded by Ancient Industry, were it spinning, or weaving, or carving, or any other art that went to make up the Home-life of long ago. All its beauty I would draw from it.[1]

Almost immediately she began spinning lessons with Mrs Pepper and her Langdale workers, establishing her own direct links with the revival of local arts and crafts, and quickly became a competent spinster. Along with her art work, that teaching was to prove the impetus for Miss Garnett to go on to other things, culminating in her own textile workshop which became widely known as The Spinnery. Certainly equal to, if not more successful than, either the Langdale or Ruskin Linen Industries, The Spinnery became a fundamental part of the local revival, and was the means by which Miss Garnett helped further to establish Lakeland's design identity, as well as the opportunity to spread both Ruskin's teachings and respect for regional handcrafts. From the very beginning, therefore, Ruskin shaped not only what would become her life's work, but her contribution to the local revival. Directly, he offered personal guidance in, among other things, her art work, and indirectly she felt his influence through St Martin's, the embodiment of his teachings.

Shortly after completing lessons at St Martin's, Miss Garnett became friends with the Brownsons of Bowness. Brownson was then curate of the local church, but was also secretary of the local art school where Simpson occasionally taught. Assuredly inspired by Simpson, and by recent events at Elterwater and Keswick, the curate proposed a more modest spinning and embroidery class for the women of Bowness. Mrs Pepper and Miss Garnett were secured to carry out the practical organisation, the former teaching embroidery, the latter spinning. In Miss Garnett's words, that early Bowness class was 'much larger' than expected and by January 1891 discussions on its development and direction were taking place with the Brownsons.[2] By 1891, just before the staging of what would be its biggest ever art and craft exhibition, south Lakeland had clearly become even more receptive to Ruskin's

---

[1] AHM, Garnett diary, 1899 (some pages of this diary do not contain precise dates).
[2] Ibid.

teachings, particularly in the practical form, and the initial response at Bowness was markedly similar to that at Elterwater and Keswick. By the time that the Bowness class had begun, local people had developed an almost overwhelming willingness to become involved in anything which even vaguely resembled the already well-received Langdale and Ruskin Linen Industries, but especially if Mrs Pepper or Miss Twelves was involved. Again Ruskin's theories and the hard work of all those involved in their realisation played a considerable part in that early success, but fortuitous circumstances (rather than any outside influences) were to play an equally considerable part in Bowness's further development.

Party to the talks between Miss Garnett and the Brownsons in early 1891 was Ernest Goddard, a house guest of the Garnetts, and he offered a sum (not disclosed in Miss Garnett's papers) which bought two extra spinning wheels—the first major acquisition for the Bowness class. Simpson was probably commissioned to make the two additional wheels since not only did he have prior associations with Brownson and Bowness Art School but he had already made wheels for Mrs Pepper, and made a number of wheels for Miss Garnett at a later date. Appropriately, in her diary, Miss Garnett chose Fleming's words from *Songs of the Spindle and Legends of the Loom* to describe how she was 'lifted into action' by Goddard's gift, resolving to develop a larger, more efficient handcraft exercise which was unquestionably and solely influenced by St Martin's.[1] Soon after, a 'grand anonymous gift' of a loom, six more wheels, a warping frame and expenses for six months was made, and it was that which finally transformed the class into a potentially commercial workshop able to make and sell finished fabrics and embroideries.[2] The gift could have come from any of several sources, including the countess of Bective, a patron of local arts, Laxey, or even Albert Fleming or Joan Severn. It was from that point that the class became known as the Windermere Industry, the name used shortly afterwards at the 1891 Kendal exhibition,[3] but it was also from that date that Mrs Pepper ceased to teach at Bowness, her place filled by Mrs Brownson and later Miss Rawson. Mrs Brownson also acted as secretary of the newly organised workshop while Miss Garnett was treasurer, taking charge of all other practical matters, including the employment of

---

[1] Ibid.; see Fleming's Foreword in H.H. Warner (ed.), *Songs of the Spindle and Legends of the Loom* (1889), 15, from which Miss Garnett quotes.

[2] AHM, Garnett Diary.

[3] The exact date when the Windermere Industry became known as The Spinnery is not clear, but the name was certainly being used by 1898.

a weaver. Fleming lent his name as president, reaffirming positive and definite links between St Martin's and the Windermere Industry, and Brownson was vice-president.

Initially based in a back room at the Crown Hotel, the Bowness spinning and embroidery workshop proved immensely popular not just because it offered a means of earning additional income, but because it offered the opportunity for the development of individual expression and creativity, all at no expense to the workers. Like their sisters at Elter-water and Keswick, and at the smaller branches of the Linen Industry then operating, Windermere Industry women, once trained, were given a wheel and materials to take home (free of charge), thus deliberately reviving traditional Lakeland domestic industry, and they too were paid on a regular basis for their work. All machinery other than that driven directly by the hand was expressly forbidden, and all the workers were actively encouraged to take pride in and receive recognition for their work, and to labour for the love of the thing rather than for profit. Similarly, they too were encouraged to express individual creativity, mainly through embroidery, the early decorating of everyday objects such as tray cloths marking the beginning of a more artistic side to the Windermere Industry akin to that witnessed in the early days of the Langdale Linen Industry. The first commercial order, which came from an American, Mrs Pierpont Morgan, in 1891, was for a rather mundane two dozen linen towels. Mrs Pierpont Morgan was the wife of banker, art collector and entrepreneur John Pierpont Morgan (1837–1913) who was also a benefactor of the Metropolitan Museum, New York, and a patron of artist and designer Roger Fry.[1] But given that Miss Garnett, her sister Winnie (also of the Crown Hotel), Miss Rawson and Mrs Brownson all exhibited silk embroideries in several needlework categories at the 1891 Kendal exhibition, a more creative side to the Windermere Industry would have been evident from the outset.

A year and a half after establishing hand spinning and embroidery at Bowness, Miss Garnett had a disagreement with the Brownsons which was not unlike that which took place between Fleming and Miss Twelves. The realisation of Ruskin's theories clearly led to success but also to much heated debate among his Lakeland devotees. Since the curacy had come to an end, the Brownsons decided to leave the Windermere Industry and Bowness, and Miss Garnett determined to take full charge of the workshop. Several rearrangements of both committee

---

[1] J.A. Garraty and J.L. Sternstein (ed.), *Encyclopedia of American Biography* (1996), 793–5.

and finances then took place before she finally became the driving force
of what she was to rename The Spinnery (affectionately known to her as
The Spin), a name more suited (like The Handicrafts) to traditional
Lakeland crafts. Not unexpectedly, given her exposure to neat
Ruskinism, Miss Garnett then began to mould her workshop yet more
closely to the example of St Martin's, her undiluted perception of Ruskin
taking full effect. The details of any changes made in working practices
and production were apparently never committed to paper, but from that
time onwards, the nature of what was designed and made evidently
brought a new and more definite identity for The Spinnery. This included
attendance at national as well as local exhibitions, a greater emphasis on
the study of nature in relation to the development of a more artistic side
to the workshop, and the award of the respected title 'art industry'. It
was also from that point that Miss Garnett developed a carefully worded
creed, outlining for the benefit of her workers the precise nature of her
beliefs concerning art and labour:

> To reach always towards the best.
> That real beauty is essential to right existence.
> That only under right conditions can workers develop to their
> utmost.
> That joy in labour is a first principle of true art.
> That work must be a living thing; the mind *and* the heart passing
> into it.
> To bring back their handcrafts into the lives of the people.[1]

Redolent of Ruskin's teachings, but also reflecting the local revival
generally, the creed hung on the wall at The Spinnery, but might just as
easily have hung at the Linen Industries, the Keswick School and The
Handicrafts, such was its potent alignment with their work practices. The
creed was never intended to be a formal contract and was never
ruthlessly enforced. Yet there was a similar willingness to abide by The
Spinnery's Ruskinian laws, and the number of women involved with the
Bowness workshop had reached a similarly satisfactory one hundred by
1899. Such was the impact of working in imitation of St Martin's that,
when she left Bowness, Mrs Brownson did not entirely abandon her
handcraft work. In 1897 the *Art Journal* reported that a Mrs Brownson,
formerly trained at Windermere, had recently established (rather than

---

[1] The creed, which is on display at Abbot Hall Museum, was written and signed by
Annie Garnett.

re-established) a hand spinning and needle-lace making class in Compton Greenfield, Gloucestershire.[1] Equally interesting is that the class never matched The Spinnery. Attempts to apply the Lakeland interpretation of Ruskin's teachings outside the region resulted in little success, which stresses the importance of place to the revival.

Although clearly equally competent in the realisation of Ruskin's theories, Miss Garnett's knowledge of Ruskin's written work is also open to doubt, particularly as, like Simpson, she appears to have left few records relating to her reading. No positive evidence survives to support a strong link with, for example, *Fors Clavigera*. It can only be presumed that, while she did record reading some Ruskin in the 1870s, her work after 1889 did have a theoretical as well as practical Ruskinian basis, but relied to a greater extent on the example set by the Langdale Linen Industry. Whether any visits to Brantwood took place after that date is also unclear. But in 1900, on hearing of Ruskin's death, she was moved to write that the country had 'lost a great and good man' who could not be replaced, concluding:

> dear old man, how much he has done to keep us in the right way will probably never be quite realised. Such a gentle influence he yielded which gathers in its folds all who read him; none can be quite the same after reading him; Everything is so beautiful; so noble; so really good; that the most prejudiced is bound to be better for having let this great man's thoughts even just pass through his brain.[2]

Miss Garnett, therefore, fell into the category of a secondary Lakeland Ruskinian. She neither joined the Guild of St George nor consulted Ruskin on any regular, sustained basis, but she clearly felt a great sense of attachment to him, fired by her earlier personal contact, and experienced a deep sense of loss at his death. The strength of her respect for both the man and his work (in practical and written form) was naturally evident from the beginning of the Bowness class, particularly as it was directly based on St Martin's, Fleming's and Miss Twelves's realisation of *Fors Clavigera*. But from 1891 the emphasis on Ruskin noticeably intensified under Miss Garnett's sole direction, with no outside influences or voices allowed to impinge on her work, and that emphasis never lessened for the remaining forty years that The Spinnery ran.

---

[1] *Art Journal* (1897), 331.

[2] AHM, Garnett Diary, 22 Jan. 1900.

Under Miss Garnett's instruction, a greater emphasis was immediately put on the role of nature in design and the study of the natural (i.e. Lakeland) environment meant that every fabric and embroidery made at Bowness would be 'an expression of nature' with 'a meaning and a history of its own'.[1] Just as Ruskin had encouraged her as an artist to go to nature, so she always deemed it 'absolutely necessary' for her workers 'to study nature; observe colours; note form; not in any hard and false way'.[2] To make that study easier, a garden was developed next to The Spinnery which, as it grew, moved into a converted stable and coach-house behind the Crown Hotel. There, 'colour effects for the woven stuffs and embroideries' could be 'grown and thought out'.[3] Her personal experiences of Ruskin, which were of fundamental importance in identifying Lakeland's individuality and separateness, had begun to surface, and to contribute to the development of the region's unique design identity between 1880 and 1920. As far as we know, neither the Keswick School nor the Langdale or Ruskin Linen Industries had a garden (although Jane Simpson did develop the garden at Littleholme specifically to inspire her similar Langdale linen-based embroidery work), and in that respect The Spinnery quickly began to add its own colour to the revival's fundamental Ruskinian basis. So successful was the garden that a separate nursery selling surplus seeds and plants was soon established, and in a leaflet listing varieties for sale Miss Garnett added the following:

An important branch of the Spinnery work lies in growing plants for the working out of original designs and colour schemes in its Textiles and Embroideries, so that the whole work may actually grow up out of the brown earth.[4]

Varieties grown in the garden and used as design inspiration included daisy, buddleia, phlox, poppies, cranesbill, violets, larkspur, campanula, dianthus, spiraea and dentaria, Miss Garnett's choice, like Ruskin's (and even Wordsworth's) before her, influenced primarily by regional conditions and local gardening traditions.

One result of The Spinnery's more intense study of nature was the production of a greater number of embroideries than at the Keswick

---

[1] A. Garnett, *Spinnery Notes* (1912), 8.

[2] AHM, Garnett Diary, 10 Dec. 1903.

[3] Garnett, *Spinnery Notes*, 8.

[4] See Miss Garnett's leaflet, *Plants and Seeds* (n.d.) (copy at AHM).

School or any of the various branches of the Linen Industry. Ruskin lace was certainly practised at Bowness, which again confirms direct links with Ruskin and St Martin's. Miss Garnett learnt the technique under Mrs Pepper and then taught some of her own workers. But embroidery took a much stronger place at all levels of decorative work at Bowness, with everything from teacloths and clothes to panelled screens speaking more vividly of the plying of the needle, the feminine plough. Since Miss Garnett trained at the site where Ruskin's vision of thread and needle was first realised in Lakeland, that vision probably provided the initial inspiration for her greater emphasis on embroidery. In 1911 the *Pall Mall Gazette* described a four-panelled embroidered screen 'nearing completion' which had 'literally grown up out of surrounding things'. While the screen's fabric was a natural coloured flax mixed with silk threads, its decoration consisted of a large bank of roses in 'a riot of summer pinks' set against the 'effect of a cloudless blue sky'.[1] The same newspaper also described one of the largest pieces of embroidery executed in 1910 as a three-panelled screen with a design based on lupins, its threads interwoven to capture the realities of nature (as Ruskin would have described it):

> The material was designed from the brilliant blue-purple petals of the flower, with a strong red-brown thread under the silk weft to give that quality of living colour one gets in so many blue flowers; the embroidery design was a hedge, literally, of the tall stately spikes of lupin with their pointed green tips aspiring to higher things.[2]

Pieces of that scale and intensity, which demanded many hours of concentrated work, were probably made largely for exhibition or on commission, and the majority of The Spinnery's more decorative output consisted of domestic goods such as tablecloths and mats, most of which were sold through the workshop or by mail order. A typical example is the embroidered tablecloth decorated with a design based on honesty illustrated in the July 1905 issue of the *Art Workers' Quarterly*.[3] Some church textiles were also produced, but not on a large scale.

In the case of fabrics too Miss Garnett applied her personal experiences of Ruskin, but also her personal preferences, determining from the

---

[1] *Pall Mall Gazette*, 22 Feb. 1911, p. 3.

[2] Ibid.

[3] *Art Workers' Quarterly*, July 1905, p. 121.

outset to produce a more expensive and luxurious range than that produced at either Elterwater or Keswick. Flax, cotton and wool were used, but so were nettle fibre, gold, silver and aluminium, materials not formerly used in Westmorland textile production. In some respects that could have been a potential disaster, since the Linen Industries, the Keswick School and The Handicrafts had already proved that the local revival thrived chiefly because of its domestic nature. In fact the innovation proved successful. Aside from linens, which were used mainly for household goods, by 1905 the hundred or so spinsters, weavers and embroiderers were producing a variety of silks, samites (silks often woven with gold or silver thread), throwans, fine throwans, coarse throwans, tweeds, and brocades (one of which, Fritillary, was specially woven for Queen Alexandra), all of which brought further widespread recognition for Lakeland arts and crafts.

Although her teaching at St Martin's provided the basic ancient techniques for the production of most of The Spinnery's fabrics, where silk was concerned Miss Garnett was entirely self-taught. Silk was introduced at Bowness around 1899 after Miss Garnett had experimented with a silk web and a loom set up in her bedroom. Twenty bobbins of silk (the first taking her seventeen hours to fill) produced shortly afterwards for a wedding dress heralded the formal beginning of its production. Miss Garnett later described The Spinnery as 'the first silk factory established in the Lake district', its products being shown 'at the exhibition of the silk manufacturers of Great Britain and Ireland, to whose association it belongs'.[1] That would suggest that, while silk was certainly used at St Martin's and St George's cottages, silk production never became a leading feature at either Elterwater or Keswick (and so they could not offer Miss Garnett any training, or claim to be a 'silk factory'), the more traditional flax taking priority. In 1899 Mrs Caine, secretary of the Utah Silk Commission, visited The Spinnery to get information on her work,[2] and in 1901 Miss Garnett was invited by the council of the Royal Society of Arts to attend a lecture on the British silk industry,[3] such was her reputation as a producer of silks. By 1912 she had resolved also to establish a rug weaving department,[4] something not generally done at any of the Linen Industry workshops.

Just as significant from the perspective of the local revival is that The

---

[1] Garnett, *Spinnery Notes*, 7–8.

[2] AHM, Garnet Diary, 21 July 1899.

[3] Ibid., Dec. 1901.

[4] Garnett, *Spinnery Notes*, 7.

Spinnery's fabrics were influenced almost exclusively by nature, specifically the Lakeland environment, and in that respect Ruskin's direct influence revealed itself again. Just as every embroidery was entirely unique, and had a development history of its own (which was a deliberate stance against modern methods), so did every fabric. As with the embroideries, inspiration for the cloths was drawn from the garden, but also from the broader Lakeland landscape in its unspoilt state, Miss Garnett capturing the myriad subtle colours of nature not only with paints and embroidery silks, but with threads and dyes, every feasible shade of blue, red, yellow, brown and orange being used to stain the hand spun, hand woven cloths. The names of the fabrics reflected the source of inspiration. Those inspired by the landscape included Heather Shadows on Skiddaw, Distant Heather Shadows and Purple Atmosphere; where more specific aspects of nature were the source of inspiration names such as Blue Kingfisher, Purple Lupin, Larkspur and Royal Lupin were used. So important was that source that it was recorded on every sample card given to customers when ordering fabrics. Even on cards of embroidery silks sold to customers and dyed to Miss Garnett's specification it was noted that the dyes were deliberately intended to 'take up the colour effects in nature', Miss Garnett reputedly sending actual flowers or leaves to assist the dyers in their work.[1] Like Simpson's carved panels, the Linen Industry's embroideries and Ruskin lace, and the Keswick School's Skiddaw trays and Ruskin vases, the fabrics spoke solely of Ruskin and Lakeland, and were a constant and deliberate reminder that their creator saw art as a means of expressing delight in God's work, but also that she believed in the value of cultivating a regional design identity. While it exhibited far and wide for more than thirty years, The Spinnery successfully retained that central Lakeland Ruskinian core and Miss Garnett never attempted to leave Lakeland or to establish a similar workshop outside the region. Neither did she ever attempt to alter her work practices or to change the nature of her textiles. Her early experiences of Ruskin and St Martin's set a pattern which would remain constant throughout her career.

Like her colleagues, Miss Garnett resolved from the outset to cultivate a commercial as well as artistic side to local handcrafts, something which had already proved to be essential to long-term survival, with even the smallest branches of the Linen Industry exhibiting locally. Like her guide, St Martin's, she exhibited on as wide a scale as possible, forming

---

[1] AHM, Cards of embroidery silks specially produced at The Spinnery for 'select clients'.

a close and successful affiliation to the Home Arts and Industries Association. At the association's 1896 exhibition Miss Garnett was awarded five gold stars for one fabric alone, while at the same time an embroidered cloth was illustrated in *The Studio*.[1] Further awards were won at the 1899, 1900, 1901, 1902 and 1903 Home Arts exhibitions, Miss Garnett arranging her own display of her prize winning textiles at The Spinnery after the 1900 exhibition. In 1901 she exhibited at an arts exhibition held in Leeds, where Arthur Simpson also showed work.[2] After the 1902 Home Arts exhibition *The Studio* reported:

> It is not too much to say that the Windermere weaving industry is producing some of the most beautiful fabrics now made in this country, and the mixtures of silk and linen, which are so distinctive a feature of the work of charm of texture and surface, were this year more than ever pleasing in the matter of colour. Under these conditions the plain self-coloured stuffs were so satisfying to the eye as to make pattern seem superfluous; but some very excellent patterns were also on view, and the embroideries, though less distinguished in design, were exquisite in needlecraft.[3]

The following year, after the 1903 exhibition, the same journal reported that the Haslemere, Windermere and Langdale industries had

> not allowed themselves to be bound by the endeavour (worthy enough in itself, but irrelevant to art) of providing remunerative employment to deserving amateurs. They have, on the other hand, developed their industries on a thoroughly practical basis, and, with the aid of enthusiastic and discriminating class-holders kept pace with the best artistic feeling of the day.[4]

This confirms not only that The Spinnery was widely accepted as an art industry, but that, whatever their lack of formal training in the arts, and irrespective of their adoption of seemingly antiquated local traditions, Miss Garnett and her workers easily competed with their fellow exhibitors.

In terms of national success, 1903 was evidently an important year for

[1] *The Studio*, July 1896, 99.

[2] *The Studio*, Jan. 1901, 253–9.

[3] Ibid., July 1902, 133–4.

[4] Ibid., July 1903, 125.

Miss Garnett and The Spinnery. Not only did she attend the Home Arts exhibition, but she became a member of the Dress Designers' Exhibition Society. Formed with the purpose of exhibiting design of all kinds relating to dress, the society's president was Walter Crane. She also exhibited textiles at the Art Work Exhibition in Bristol, the fifth exhibition of the Bristol and Clifton Arts and Crafts Society where the highly acclaimed work of Ann Macbeth, Howson Taylor and the Canterbury Weavers appeared. Spinnery textiles were also shown as part of the Arts and Crafts Exhibition in London, Miss Garnett's first (as far as can be ascertained) appearance at the Exhibition Society's exhibition, with other textiles appearing in the 1906 and 1910 Arts and Crafts exhibitions. Given their rather irregular nature, her appearances were less a statement of association with the Arts and Crafts movement than evidence of the standard of The Spinnery's work. In 1905 Miss Garnett was invited to take part in The '91 Art Club Exhibition, and in 1906, following an article devoted to The Spinnery in the *Art Workers' Quarterly*, she showed textiles at the Society of Artists at Work Exhibition held in the Grafton Gallery.[1] Afterwards, it was reported that 'Miss Garnett, the weaver of the Windermere linens, is a nature worshipper after the pattern of the Greeks. She draws all her inspiration from what she sees out of doors'.[2] Her work also appeared at the Montague Fordham Gallery, London, in 1906, and at the Lyceum Club in 1907 in connection with its Crafts Guild.[3] Elsewhere, she exhibited at the Society of Women Artists (1902–7), becoming an associate of the society in 1905 (until 1908). Internationally, she experienced similar success at the 1893 World's Columbian Exposition held in Chicago (exhibiting alongside St Martin's), at the 1909 Deutsch Kunst und Dekoration in Berlin,[4] and at the 1927 Leipzig Exhibition of English Craftsmanship.[5]

While successfully maintaining a national profile, The Spinnery remained at heart a carefully nurtured local exercise which made a concerted effort to adhere to local tradition and to support its revival colleagues. The Spinnery's place in the local revival was vividly outlined by Rawnsley in *Ruskin and the English Lakes* in 1901, its inclusion in

---

[1] *Art Workers' Quarterly*, April 1906, 56–7, 68–9.

[2] *The Studio*, Dec. 1906, 248.

[3] *The Times*, 24 Oct. 1906; *Daily Chronicle*, 23 May 1907.

[4] *Westmorland Gazette*, 14 Oct. 1983.

[5] AHM, Letter to Annie Garnett from the Design and Industries Association, 4 Jan. 1927.

his assessment of Lakeland's home arts industries verifying its important links with Ruskin's presence in the Lake District, and even its secondary nature as a product of the Langdale Linen Industry:

> This weaving and spinning and embroidery school cannot be said to be directly connected with Brantwood, but it was the direct resultant of the Langdale linen experiment, and none the less does it appear, as one talks with the promoter, that here too is an example of the subtle way in which Ruskin's known wishes in the day of his health and hopefulness brought it about that in the day of his weakness and heart sadness, when he had retired from the world of action, there came to him cheer from loyal followers in the Lakeland vales.[1]

The Spinnery's part in the revival was confirmed just as clearly by its strong support of local exhibitions, which represented a positive contribution to Lakeland's collective statements of unity and indepen-dence. At the 1891 Kendal Arts, Crafts and Loan Exhibition, when the Windermere Industry was still in its earliest stages, its chief figures were already exhibiting embroidery work. Miss Garnett showed work under her own name in no fewer than nine categories, clearly stating her independence as a local craftswoman, and winning a first prize in one of them.[2] As she recalled, that caused something of a stir locally, but once again the overriding sense of local camaraderie born of a shared objective (the revival of local crafts under Ruskin's influence) meant that competition was never taken to extremes. The appearance of John Bell's name at the exhibition in connection with both Langdale and Bowness shows that Miss Garnett even employed the same weaver as St Martin's:

> When discussing the yarn that had been awarded the first prize at the Kendal Exhibition of 1891 a group of Ellterwater spinsters, bemoaning the fact that the prize had not fallen to their lot, were quite consoled in remembering the part they had taken in making the thread, 'but we larned her' they were overheard to remark quite cheerfully. And so the traditional spinning has been handed

---

[1] H.D. Rawnsley, *Ruskin and the English Lakes* (Glasgow, 1901), 147–8.

[2] The nine categories were: Embroidery Worked in Silk, Linen—Embroidered or Drawn, Embroidery Worked in Cotton or Linen in White, Article Showing Greatest Ingenuity and Taste with Least Comparative Expense, Piano Back or Centre for Dinner Table on Langdale Linen, Langdale Linen—Embroidered or Drawn, Embroidered Curtain, Hand Spun Flax Yarn, and Hand Spun and Woven Linen, Grass Bleached.

on from one to the other.[1]

By the time of the 1899 Kendal Exhibition of Pictures and Decorative Art, The Spinnery was employing four weavers and at least a hundred part-time spinsters and embroiderers. In her diary Miss Garnett notes that by then about a hundred additional women whom she had taught were practising spinning or embroidery (or both), but no longer in connection with the industry. Textiles submitted on that occasion naturally reflected the considerable developments within the industry over the previous eight years, with a greater variety of fabrics (including throwans, silks and linens) as well as embroideries being shown. Miss Garnett's textiles also appeared at Arthur Simpson's annual exhibition, certainly in 1903, and as late as 1921 at the Grasmere exhibition,[2] which was probably her last appearance locally. A number of silks and embroideries, including 'Honesty', 'Wistaria', and 'Periwinkle', were shown at the 1910 Coniston exhibition. Other Spinnery exhibits shown at Coniston were: a tea cloth, 'Herb Paris'; silk, pale blue herring-bone; silk, pink seeded; silk, 'Cream Trellis'; brocade sprig; motor scarf, 'Begum'; throwan, finest blue; blouse front, 'Roses and Rings'; Table-cloth, 'Warmensteiner Stole'; and a table-centre, 'Privet'.[3]

During its lifetime a considerable number of people called at The Spinnery to buy its textiles, but also to see the seemingly antiquated methods of production in action. Visitors, including Mrs King of the Haslemere Weaving Industry, came from far and wide, including America and Canada, but in terms of the local revival some of the most significant names are Arthur and Jane Simpson, Edith and Hardwicke Rawnsley, Albert Fleming (on numerous occasions), Mr and Mrs Rupert Potter (parents of Beatrix and friends of the Rawnsleys) and C.F.A. Voysey. Miss Garnett visited Voysey's house, Broadleys, in 1900, recording in her diary that she 'called on Mrs Currer-Briggs at her new house which Voysey has built; it is delightful … The grandest feature of the house I nearly missed is the great hall, just such a one as our ancestors would have built'.[4] Simpson was commissioned to make a number of spinning wheels and possibly several looms for The Spinnery over the years, all of which were based on those traditional to Westmor-

---

[1] Garnett, *Spinnery Notes*, 9–11.

[2] *Kendal Mercury and Times*, 27 Nov. 1903; *Westmorland Gazette*, 23 July 1921.

[3] *Catalogue of the Seventh Annual Coniston Exhibition: Coniston Institute* (1906) (copy in Ruskin Museum, Coniston).

[4] AHM, Garnett Diary, 7 Sept. 1900.

land, as Miss Garnett stressed in her booklet *Spinnery Notes* in 1912:

Weaving is taught on looms that are models of the Westmorland ones in use since the fourteenth century without any addition, excepting a contrivance of string and buffalo hide to increase the speed of the shuttle as it is 'shot' across the web. And the spinning is taught on wheels that are either reproductions, or the actual old ones that have been in use for the last two or three hundred years.[1]

In *Notes on Hand-Spinning* (1896) she had already drawn attention to her awareness of Lakeland's textile history in relation to the value of handwork, echoing Ruskin's earlier observations in *Fors Clavigera*:[2]

The spinning wheel never quite disappeared from our midst. In this Lake District, our grandmothers still spun their own linen, and though their daughters preferred, I think only for novelty's sake, machine-made linens, their grandmothers have returned to the old ways, for the sake, I hope, of something more beautiful than can be found in the sameness of machine-made things, for the real love of hand work, 'the record of thoughts and intents and trials and heart-breakings, of recoveries and joyfulnesse of success.'[3]

The Spinnery therefore made a positive and direct contribution to bridging the gap made in local tradition by the introduction of machinery, reaffirming its rightful place in the local revival. Appropriately, immediately after the paragraph just quoted, Miss Garnett added a quotation:

After long pondering over Wordsworth's sonnets and Mr Ruskin's eloquent appeals in *Fors*, I was lifted into action by the homely speech of one of my poor neighbours, 'When t'ould wheels died out,' said she, 't'gude times went too; m'happen they'd come back if t'wheels did.'[4]

---

[1] Garnett, *Spinnery Notes*, 15.

[2] Above, p. 18 for Ruskin's remarks in Letter XL of *Fors* concerning Cumberland's lost spinning tradition.

[3] Garnett, *Notes on Hand-Spinning*, 12.

[4] Warner, *Songs*, quoted by Miss Garnett in her diary for 1899.

Taken from Fleming's foreword to *Songs of the Spindle and Legends of the Loom* and often repeated by Miss Garnett, this quotation clarifies without doubt that she saw her work as directly based on the Langdale Linen Industry, but just as significantly as the continuation of local tradition. In 1913 additional evidence of that continuity appeared in the form of a new Spinnery workshop which was built next to the old coach-house. Under Miss Garnett's influence, its design was based on the traditional Westmorland cottage, with 'deep window seats and panelled walls, casement curtains, and round chimneys'.[1] Devised to house a small museum of antiquities related to spinning, weaving and embroidery, it also provided additional space for spinning and teaching. Miss Garnett saw her new workshop as

> the fulfilment of desires borne of a visit some 25 years ago to the little spinning home at Elterwater, where the old-world atmosphere, the peace, the restful labour, the purring of spinning wheels, and the music of a loom must have entered into the hearts of most of those privileged to visit it.[2]

Even after a quarter of a century St Martin's and all that it represented clearly remained her central focus.

The Spinnery's place as first and foremost a local revival industry was made yet clearer by Miss Garnett's lifelong and unflinching devotion to Ruskin's teachings, her work always relaying that same curious and yet highly compatible mix of Ruskin and Lakeland which lay at the heart of the revival. Under Ruskin's influence, she always upheld spinning and embroidery as 'proper women's acts',[3] and, while The Spinnery kept a small permanent staff, a concerted effort was made throughout its existence to keep most of the women very much in the domestic environment:

> It [The Spinnery] gives employment to women and girls in their spare time on the understanding that it *is* spare time work only, and is not to interfere with their allotted work in life. They may thus add to their incomes by industriously filling their spare moments, but are not permitted to make a living by it.[4]

---

[1] A. Garnett, *Spinnery Notes* (1912), 14.

[2] Ibid., 5.

[3] AHM, Garnett Diary, 11 July 1899.

[4] Garnett, *Spinnery Notes*, 6.

In her diary for 1900 she drew particular attention to her understanding of Ruskin's concentration on 'Truth; and Beauty; and Moral worth', agreeing that the gospel of the day was 'gain' and 'self'.[1] As an equally devout (but also questioning) Christian, Miss Garnett always shared the writer's (and the revival's) view that 'all things beautiful suggested God'. She debated the implications of a godless existence but maintained throughout her life that Nature as God's creation was an essential part of life: 'A country life is the life to live; in touch with God, Nature controlling; surrounded with Nature; in the very midst of nature; part of nature'.[2] Her diary suggests that Miss Garnett, like Marian Twelves, encouraged her workers to read Ruskin, believing that the stimulation of the mind was as beneficial to the individual as practical labour unhindered by machines.

While The Spinnery kept its female workers in the home, their traditional place, it clearly presented Miss Garnett with the opportunity to establish herself as both an independent craftswoman and a businesswoman who openly rejected marriage in favour of 'the joys of labour', which earned her the title of 'black sheep' of the family.[3] Unlike Marian Twelves, without the presence of the Guild of St George or any other potentially restricting body, Miss Garnett was free to profit from her work and to apply her understanding of Ruskin to a degree entirely suited to herself. This suggests a rather freer interpretation of Ruskin in the revival's leading secondary Ruskinians, although it does not imply that their devotion was any less deep. While remaining a committed Ruskinian, she saw a simultaneous need to raise awareness of women's issues which, given that she was some years younger than Marian Twelves, were coming more to the fore during her later career. Over the years she became vice-president of the Westmorland Women's Liberal Association (which indicates that, like Simpson, she had a definite interest in politics), gave lectures to groups including the Lancashire Federation of Women's Institutes, and regularly gave advice to various societies and committees, including the Women's Advisory Committee, on the employment of disabled nurses and unemployed women. She also attended events such as the Women's Exhibition held in Earls Court (sending some 70 exhibits in 1900) which were aimed specifically towards the promotion of women's crafts. Less surprisingly, she took an active part in the Home Work Co-operative Society which

[1] AHM, Garnett Diary, 22 Jan. 1900.
[2] Ibid., 23 Sept 1899.
[3] Ibid., 9 July 1899.

was formed with the intention of helping women to increase their incomes. How Miss Garnett reconciled these two seemingly opposing schools of thought is not clear, but all her life she achieved personal and financial independence, and expressed a degree of pre-feminist thinking, while remaining one of Ruskin's most loyal queens of domesticity. In 1913 she demonstrated the depth of her commitment to bringing back the 'old-world life' of Westmorland by building the second centre specifically designed to house local, traditional crafts (the Keswick School being the first).[1]

The building of the new workshop symbolised the peak of Miss Garnett's career and, at that time, she had successful outlets at Liberty's and Waring & Gillow. Then war began and restrictions were imposed. She became honorary secretary of the Windermere War Hospital Supply Depot which brought her into contact with Rawnsley's friend and fellow Lakeland defence campaigner Gordon Somervell. In 1916 she received Queen Mary's Needlework Guild badge certificate for voluntary work and later became a member of the Westmorland Red Cross Demobilisation Committee. In July 1919 she was invited to a Buckingham Palace garden party in honour of her hard work. Shortly afterwards her health began to deteriorate and, like The Handicrafts, The Spinnery went into a slow decline. Unlike Marian Twelves, who had the Misses Adamson to carry on her work, Miss Garnett apparently had no-one willing to take over her work, despite the hundreds of women taught and employed by The Spinnery over the previous four decades. By the 1930s the Bowness workshop had closed, and in 1942 Miss Garnett died in a Carlisle nursing home. In 1952 pieces of her work were shown at the Decorative Arts Exhibition at the Victoria and Albert Museum,[2] which served as a brief reminder of what has since been largely forgotten.

[1] Garnett, *Spinnery Notes*, 5.

[2] AHM, Annie Garnett papers.

10

THE CONTINUED REVIVAL
OF HANDCRAFTS
IN LAKELAND

One direct consequence of the overwhelming success achieved by the considerably larger Langdale and Ruskin Linen Industries, the Keswick School, The Handicrafts and The Spinnery, in which the realisation of Ruskin's teachings proved abundantly fruitful, was the establishment of a number of smaller handcraft classes and workshops in south Lakeland, Ruskin's influence filtering down to even the least populated areas of the region. Like The Spinnery and The Handicrafts, they were 'secondary' Ruskinians with no obvious connections with the Guild of St George, and only minimal direct contact with Ruskin, but with direct and sustained association with those at the forefront of the revival.

Although based exclusively on the examples already established, these smaller groups were markedly less ambitious, yet they were just as successful in terms of realising Ruskin's theories and in reviving local, traditional handcrafts, and contributed to the spread of the revival. Lacking almost any outside contact, they thrived solely on their regional nature and show how the revival dispersed, its extent and impact locally, the direction it took as time passed, and its true nature as a domestic revival. Although small, they were concentrated pockets of the revival's unique mix of Ruskin and Lakeland, again reflecting a regional positivity which successfully defied the destruction of regional arts and crafts. They also reflected a willingness in the people of Lakeland to retrieve and continue their regional heritage in accordance with a specific set of Ruskin-based teachings. None of the smaller classes and workshops had any connections with any Arts and Crafts developments, although there were ties with the Home Arts and Industries Association in two instances. Other than that, local exhibitions were their main source of publicity and Ruskin's teachings, combined with local tradition, their principal fuel.

By the time the revival had established itself in south Lakeland, with widespread success achieved by its leading forces, the picture of local arts and crafts had become very complex. With their appearances at national as well as local exhibitions, it would be difficult to overlook the Linen Industries and the Keswick School as the leaders of a new wave of art and design in late nineteenth-century Lakeland, but it is only by looking much more closely at local exhibitions from a local perspective that the true extent of the spread of the return to regional arts and crafts in Lakeland can be fully assessed.

Within two years of the founding of the Keswick School and the Langdale Linen Industry, The Handicrafts had come into existence, and no fewer than five other related classes and workshops had been founded, albeit on a much less ambitious scale, directly as a result of the examples set by Fleming, Marian Twelves, Simpson and the Rawnsleys. Three classes—Burneside, Gatebeck, and Milnthorpe—have already been mentioned in connection with Simpson, whose involvement can be linked to their beginnings in 1885, the year when he established himself as a local craftsman. It is highly probable that Simpson founded or contributed to the founding of the classes, and his influence clearly dominated throughout, although the Keswick School would also have exerted some influence. While leather work (taught by Alfred Bowers, also of The Handicrafts) and needlework were carried on, woodcarving—a local handcraft once as popular as spinning—was always the chief subject taught, and all three classes proved successful, running well into the 1900s. Since there were no woodcarving or leather work classes of any description before 1885 at any of the three sites (the crafts having formerly been taught and practised only in the home), and given their close associations with Simpson, their birth and growth must be attributed to the Ruskinian Lakeland revival and its prominent figures, the more ambitious examples already established providing a successful model to follow.

Already described as the epitome of Ruskin's (and Rawnsley's) vision of a parish workshop, Burneside, Gatebeck and Milnthorpe ran strictly as amateur evening classes and never developed ambitions which took them beyond the parish boundaries. Formed solely to teach Westmerians the joys of hand labour as an occupation outside working hours and inside the home, their local domestic nature was particularly evident. Under Simpson's guidance, all three proved immensely popular and produced work of an exceptional standard, the pinnacle of which was the Burneside reredos, but all exhibited strictly within Lakeland's borders. Locating names of students and teachers (other than Simpson and Alfred Willink) has proved difficult and exact numbers who attended are not known. Given his later more prominent role as chairman of the Westmorland Education Committee, Willink was probably the central figure in all three classes, supported by visiting teachers such as Simpson, and probably also W.G. Collingwood and the Rawnsleys. Exhibition catalogues give some indication of size and names. Students linked to Burneside who exhibited at the 1891 Kendal exhibition, for example, included Richard Davis, Thomas Jones, Miss E.M. Love and John Marsh.[1] Exhibits submitted by Burneside (including its separate beginners' class) included various pieces of furniture and a considerable number of carved decorative panels which were highly suggestive of Simpson's influence. Since twelve Burneside carvers (excluding Willink) had already been attributed with working on the local church reredos when finished portions were shown at Simpson's 1887 exhibition (A. Bigland, W. Case, S. L. Clarke, T. Davis, B.A. Willink, R. Davis, T. Jones, W.P. Line, E.M. Love, J.C. Pittaway, W. Roper, and J. Todd),[2] it may be supposed that at least ten carvers worked in association with that class at any one time, a portion being women. How many trained with the class and then left to continue with their craft strictly in the home, acting as independent craftsmen and women and never exhibiting, cannot be known. Numbers associated with the Milnthorpe class around 1891 appeared to be similar to Burneside (including John Spencer, Miss C. Semple, G.E. Cary, W. Nelson, J. Atkinson, George Nelson, John Dobson and George Shaw), while Gatebeck was clearly a smaller class which exhibited less frequently. The catalogue of the 1891 Kendal exhibition shows that noticeably fewer students from Gatebeck showed work, and the local newspapers reported fewer names in connection with the class when writing on Simpson's annual exhibition.

Joining the Burneside, Gatebeck and Milnthorpe classes, and beginning at almost the exact same time (only weeks or even days before), were the Coniston and Kirkby Lonsdale classes, of which the latter was arguably the most substantial and sizeable of the 'secondary' revival amateur classes (rather than workshops). The Coniston woodcarving class, formed in May 1885, was again an entirely amateur exercise which aimed to restore local crafts to the home and benefitted from Simpson's tuition. Given its close proximity to Brantwood, and the fact that it clearly echoed the Rawnsleys' Wray and Keswick carving classes, Ruskin and the revival were at its core also. The Coniston class was originally begun by a Capt. Wodehouse, with the same fundamental aim of teaching local men and women a traditional domestic craft once

---

[1] *Catalogue of the Kendal Arts, Crafts and Loan Exhibition* (1891) (copy in Kendal Library).

[2] Names of students in 1886 taken from church reredos.

prevalent in Lakeland, and woodcarvings made were of a similarly high standard.[1] Its most prominent member was Robert W. Redhead (possibly Wodehouse's successor), whose work appeared locally as late as 1915 at the Coniston exhibition. This suggests that here was another local craft class which survived and thrived for some years, drawing on seemingly outmoded methods. It is thought locally that Ruskin and Collingwood also contributed to the class, and the making of spinning stools would certainly indicate a potent Ruskinian as well as Lakeland influence. The Keswick School, of course, was already producing such stools by 1885 as a direct result of Ruskin's influence, and Ruskin himself had by that time glorified the image of the spinster sat by the hearth on her spinning stool.[2]

Like its smaller contemporaries, the Coniston class appears never to have exhibited outside Lakeland, but made a definite contribution to local exhibitions. No fewer than ten carvers showed specimens of work, including wall brackets, footstools and handkerchief boxes, at the 1891 Kendal exhibition, a range of domestic goods befitting its domestic status. Students at that time included John Mather, John Mason and William Tyson, but also Fred Raven, the son of Ruskin's former housekeeper.[3] Given the close proximity of the class to Brantwood, it would not be remiss to suggest that carvings by those such as Fred Raven were kept at the house, or that Ruskin gave direct guidance of some sort in relation to those carvings between 1885 and 1900, particularly since there was a strong reliance on nature as design source. Coniston's reverence for nature would have been enhanced by Simpson's teachings, even the most basic of household items such as decorated bookshelves reflecting his typical simplicity in design, and also his masterly use of nature as a design source, of which Ruskin had already personally approved.

Ably capturing the realities of nature under Ruskin's influence (which the Pre-Raphaelites, with all their professionalism, arguably failed to do), the success of the Coniston class illustrates the spread of the revival, the considerable time and effort invested by Simpson in reviving local woodcarving, and the extent of his impact on the region artistically as a

---

[1] The *Catalogue of the Ruskin Museum, Coniston* (ed. W.G. Collingwood) (5th edn, 1919), 29, shows that the museum then contained a letter of 7 May 1885 from Ruskin to John Bell asking him to start the carving class at Coniston under Capt. Wodehouse.

[2] In *Fors Clavigera*, Letter XXXII (*Works*, xxvii. 596) Ruskin referred to Scott's description of 'the grandmother spinning, with her stool next the hearth', as the epitome of rewarding labour.

[3] *Catalogue of the Kendal Arts, Crafts and Loan Exhibition* (1891).

Ruskinian.[1] Although the Keswick School played its part, as an individual craftsman Simpson did perhaps more than any other individual locally to reintroduce woodcarving, probably creating as many self-sufficient carvers across south Lakeland as the Keswick School between 1880 and 1920. In Coniston too he assisted in bridging the gap wrought by mechanisation, often teaching several members or generations of one family, just as the Keswick School and the Linen Industries did, and employing the same approach to do so. Coniston also rejected machinery outright, with hand work taking pride of place; nature was the dominant theme, and the concentration on domestic goods remained. The size of the class was similar to Burneside and Milnthorpe, never becoming unmanageable, so that individual tuition was possible. In this case, however, the class remained largely male, the local women perhaps being more preoccupied with Miss Twelves's Coniston Greek lace class.

Coniston's success led to the founding of a smaller woodcarving class at nearby Torver, showing how the dispersal of the revival touched even the smallest hamlets. Little remains of Torver other than a few references to its appearances at the annual Coniston exhibition between 1906 and 1918. In 1910 H. Barrow, W. Bell and W.H. Redhead exhibited under the Torver name. Torver was joined on that occasion by Miss Twelves's Coniston Greek lace class and Junior Coniston Greek lace class which by 1910 had been taken over by Ada Hooper.[2] Given that Ruskin and his Lakeland home were at the core of the revival, a concentration of Ruskin linen and lace classes would have been expected around Brantwood, but more generally the revival proved to be largely consistent in its spread across south Lakeland, also reaching Kirkby Lonsdale relatively early on. With its slightly larger population, Kirkby Lonsdale proved to be the most diverse of the 'secondary' revival classes, offering a wider range of crafts than any other to both men and women, and the opportunity to exhibit not only locally but nationally at the annual Home Arts and Industries Association exhibition.

Begun in 1885, like the Langdale Linen Industry and the Keswick School, Kirkby Lonsdale was founded by outsiders, the Harris family, who, like Fleming and Rawnsley, moved into the region and became wholeheartedly involved in reviving its heritage. The head of the family was Alfred Harris from Bradford who in 1869 bought the 40-acre

---

[1] Ruskin eventually became somewhat disillusioned with the Pre-Raphaelites, concluding in *Modern Painters* (*Works*, vi. 30) that their almost laborious attention to detail in nature was a 'morbid indulgence of their own impressions' of their natural surroundings.

[2] *Catalogue of the Eleventh Annual Exhibition: Coniston Institute, 1910* (copy in Ruskin Museum, Coniston).

Lunefield estate in Kirkby Lonsdale, skirted by the river Lune, close to the site of one of Ruskin's favourite views. In 1870 he commissioned Alfred Waterhouse to design a new Lunefield House (now demolished), replacing the older one on the site. Largely due to the work of Harris's wife and daughters, by the mid 1880s pottery, drawing, spinning, woodcarving, repoussé and leather work classes had been established in the town. Students met five evenings a week, on Wednesday afternoons and Saturday mornings. Indications are that an annual exhibition of work may have been held, including designs, drawings and plaster casts.

Given that the family had lived locally for over fifteen years by 1885, and had made no efforts to establish any classes before that, it seems likely that the example set by the Langdale Linen Industry and the Keswick School once again provided the inspiration and format, particularly since Marian Twelves was originally engaged to teach spinning. Simpson probably provided some tuition in woodcarving in the early days and the Kirkby Lonsdale carvers showed work alongside the Burneside, Gatebeck, Milnthorpe and Coniston classes at his annual exhibition. In 1888 Robert Redhead of Coniston exhibited a carved panel representing Christ at the well (which had won a first prize at the 1887 Manchester exhibition) alongside leather work, woodcarvings and pottery from Kirkby Lonsdale. Although Redhead exhibited independently a few times outside Lakeland, the Coniston class as a whole appears to have exhibited only in the region. Canon Rawnsley made several visits to Lunefield, penning a poem in honour of the valley in which the house was situated:

Of northern valleys in luxuriant June,
For English eyes no fairer vale I know
Than where the Oak and Ash together throw
Abundant shadow by the banks of Lune;
There race the fillies, there at lazy noon
The lambs make sport, kine musically low,
And where the swallows skim, with southward flow
The yellow freshets chime their river-tune.
There, larger-limbed, the shepherd plies the games
At shearing time, and, as he drives the sheep
Back to the cloud-empurpled Yorkshire fells,
His rough hands full of Canterbury Bells,
He sees by stately lawn and towery steep

A silver vision of the royal Thames.[1]

He also visited the Harrises' classes, writing in 1901:

Anyone who had the privilege, as I had on more than one occasion, of seeing the youth of Kirkby Lonsdale gathered together under the teaching of Miss Harris at the drawing school there, would have realised how truly Ruskin's mind was over all.[2]

While Ruskin's personal influence at Kirkby Lonsdale is open to question, and visits to Brantwood may never have taken place, indirectly, through his most loyal Lakeland devotees and their realisation of his teachings, his impact was considerable.

Although the extent of the Harrises' arts training is uncertain, Marian Twelves, Simpson and Rawnsley all played some part in shaping the Kirkby Lonsdale classes. In what was by 1885 a tried and tested format, the revival of handcrafts once prevalent in Lakeland took priority, strictly as a means of returning them to the domestic environment and not to create financially independent, full-time craftsmen and women. Nature was again the primary source of inspiration, and the response was positive and sustained, with similar long-term success. The classes were held in several local buildings and by 1903 there were ten classes in operation with a total of over 70 students. They were financed largely by subscription with additional support from the higher education committee of the county council for a while.

As well as appearing on a regular basis at Simpson's annual exhibition, the Kirkby Lonsdale craft workers contributed to other local exhibitions, particularly those held at Kendal in 1891 and 1899. At the 1891 event Harris, also a magistrate, acted as a guarantor, and took an active role on the organising committee. Mrs Harris exhibited several paintings, drawings and illuminated designs, while other members of the family (under the title of Kirkby Lonsdale) exhibited various specimens of art and design work. In more direct relation to handcrafts, Lilian Harris, Enoch Archer, Walter German, Louis Drake, Denby Preston, Albert Bowers, J. Willan, A.C. Goddard, William Atkinson, Jeremiah Shepherd, Luke Lupton, Percy Rallinshaw, John Thornburrow, Thomas D. Hadwin, Harold Wolfenden and Miles Cornthwaite all contributed specimens of woodcarving. The list of names suggests a considerable

[1] H.D. Rawnsley, *Sonnets at the English Lakes* (1881), 118.

[2] H.D. Rawnsley, *Ruskin and the English Lakes* (Glasgow, 1901), 146.

number of successful carvers were working in association with Kirkby Lonsdale within six years, as well as the wide age-range covered by the classes (with some ages given in the exhibition catalogue), and also that some women were involved in woodcarving. Lilian Harris was probably instructing the carving classes as Edith Rawnsley was doing at Keswick. The youngest students associated with Kirkby Lonsdale, who exhibited in the junior classes of the 1891 Kendal exhibition, were aged between thirteen and sixteen. No fewer than ten 'juniors' from Kirkby Lonsdale exhibited in the woodcarving and design categories.[1]

By 1891 even the vicar of Kirkby Lonsdale, the Revd J.N. Williams, had become involved, submitting a design for a coloured hearth-rug and two flower drawings to the Kendal exhibition, undoubtedly inspired by the example set by his parishioners and reaffirming the strong links between the revival and the Church. Not surprisingly, Kirkby Lonsdale also contributed to other categories of the 1891 exhibition, with specimens of metalwork by Ernest Woodhouse, Ernest Bowers and Richard Mayor, and no fewer than 28 specimens of leather work by the local women. Another 39 exhibits were shown in various categories relating to textiles, all of which indicated the influence of Marian Twelves's teaching, and the speedy effect the revival had in Kirkby Lonsdale. At the 1899 Kendal exhibition, however, at what was a noticeably smaller event, the class submitted only a few exhibits, including an oak settle priced at £9 9s.[2]

Such was the success of the Kirkby Lonsdale classes that they became almost a model for the repercussions of Ruskin in Lakeland, with local people willingly taking up the revival of local arts and crafts under his influence. Within six years of their founding, the classes had become the epitome of Ruskin's vision of a parish workshop, an integral part of everyday life in the town, with all generations involved and respect for nature restored. So important was the role of nature to become in Kirkby Lonsdale that in 1887 the *Manchester Guardian* observed that the Kirkby Lonsdale carvers, exhibiting at that year's Home Arts Exhibition, had 'evidently studied the blackberry spray and the oak-leaf branch and the oxeye daisy's growth', while wood carvers from elsewhere had failed to show that they had 'gone to nature'.[3] Again the willingness to embrace Ruskin's teachings and the revival indicates that in Kirkby Lonsdale

---

[1] *Catalogue* (1891).

[2] *Catalogue of the Exhibition of Pictures and Decorative Art* (1899) (copy in Kendal Library).

[3] *Manchester Guardian*, 9 Dec. 1887.

some form of pre-conditioning to the writer had taken place which could only have come from his presence in the region before (in this instance) 1885, and to his being accepted by the 1880s as an integral part of Lakeland's unique heritage. But its success was due equally to the dedication of those at the helm, but particularly the Harris family. Their dedication was to be suddenly curtailed in 1901 when the family moved to Wharfenden, although the handcraft classes appear to have continued after their departure.

By 1901 the Kirkby Lonsdale classes had been running most success-fully for around sixteen years and had made a considerable contribution not only to the spread of the local revival, but also to the wider view of Lakeland as an important centre of arts and crafts, principally because they chose to attend national as well as local exhibitions. Unlike Burneside, Gatebeck, Milnthorpe and Coniston, which remained strictly local exercises, Kirkby Lonsdale was large enough by at least 1887 to consider exhibiting at the Home Arts Exhibition in London. Since the classes had close ties with the Linen Industry (in the form of Marian Twelves, its original teacher of spinning) and the Keswick School (in the form of Rawnsley), the initial idea to attend the Home Arts Exhibition probably came from their example. Work appeared there almost annually between 1887 and 1901, and was mentioned in *The Studio* in 1894 in an article entitled 'Provincial Arts and Crafts' (which hints that there was some wider recognition of place as significant to some late nineteenth-century arts endeavours), along with that of the Keswick School and the Linen Industry among others.[1] However, Kirkby Lonsdale appears never to have exhibited at the Arts and Crafts Exhibition in London which calls into question any categorisation of its work as Arts and Crafts derived.

As with the Linen Industry and the Keswick School, Kirkby Lonsdale produced a small number of outstanding craftsmen and women, and it was their work which appeared most frequently at national as well as local exhibitions. In relation to pottery, John T. Firth made arguably the greatest impact. Although strictly an amateur, Firth exhibited under the Kirkby Lonsdale title for a number of years, including Simpson's annual exhibition from 1887 where the work of wood carvers Enoch Archer (also of Kirkby Lonsdale) and F. Towell of Gatebeck (who also produced nature inspired panels under Simpson's influence) won considerable praise in the local press.[2] Firth, a protégé of the Harrises' classes, was

---

[1] *The Studio*, Nov. 1894, 147.
[2] *Westmorland Gazette*, 28 May 1887.

also the dominant Kirkby Lonsdale exhibitor of pottery at the 1891 Kendal exhibition, contributing both glazed and unglazed ornamental wares, and exhibited at least nine specimens of pottery at the 1899 Kendal exhibition (under his own name rather than Kirkby Lonsdale). His pottery was at the corner of the Horsemarket and Mill Brow where he had a kiln. He was assisted by his son and daughter, Sidney and Ellen. Firth became best known for his revival of the solid black ware of Etruscan origin, and it was that which was shown most often at the Home Arts Exhibition in London. Other members of the Firth family were linked to pottery production at Kirkby Lonsdale, including Susannah Firth, probably his wife. She also excelled in leather work, some of which was carried out in collaboration with Mrs Harris and shown at the Home Arts Exhibition. The Firths evidently became a leading artistic force in the town, and were long-associated with the local classes until the family moved to the West Riding. Although they were classed as 'amateur' at the 1891 Kendal exhibition, the family were clearly talented, and doubtless went on to teach alongside Lilian and Marion Harris. Firth later worked for the Royal Lancastrian Pottery, followed by another pottery, possibly the Leeds Art Pottery and Tile Company. He died in Liverpool where his daughter lived.

As a result of Lilian and Marion Harris's interests in pottery and leather work, Kirkby Lonsdale always excelled in those two fields. But given that the classes were run principally by females, a number of local women were particularly encouraged to come forward and contribute to the development of the leather work classes. Women students at Kirkby Lonsdale appeared always slightly to exceed the number of men, and without any potentially restricting input from any outside body such as the Guild of St George (which the Harris family, as 'secondary' Lakeland Ruskinians, never felt compelled to join), it was always more likely that women would make an equal, if not greater, impact than men. As a domestic exercise Kirkby Lonsdale rarely encouraged its teachers or students to develop professional careers in the arts (something which, as a Lakeland revival handcraft female, Annie Garnett perhaps came closest to doing) but, like its revival colleagues, it always sought to give as much creative freedom to women as to men, which brought some of its participants close to becoming self-supporting craftsmen and women. Such were the talents of the Kirkby Lonsdale leather workers under Marion Harris that in 1897 they contributed to the highly successful First Exhibition of Women's Bindings held in London. As a result, a small number (probably including Marion Harris and Susannah Firth) became members of the Guild of Women Binders when it was founded shortly after the exhibition. The guild was a nationally important group of 67 women who established females in a formerly exclusively male craft and went on to hold other exhibitions. Most of its members came from the Chiswick Art Workers' Guild, the Edinburgh Arts and Crafts' Club, the Gentlewomen's Guild of Handicrafts, the Royal School of Art Needlework and the Kirkby Lonsdale handcraft classes. As if to verify their theoretical basis, at the guild's second exhibition, held in the winter of 1898–9, the Kirkby Lonsdale women showed a binding for Ruskin's *The Crown of Wild Olive*, and they were probably responsible for a surviving leather binding which was kept at Brantwood during Ruskin's time. Although little work produced by the Kirkby Lonsdale classes has been traced, a Book of Common Prayer with an elaborate repoussé upper board worked by Marion Harris in October 1891 has recently been rediscovered.

Despite the departure of the Harris family in 1901, Kirkby Lonsdale remained an important offshoot of the local revival, and, like Annie Garnett, even introduced a hint of pre-feminist thinking to local art and design which suggested that changes were under way for some of the poorer local women. Like her Spinnery contemporary, Lilian Harris managed to bring her own pre-feminist edge to Lakeland whilst working in the name of Ruskin, acting as cashier of the Women's Co-operative Guild from 1893 and as its secretary from 1901. The guild was largely developed by Margaret Llewelyn Davies, a social reformer, and for a time was based at the vicarage at Kirkby Lonsdale. In contrast to the domestic nature of the Lakeland revival, which the Harris family clearly supported, the guild had considerable success in establishing women's rights. Once away from Lakeland, however, and out of reach of the revival, the Harris women (like Mrs Brownson of Bowness) also faded into obscurity, and never made the same impact anywhere else after 1901. This again suggests that Lakeland was a particularly fertile ground for sewing the seeds of Ruskin, primarily because of his presence and the form which the realisation of his teachings took in the region after 1883. The Kirkby Lonsdale classes continued into the 1920s and 1930s, but took on a different form after the Harrises' departure, losing their national appeal, with what appears to have been a final appearance at the 1901 Home Arts exhibition. Unfortunately for the Harrises, the annual Coniston exhibition did not begin to include handcrafts until 1906, by which time they had long since gone.

Slightly later than Kirkby Lonsdale, but of similar importance as an example of the effect of Ruskin in Lakeland, was the Heversham metalwork class. In true revival mode, Heversham began as a spare-time occupation for local men and boys, originally run by a blacksmith, Henry Varley, and Percy J. Hibbert, resident of Plumtree Hall. It followed the pattern of the local revival set by Fleming, Rawnsley and others, teaching the joys of hand labour in an age of mass mechanisation, a respect for nature as both God's creation and design source, and the value of passing on traditional crafts. The choice of metalwork was clearly Hibbert's since he excelled in copper, silver and wrought iron, but also practised leather and basket work, the latter another craft once prevalent in Lakeland. As one of the district secretaries for the 1891 Kendal exhibition, and as a member of the general committee for the 1899 exhibition, Hibbert came into close contact with those at the heart of the revival and would have taken his inspiration from the likes of the Keswick School and Kirkby Lonsdale. Run in the Old School, the Heversham metalwork class had barely begun by the time of the 1891 Kendal exhibition, but already Hibbert and Varley were taking an active part as exhibitors along with Wright Laycock, one of Heversham's earliest associates. At the 1899 Kendal exhibition Hibbert contributed specimens of metalwork which were displayed between Arthur Simpson's 'Iris' panel, leather work by Alfred Bowers, and pottery from Kirkby Lonsdale, firmly marking his rightful place alongside his revival colleagues.[1]

One of the slightly later revival classes, Heversham was founded at around the same time as The Spinnery and several of the smaller branches of the Linen Industry, and was part of the particularly strong wave of 'secondary' Ruskinism in south Lakeland which culminated in the 1891 Kendal exhibition, the largest to be held in the south of the region between 1880 and 1920. No less dedicated to a specific set of Ruskin-based teachings compatible with Lakeland than its earlier revival associates (although lacking any direct contact with Ruskin), Heversham also achieved long-term success without ever losing its local, domestic flavour. Aiming to be similarly self-sufficient from the outset, local exhibitions were one of the primary outlets for selling its mainly domestic wares, although, given the high standards which Heversham reached within a few years of its founding, it seems likely that the class would have attended the Home Arts Exhibition in the 1890s.[2] Unlike Kirkby Lonsdale, Heversham was able to take full advantage of the annual Coniston exhibition as a source of sales and publicity, and appeared there regularly between 1906 and 1918. In 1907, the class submitted twelve exhibits, including a brass palm pot by Herbert Kilshaw

---

[1] *Catalogue of the Exhibition of Pictures and Decorative Art* (1899).

[2] Catalogues have not been located for all the exhibitions of this period to establish this for certain.

(sold for 13s. 6d.), a brass muffin stand by H. Thompson (sold for 12s. 6d.), and two copper candlesticks by Fred Sisson (sold for 4s. 6d.), a range of goods typical of the Keswick School and Kirkby Lonsdale.[1] To give some idea of the size Heversham reached, 35 exhibits appeared in the 1908 Coniston exhibition executed by fourteen men including Varley, a considerable number of both exhibits and students for what was one of the least populated sites of a revival workshop. After the 1912 Coniston exhibition the local newspaper reported:

> The Heversham metal class is so generally good that it is not easy to name special workers. Representative pieces of work are a brass jug by Mr W. Varley; a square copper bulb pan by Mr Sidney Hodgson; a copper candlestick with glass by Mr Herbert Kilshaw; a copper shaving pot by Mr Percy Shaw; a copper tumbler holder by Mr Fred Sisson; a copper tray, with wood stand by Mr J. Sisson; a brass coal box (404), of good design, by Mr E.P. Birkett; a brass letter rack by Mr P. Shaw; and large brass jardiniere, very well conceived, by Mr W. Thompson.[2]

Heversham also made occasional appearances at other local exhibitions including the 1901 Milnthorpe Art and Industrial Exhibition. Inexplicably The Handicrafts was never approached as a possible venue for sales or exhibitions, despite its obvious suitability.

Although, in contrast to the Keswick School, Heversham never employed any outside professional figures, it too maintained a consistently high standard of workmanship, and became known locally as an 'art industry'. By 1910 the class had been taken over by later resident of Plumtree Hall, Thomas Carrick Watson, and under his guidance a permanent showroom was established in 1914 in the Old School. Carrick Watson continued the Heversham (and revival) emphasis on simplicity in design, encouraging the individual both to design *and* execute, and to seek inspiration from nature. Pieces such as matchbox covers and ashtrays are more typical of Heversham's later phase under Carrick Watson and reveal his influence in style and design, but also indicate that the class added its own particular colour to the revival, enhancing local design yet further. Carrick Watson also saw that links were maintained with the local church, St Peter's, for whom the class made a magnificent

---

[1] *Catalogue of the Eighth Annual Exhibition: Coniston Institute* (1907) (copy at Ruskin Museum, Coniston).

[2] *Westmorland Gazette*, 27 July 1912.

jug. Heversham continued to run successfully until 1927, the time when the various branches of the Linen Industry were coming to an end commercially, and was affected chiefly by the building of the village bypass which halted trade almost overnight. But that was not before King George V and Queen Mary had visited Westmorland and bought a copper coal scuttle made by the Heversham metal workers.

The spread of the revival did not end with its 'secondary' phase, for it went on to create a third phase which saw yet further diffusion of Ruskin's teaching under the influence of the revival's primary and secondary leaders. Such was the revival's potency that its influence affected yet smaller local classes and workshops, all of which appeared between 1883 and 1920, the period in which Ruskin's teachings were at their most effective in south Lakeland, and encouraged numerous other individuals who felt compelled to partake in some minor way. With the success of Burneside, Gatebeck and Milnthorpe, Arthur Simpson began to teach further afield in Hawkshead (probably in association with the Keswick School), Bolton-le-Sands, Sedbergh and probably Kirkby Fell. These classes remained modest efforts, rarely exhibiting and surviving with only a small number of pupils, but nonetheless producing successful craftsmen and women. Following his success with the Keswick School, Thomas Sparks began to work in collaboration with metalwork classes at Morecambe School of Art, spreading Rawnsley's perception of Ruskin's teachings to the very edge of Lakeland, and later, a breakaway faction of the Keswick School founded the Borrowdale metalwork industry, producing decorative wares by hand in modern materials, including stainless steel.

At Charlotte Mason College at Ambleside, Ruskinian Julia Firth (d. 1919), who also had links with the Langdale Linen Industry, encouraged the addition of woodcarving to the curriculum for student teachers. Charlotte Mason herself took part and carved her own spinning chair, which is now in Abbot Hall Museum, Kendal. The widow of Thomas Firth of Sheffield, Mrs Firth lived at Seathwaite Rayne, Ambleside. She translated Jeremiah Gotthelf's *Ulric the Farm Servant*, edited by Ruskin (1886–88).[1]

Countless other individual craftsmen and women practised their craft in the home without maintaining any formal associations with a place of learning, their number running into several hundred by the early 1900s. There was a noticeably strong return to family involvement where the revival was concerned, the restoration of lost handcrafts to the home

---

[1] Information from the Ruskin Museum, Coniston.

bringing back what were once seen as family, rather than individual, activities. Where entire families had once taken an active part in cloth production, now they all took part in the revival, often learning and practising the same craft through several generations. One of the more important families involved were the Peppers: Mrs Heskett (grand-mother), Elizabeth Pepper (mother), Alfred Pepper (husband), Abigail Pepper (daughter) and Mary Ellen Pepper (daughter) all took part in revived local handcrafts in the home. Others who followed suit included Mrs Bownass (wife of the honorary curator of Coniston Institute, Herbert Bownass), Mrs Willink of Burneside (an embroideress), Barbara, Dora and Ursula Collingwood (daughters of Dorrie and W. G. Collingwood), several generations of the Sisson family of Heversham, and various members of the Redhead family (father, brother and daughter) of Coniston and Torver. With their appearances at local exhibitions until at least 1918, the revival clearly managed to generate and regenerate local enthusiasm across south Lakeland for over 35 years, a testament to the long-term acceptance of, and absorption of, Ruskin's teachings in the Lake District.

11

W.G. COLLINGWOOD
AND THE REVIVAL
OF LAKELAND ART

While local handcrafts became prolific once again across south Lakeland under the influence of Ruskin, local art also experienced a healthy revival between 1880 and 1920, its chief events again orchestrated by a devout Lakeland Ruskinian, W.G. Collingwood. The revival of local art was inextricably linked from the outset with the revival of local crafts. The worship of nature and a respect for Lakeland's history and tradition were combined with Ruskin's direct input in order to retrieve an equally important aspect of local arts and crafts which had also diminished before Ruskin arrived in Lakeland. For the local artist too, Lakeland once again became a rich and fertile ground, inspiring not merely the individual but the collective founding of the Lake Artists' Society, one of the most important and long-lasting schools of art. Like its local handcraft fellows, the Lake Artists' Society was most definitely the product of Ruskin in Lakeland and was quite distinct from anything outside the region, its members making an equally valid statement about the value of nature, but more particularly regionalism, in art. With a small number of female members, the society also drew attention to the work of several leading women artists active in Lakeland between 1880 and 1920, offering them one of the first opportunities to exhibit their work collectively in the region. The very first opportunity, however, came through Arthur Simpson who exhibited the work of Lakeland's male and female artists in 1886 alongside local crafts, a fitting and early gesture of unity in local arts.

Like Fleming and Rawnsley, Collingwood was originally drawn to the Lake District because of Ruskin and Brantwood. He too had known the writer before his own move to the region, having studied drawing under Ruskin at Oxford in the early 1870s. In 1873 he visited Brantwood for the first time, and so was one of the earliest revival figures to call at the house. He did not move to the Lake District until around 1880, from which time he acted as Ruskin's assistant in geological matters, initially working alongside another gifted artist, Laurence Hilliard. As time progressed, he became more of a confidant and secretary, and lived for a short time at Brantwood. By the close of 1881 he had begun to find life at the house difficult, not least because of Ruskin's bad temper and insistence on four long meals a day,[1] and by 1882 had moved into a cottage at Gill Head, Windermere, which in 1891 was taken over by the Simpsons. From the outset Collingwood continued with his own studies in art and archaeology, guided in the former by Ruskin (who resolved to cure his 'Pre-Raphaelite measles').[2] In 1903 Collingwood recalled that in the early 1870s he had 'the pre-Raphaelite measles badly', and that Ruskin resolved to show him that: 'the virtue of real pre-Raphaelite draughtsmanship was in faithfulness to natural form, and resulting sensitiveness to harmony of line; nothing to do with sham medievalism and hard contours'.[3]

Over the next five decades Collingwood worked on a number of important archaeological sites in Lakeland as well as producing countless watercolour studies of the region which, in number, probably exceeded Ruskin's. He also wrote 30 literary works, many of which (like Rawnsley's writings) took Ruskin or Lakeland as their subject matter. Those included *The Poems of John Ruskin*, edited in 1891, *The Lake Counties* (1902), *Ruskin Relics* (1903) and *Lake District History* (1925). His last book was *The Bondwomen: A Saga of Langdale*, published in 1932, the year of his death. His decision to remain in Lakeland for the rest of his life (which mirrored that of his revival colleagues), to be buried there and to keep his focus chiefly on the region in an archaeological, artistic and literary sense, suggests that again there was a deliberate and concerted effort to adopt Lakeland as his own. It also suggests the strength of his affection for Ruskin, and his support of the revival of local arts and crafts as a product of Ruskin's teachings was total from the outset.

For almost twenty years Collingwood's work as Ruskin's secretary gave him the opportunity of meeting many of the writer's associates, including Kate Greenaway, and also brought him into close contact with those at the heart of the revival. Rawnsley had been a visitor at the house since 1877, joined in 1878 by Edith. In 1883 Albert Fleming began his visits, joined by Marian Twelves in 1884 and Arthur Simpson in 1885; he probably even met Annie Garnett and her father on their

---

[1] AHM, Collingwood to Dorrie Isaac, 10 Oct. 1881.

[2] W.G. Collingwood, *Ruskin Relics* (1903), 7.

[3] Ibid.

occasional visits to Brantwood. Along with Rawnsley, Collingwood was to play a particularly active role in the Cumberland and Westmorland Antiquarian and Archaeological Society, founded in 1866. Rawnsley's contributions to the society included 'Chrism Crosses at St Kentigern's Church, Crosthwaite', a lecture originally delivered in Ambleside in September 1915 and published in the society's *Transactions* for 1916. Collingwood edited the *Transactions* from 1901 until his death. In 1900 he also became the society's president and was a member for 42 years, contributing some 60 articles to its journal, including 'An Anglian Cross at Tullie House' (1914), which revealed his sustained interest in Lakeland art and archaeology.[1] At the same time he was a member of Coniston parish council, becoming firmly embedded in life around, as well as at, Brantwood. As with Simpson, Collingwood frequently played the part of intermediary between Rawnsley and Ruskin, conveying not only Ruskin's teachings and advice, but passing on more personal messages at times of ill-health. When he lectured on Ruskin at the Keswick School in 1897 Collingwood wrote to Rawnsley: 'I gave Mr Ruskin the message entrusted to me at the meeting of your School, and he was much pleased with the good account I was able to render of the success of your work'.[2] In return the cleric thanked Collingwood for his personal help and in his *Round the Lake Country* (1909) included Collingwood's name in the preface. Given Ruskin's age and poor health after 1889, Collingwood clearly played an immensely important role for those at the centre of the revival. Like Mrs Severn he was Ruskin's ambassador and a personal link with Brantwood, sustaining his influence long after the writer's death. He also made a more direct contribution to the revival, adding his own particular flavour to local art and design.

In terms of local art, Collingwood's associations with Simpson were to prove the most fruitful, with the Kendal wood carver providing the impetus for his revival of Lakeland painting and later for his co-founding of the Lake Artists' Society. Collingwood spent his first five years in Lakeland producing paintings as an independent artist, observing Ruskin's own example and teachings, but showing no signs of exhibiting the results locally. In 1883 he married artist Edith Mary Isaac, always known as Dorrie or Dorothy, and she joined him at Gill Head. Originally from Essex, Mrs Collingwood was a keen landscape, portrait, flower and miniature painter who in 1901 was elected a member of the Society of

[1] *Transactions of the Cumberland and Westmorland Antiquarian and Archaeological Society*, xiv (1914).

[2] CROC, DB 111, Collingwood to Mrs Rawnsley, 4 Feb. 1897.

Miniaturists. Although she trained in London she remained in the Lake District for the rest of her life and like her husband was quite happy to become recognised as a Lakeland artist. It was evidently only after coming into contact with Simpson in 1885 that the Collingwoods began to exhibit alongside other regional artists and to become involved more directly with the local revival, although Collingwood may have taken some part in Fleming's founding of the Langdale Linen Industry in 1883. That year Collingwood told his wife that 'The woodwork of the loom has at last come: and when I've a little time I'll set it up: and then marvels will happen'.[1] The Collingwoods' friendship with the Simpsons was of a much more personal and intimate nature than that with the Rawnsleys, and culminated in W.G. Collingwood writing Simpson's obituary in the Antiquarian Society *Transactions* in 1922. The speed with which the friendship developed perhaps best revealed itself when Simpson invited the Collingwoods to exhibit at his first exhibition of local arts and crafts in 1886, no more than eighteen months after his return to Kendal, presenting them with an opportunity to show the people of Lakeland exactly what was occurring in terms of art as well as craft.

Given Simpson's strident participation in the revival of local arts and crafts under Ruskin's influence, the Collingwoods could have been under no misapprehensions about the nature of his annual exhibition as a forum for revival-associated artists, craftsmen and craftswomen, or the statement they were making as like-minded Ruskinians by contributing. At that stage, their conversion to the Lakeland theme was already beginning to show itself, with W.G. Collingwood exhibiting a few Pre-Raphaelite-influenced studies alongside *A Summer Storm on Windermere* and an unfinished study of a stretch of ground at Gill Head. Mrs Collingwood exhibited studies of Swiss scenery and *Lady's Face*.

To some, Simpson's first exhibition might have been little more than a modest display of locally produced woodcarvings and paintings, and it won not a single mention in the national press. In terms of the local revival it was immensely important, establishing a very different style in local exhibitions which mirrored the Keswick School's own declaration of regional independence, acting as the earliest collective statement of unity among Lakeland's Ruskinians. Such was the impact of that statement that Simpson repeated the exercise in May 1887 on a larger and more professional scale. The Collingwoods were joined by some 23 other local artists who had seemingly appeared from nowhere, all keen to contribute to a Lakeland-focused exercise. Again the Collingwoods

[1] AHM, Collingwood to Dorrie Collingwood, 18 April 1883.

contributed Lakeland-inspired paintings, including *In a Day of the East Wind* in which W.G. Collingwood set a solitary figure in a landscape of Windermere, Wetherlam and Bow Fell. The *Westmorland Gazette* noted that, while the figure was of no consequence, the landscape depicted was 'very charming—full of light and distance and delicate effects of colour', which suggests most aptly the direction towards the portrayal of the Lakeland landscape (under Ruskin's guidance) which his work was beginning to take.[1]

To the advantage of local art, the Collingwoods were joined at the 1887 exhibition by Cuthbert Rigby, another close friend of the Simpson family and a local artist who had taken up the return to Lakeland as subject matter, but this time beginning in the 1870s under the influence of J.W. Bishop rather than Ruskin. Following in the footsteps of Matthias Read and William Green (already noted as the fathers of Lakeland landscape painting), Rigby was another outsider to make the decision to adopt Lakeland as his own, particularly as a painter, helping to end the artistic lull which had begun after Green's death in 1823. Although not a devotee of Ruskin to any noticeable degree, through Simpson Rigby was firmly drawn into local events and might be best described again as part of the knock-on effect of Ruskin in Lakeland. Nationally he was already exhibiting at the Royal Academy in 1875 and in 1877 became an associate of the Royal Society of Painters in Water Colour. He later moved from Southport to Kendal before finally settling at Skelwith Fold, Ambleside, close to Fleming. His reputation as an artist was well-established before he began to exhibit in Lakeland, but the fact that his work was noticeably Lakeland inspired even before he moved to the region suggests that he had a particular affinity with the area, which may explain his willingness to contribute to local as well as national exhibitions. While exhibiting as one of a considerable group of local artists at Simpson's second exhibition, Rigby stood apart from his regional colleagues for several reasons. His close friendship with Simpson resulted in one of Rigby's sons serving his apprenticeship with the Kendal wood carver; and in return Rigby presented Simpson with a painting of *Little Langdale from Stang End* (1891), where the Rigbys and the Simpsons shared a holiday cottage, and a drawing of himself at work.

Rigby became so entrenched in local life that he—like Collingwood and Rawnsley—began to write extensively on Lakeland, one of his few published works being *From Midsummer to Martinmas: a West Cumberland Idyl* (1891). Through his appearances at Simpson's

---

[1] *Westmorland Gazette*, 28 May 1887.

exhibition, Rigby developed an equally strong friendship with the Collingwoods, and in 1902 was asked to produce 42 sketches for W. G. Collingwood's *The Lake Counties*. In the same year, he and the Collingwoods organised a second joint exhibition of their work at Coniston Institute, the first having taken place in 1901. Collingwood had begun the Coniston exhibition in 1900 as a memorial to Ruskin but its success meant that it became a more general annual event until at least 1919. Along with Simpson's exhibition, the Coniston exhibition became one of the most important vehicles for promoting the local revival and one of the strongest signs of Lakeland's recognition of itself as artistically independent. Rigby exhibited his art work in Lakeland for over forty years, one of his last appearances being at the 1927 Hawkshead exhibition. There he showed works including *Ullswater and Glenridding* and *Spring at Pull Scar*. The exhibition marked his fortieth year of exhibiting as a Lakeland artist and his fortieth year since first exhibiting at Simpson's annual exhibition.

The appearance of so many local artists at Simpson's 1887 exhibition (when in 1886 there had been only the Collingwoods) suggests that changes were already well under way in local art, but that it was Simpson who drew attention to those changes and brought together what were previously isolated individuals. Until 1887 south Lakeland had held comparatively few collective exhibitions. It was undoubtedly the scale of that response in 1887 which drew Collingwood's attention to the need for a more regular and specialised exhibition to promote the work of artists who followed his own return to local traditions, and he may also have been influenced by the Keswick School's successful annual display of local craft work. The 1891 and 1899 Kendal exhibitions added to that need, with Collingwood and Rigby both contributing to those events as organisers and exhibitors. As at Simpson's exhibition, at Kendal the same artists' names appeared and reappeared, indicating that a core group was developing, including Harold Moss of Ulverston, Frederic Tucker of Windermere, Arthur Tucker of Windermere, Cuthbert Rigby of Kendal, Hubert Coutts of Windermere, Arthur Severn of Brantwood and Sydney Scott of Ulverston, all of whom later joined the Lake Artists' Society. In his inaugural address to the 1899 exhibition, Rawnsley referred to those artists as 'the present School of Lake District artists' which confirms that there was local recognition of a collective arts effort.[1]

The first Coniston exhibition was arranged within a short time of the

---

[1] *Westmorland Gazette*, 8 July 1899.

1899 Kendal exhibition and was originally Collingwood's personal response to Ruskin's death. Held in the Coniston Institute from 21 July to 15 September 1900, it was intended, according to Collingwood:

> to give those who have known Mr Ruskin personally here in Coniston, and any who have read his books or taken an interest in his teachings, some further glimpses at his life's record, and at his studies in nature and art.[1]

Admission was 6d. and some 10,700 visitors attended, profits reaching £600. Exhibits consisted of a small number of original drawings by Ruskin which were for sale, numerous other Ruskin drawings and paintings (some borrowed from Brantwood), drawings by those associated with Ruskin (including Collingwood's portrait of Susie Beever completed in 1893), and paintings by those whom Ruskin admired such as Turner and Burne-Jones. Paintings by Arthur Severn and some of Ruskin's 'Personal Relics', such as his geological hammer, his walking stick and a miniature of Joan Severn painted by Mrs Collingwood, also appeared. Drafts of *Fors* were also on display along with early poems and various notebooks. Photographs included one of the Brantwood bedroom where the writer had died and one of Coniston churchyard where he was buried. A limited number of 'large-paper proofs' from three original etchings by Ruskin used in *Modern Painters* were also on sale, as were colour plates of a picture of Ruskin in his study (priced at 3s. 6d. each),[2] one of which was bought by Marian Twelves and hung in St George's Cottage. From the beginning, therefore, there was a strong regional flavour to the Coniston exhibition.

As chairman of the Coniston Museum and Exhibition Committee (formed after the museum opened in 1901 next to the institute), Collingwood repeated the exhibition in 1901 and 1902, this time using it as a forum for his own paintings and those of Mrs Collingwood and Rigby. By 1902 all three artists had become absorbed in Lakeland and its natural assets, showing the largest collection of their locally-infused work in south Lakeland to date. Always preoccupied with the Lake District, Rigby showed over 80 paintings, including *Scandale Beck*, *Sunset in the Brathay Valley*, *Arnside Knott* and *Rydal Water*, while Collingwood showed *Head of Coniston Water*, *Borrowdale*, *Honister Crag* and *Green Coniston*, along with more than 80 other studies, mostly

---

[1] *Catalogue Ruskin Exhibition. Coniston, 1900* (copy at Ruskin Museum, Coniston).
[2] Ibid.

relating to Lakeland. Mrs Collingwood showed a similar number of studies, including *Cherry Blossom* and *In Her Garden*, which also suggested observation of her natural surroundings.[1]

In 1903 the Coniston exhibition reverted to its original theme, consisting of a collection of works by Ruskin and by those who had worked under him, including Laurence Hilliard, Arthur Severn and Kate Greenaway. By 1904 the Lake Artists' Society had come into being and its members' work was exhibited as a declaration of the formalisation of a new local school of art. A more permanent statement of artistic unity among those whom Simpson had originally brought together, the society was to have a lasting effect, as did all those developments which took place around Brantwood between 1880 and 1920, and was to give a much needed public voice to future generations of Lakeland artists, including Francis (Frank) Reiss (1893–1973), an amateur whose engravings won national acclaim from the 1920s onwards. Original members and early exhibitors at Coniston included Hubert Coutts, Arthur Tucker, Cuthbert Rigby, the Collingwoods, Arthur Severn, Sydney Scott and Harold Moss, all of whom had been exhibiting together locally (but informally) for around seventeen years by 1904, often alongside craftsmen and women directly associated with the revival of local traditions. Rigby was one of the society's longest serving original members, and eventually became its treasurer.

The 1905 Coniston exhibition was again centred on the Lake Artists' Society and revealed the society's role in promoting not only Lakeland artists but Lakeland itself as an environment conducive to good art. Like their regional craft fellows, every artist proclaimed a personal love of the region, and used art as a means of expressing that love, glorifying what had remained largely unchanged since before Read's time, the collective scale of which had never been witnessed before in south Lakeland. Ruskin may have had no obvious role in drawing out that love in some instances, and may not have directly contributed to the founding of the Lake Artists' Society, but through the Collingwoods the application of his teachings would have been evident, particularly in relation to the study of nature and respect for those who had gone before (such as Read and Green). Since the society's existence can be traced back to Ruskin's initial insistence that Collingwood move to the Lake District and remain there (even finding him Lanehead in 1891), he clearly played some part in the founding of the society, acting once again as a catalyst, his

---

[1] *Catalogue of the Third Annual Exhibition: Coniston Institute, 1902* (copy at Ruskin Museum, Coniston).

presence and influence in Lakeland inspiring others to realise his teachings.[1] It might even be said, somewhat lyrically, that the work of the Lake Artists' Society was the visual mirror not only of Ruskin's art teachings but of Wordsworth's poetry, recreating images of Lakeland redolent in his works written a hundred years earlier. Like Collingwood, Fleming and Rawnsley, a number of the society's members, besides Rigby, were not Westmerians or Cumbrians by birth, but had taken up the Lake District as both home and work place. In that sense they had a bond with those at the core of the revival and their commitment to the region was arguably even stronger than that shown by Simpson or Annie Garnett.

In 1906 the Coniston exhibition took a significant change in direction, the origins of which might again be attributed to Collingwood's close association with Simpson, Rawnsley and others. By then the revival had been firmly established in south Lakeland for at least 20 years, and there was always evidence of a unity between local art and craft, with active participation in both by many of those involved. The Keswick School and Kirkby Lonsdale always ran drawing classes (although with a view to creating designer-craftsmen rather than artists) and various individuals, including Edith Rawnsley and Annie Garnett, developed their artistic skills (under Ruskin's direct guidance) to assist in their practical craft work. Similarly Arthur Tucker's drawings were used to illustrate *Songs of the Spindle and Legends of the Loom* in 1889, including a frontispiece showing the Langdale valley.

Although Simpson's exhibition had combined local art and craft from 1886, 1906 proved to be the first attempt to combine the two at Coniston. Like Simpson's exhibition, Coniston now also spoke predominantly of changes which had taken place under Ruskin's influence and, with the exception of the 1913 and 1919 exhibitions, continued to do so until 1918. In that first attempt, Collingwood's designs for memorial crosses were displayed alongside woodcarvings by Arthur Simpson, Robert Redhead and Fred Raven, textiles from St Martin's at Elterwater, the Flaxhome Industry at Grasmere and the Ruskin Linen Industry at Keswick, and metalwork from the Keswick School.[2] Despite his absence

---

[1] In 1891 Collingwood told his father that Ruskin and the Severns had requested that he and Dorrie move to Lanehead in order to be closer to Brantwood: 'They all seemed anxious to have us there: and they have planned everything for us, and talked it over—seemingly as a fait accompli'. AHM, W.G. Collingwood to W. Collingwood, 12 May 1891.

[2] *Catalogue of the Seventh Annual Exhibition: Coniston Institute. 1906* (copy at Ruskin Museum, Coniston).

between 1900 and 1910, when he was professor of fine art at University College, Reading (where he taught Arthur Simpson's son, Ronald, and where he probably secured a post for Herbert Maryon after his departure from Keswick), Collingwood revealed his continuing commitment to Lakeland not only by co-founding the Lake Artists' Society, but by delivering a specially composed lecture at the 1906 exhibition. Entitled *Aids to Design*, the lecture revealed his complete absorption of Ruskin's teachings and his fundamental alignment with the revival's philosophical basis. Also mirroring Simpson's writings, the lecture noted that:

> If craftwork is to sell, it must have this artistic quality. It must not be a merely mechanical reproduction. It need not be perfect, technically, but it must have the fire of life and other warmth of feeling in it, which make art of any kind worth notice and remuneration.

and:

> Ornament must be based on nature, but adapted to material and to use. Let us first see how we can base our patterns on nature. We can't make something out of nothing, and no decent design is likely to be invented without some hint from actual forms and colour.[1]

Both observations indicate that the voice of Ruskin was still clearly audible in south Lakeland. In other lectures given locally Collingwood revealed more subtle signs of Ruskin's influence. In 1890 he delivered a talk to a group of ladies at Levens Hall on 'Carlyle's Mohammed',[2] Carlyle being one of the most influential figures in Ruskin's early years.

After 1906 the Coniston exhibition became an even more intense, varied and sizeable display of work from all parts of south Lakeland, much—but not all—of which could be directly attributed to the Lakeland Ruskinian revival. Individuals, groups, schools, workshops and classes representing all aspects of the arts took part, and to some degree Coniston became a measure not only of the development and direction of the revival after 1906 but of developments in local arts generally.

---

[1] W.G. Collingwood, *Aids to Design, a lecture delivered at the Coniston Crafts Exhibition, September 1906* (copy at AHM).

[2] AHM, W.G. Collingwood to his father, 23 Oct. 1890. Carlyle does not appear to have written a separately published work on Muhammad.

Kendal School of Art exhibited at Coniston regularly, recognising it as a valuable source of promoting its own local students, the most promising of whom in the early 1900s was Isabel Airey, one of several members of a family involved in local arts and crafts who exhibited at Coniston.[1] A proficient metalworker and wood carver, Miss Airey was yet another female design force in Lakeland. By 1916 she was exhibiting in her own right locally and nationally. Her glove box in walnut with coloured panels was praised at the National Competition of Schools of Art in 1914 and was mentioned in *The Studio*.[2] Although Kendal School of Art was not necessarily Ruskin-inspired, it seems that Miss Airey too followed the local Ruskinian movement, producing such things as brass hyacinth bowls. The intermingling of those involved in the revival and those not thus resulted in the further dispersal of Ruskin's teachings.[3] Local regard for Ruskin was always paramount and one of the most regularly displayed items was Ruskin lace made by local women from various towns and villages. In 1913 Coniston reverted to being a showcase purely for the Lake Artists' Society which then had 24 members, three of whom were women. In 1919, at the last exhibition held, there was a total return to Ruskin with the Ruskin Centenary Exhibition, a final declaration of allegiance. It was appropriate that the exhibition should end as it had begun, with Ruskin, and that the majority of those involved over the years were his Lakeland followers. Why the exhibition came to an end remains unclear, particularly since it had survived the First World War, but it was a fundamentally important vehicle through which to publicise all that had occurred in south Lakeland arts under Ruskin's influence.

The Lake Artists' Society was important not merely for local artists, but for local women artists. Although only three of the society's early members were female—Dorrie Collingwood, Barbara Collingwood and Edith Rawnsley—each made an important contribution to improving the perception of women artists both inside and outside Lakeland, if not helping to create a large number of new local women artists.

Edith Rawnsley was the first true local female artist associated with

---

[1] According to the catalogues at the Ruskin Museum, Coniston, for 1900–19, Miss Airey exhibited a number of times at the annual Coniston exhibition, initially under the heading of the Kendal School of Art, as did 'Mrs E.E. Airey, metalworker', and 'Miss Jennie Airey, embroideress'. All three were listed as living at Kendal and the two latter were presumably Miss Airey's mother and younger sister.

[2] *The Studio*, Sept. 1914, 281–2.

[3] *Catalogue of the Thirteenth Annual Exhibition, Coniston Institute. 1912* (copy at Ruskin Museum, Coniston).

the revival. She was born in the region, remained there, produced much of her art as well as craft work there, and joined the Lake Artists' Society. She was also one of the earliest revival artists to exhibit Lakeland subjects nationally, beginning around the same time as Cuthbert Rigby. Although much of her career was devoted to the Keswick School, where her influence was felt most keenly, her skills—had her involvement in the arts taken a different direction—could have given her the opportunity to develop a career as an independent artist. Her devotion to Ruskin and to Lakeland, however, took priority, although her talents proved invaluable in her design and craft work. The domestic nature of the revival in Lakeland meant that the Keswick School never produced any notable artists, although it did deliberately set out to improve drawing skills in its students by employing a drawing master. Art could not be considered a remunerative pastime in itself, and so was never encouraged as a subject in its own right, or one which would produce additional income. Nonetheless, Mrs Rawnsley's contribution to art as well as craft helped to enhance the general perception of Lakeland as a centre of excellence in the arts around 1900. Rawnsley's *Flower-Time in the Oberland* (1904), to which his wife contributed twelve pencil sketches, suggested that she continued with her art work in her later years at the Keswick School. Like Marian Twelves and Annie Garnett, she also set a generally positive and long-lasting example to the women of Lakeland which was enhanced by Mrs Collingwood's similarly lengthy career.

Although born in Essex and trained in London, Dorrie Collingwood (née Isaac) proved an influential force in south Lakeland at the time of the revival, establishing her national reputation slightly later in 1901 when she exhibited *Portrait of a Lady* at the Royal Academy and joined the Society of Miniaturists. Working strictly as an artist rather than as a craftswoman, Mrs Collingwood lived and worked in the Lake District for 45 years, and achieved further success at the Royal Academy with *Blossom* in 1902 and with portraits of two of her four children (Robin and Ursula) in 1910 and 1911. In March 1907 sketches by her and her husband were also exhibited at Dickinson's Galleries, New Bond Street. Her artistic talents took her far and wide, her landscape studies of Switzerland among other places winning her further national recognition. Closer to home, one of her best known commissions was the completion of the flower panels at Wallington Hall, Northumberland, to which Ruskin had contributed. Like her husband, her Lakeland work, which consisted mostly of portraits and flower studies as time progressed, was arguably her largest contribution to the art world, and was mostly executed in her specially designed studio at Lanehead. Her flower studies in particular always reflected a Ruskinian respect for nature, but particularly Lakeland nature, showing a detailed observation of what grew around Gill Head and Lanehead. Lakeland also proved to be the place where she exhibited most consistently, her work appearing in the majority of exhibitions held in the south of the region after 1885, although her husband exhibited for longer, showing seven studies of 'Pre-Norman Crosses of Lancashire' and a painting of *Top of Wetherlam after a storm, from Hawkshead Moor* at the 1927 Hawkshead exhibition.[1] At the annual Coniston exhibition Mrs Collingwood showed that her considerable output easily matched that of her fellow Lake Artists' Society members and in 1913 she became a member of the society's council, along with Harold Moss and James H. Crossland. Doubtless under the influence of their parents, Dora (b. 1885) and Barbara Collingwood (1887–1961) both took up the arts, Barbara succeeding her father as president of the Lake Artists' Society in 1932. Her plaster bust of Ruskin is well-known locally and her work appeared regularly at the annual Coniston exhibition. Two generations of the Collingwoods thus combined to make a strong declaration of belief in the value of regional arts exhibitions.

While Dorrie Collingwood concentrated solely on her art work, during his time in Lakeland W.G. Collingwood also ventured into design, the results of which had other lasting implications for the region. Along with the 1900 Coniston exhibition, Collingwood's response to Ruskin's death was to design a memorial cross in Coniston churchyard, marking the spot where the writer chose to be buried. Arguably one of his most challenging Lakeland projects, the 9 ft high cross towers over the graves of the Beever sisters, each of its four sides a lyrical narrative of Ruskin's life and work. Among other texts, visual references are made to *The Poetry of Architecture*, *Modern Painters*, *Sesame and Lilies* and *Fors Clavigera*, while St George and the Dragon represents the Guild of St George which certainly had some impact on late nineteenth-century Lakeland. A unique tribute to Ruskin in Lakeland, the cross was carved by H.T. Miles of Ulverston who had previously worked under Ruskin, the shaft and head cut from a single stone from Moss Rigg quarries at Tilberthwaite, while the base came from Elterwater. Like Rawnsley's Ruskin memorial put up at Friar's Crag, Keswick, in 1900 (unveiled by Mrs Severn in October of that year), the Coniston memorial is a permanent reminder of the depth of local respect for the writer, and that Ruskin considered the region to be his rightful resting place. It is an equally potent reminder of

---

[1] *Westmorland Gazette*, 6 Aug. 1927.

Collingwood's place in local history, and the first of several Lakeland memorial designs executed by him, including those at the churches at Hawkshead and Penrith. With Simpson, Collingwood had designed several pieces of furniture for Lanehead in 1891, and so had some involvement in design prior to the Coniston memorial, but the tribute to Ruskin was arguably his finest piece of local design, and one which aptly portrays Ruskin's full and active life.[1] The lettering for Rawnsley's Ruskin memorial was also designed by Collingwood, incorporating Ruskin's words: 'The first thing that I remember as an event in life was being taken by my nurse to the brow of Friars Crag, Derwentwater', potent words for his Lakeland followers.

Like Ruskin and the Rawnsleys, the Collingwoods also elected to be buried locally, next to Ruskin and the Beevers in Coniston churchyard, within sight of Lanehead and Brantwood across Lake Coniston. In recognition of their contribution to local art, in 1971 Abbot Hall Art Gallery, Kendal, held an exhibition of work by the Collingwoods, a considerable portion of which recorded the area around Lanehead and Brantwood, reflecting an intimate knowledge of a landscape which— thanks largely to Ruskin and Rawnsley—still remains virtually unchanged.

---

[1] AHM, Collingwood letters show that on 23 Oct. 1890 Mr Cropper of Burneside asked Collingwood to design a public fountain for Kendal. It is not clear whether the design was ever completed.

12

THE ART EXHIBITION IN LATE NINETEENTH-CENTURY LAKELAND

Arguably the most successful by-product of the revival of Lakeland arts and crafts under Ruskin's influence, and one of the most suitable means of declaring the revival's uniqueness and independence after 1880, proved to be the local exhibition. Exhibitions were not new in south Lakeland, the first sizeable one having been held in Kendal in 1859. That, and another six-week event held in the town in 1872, had a distinctly industrial flavour reminiscent of the Great Exhibition of 1851. But they were few in number before 1880 and of little direct relevance to most Westmerians. With the revival of local arts and crafts, south Lakeland began to see a dramatic change and growth in the local exhibition, the scale and frequency of which was unlike anything seen before in the region. Gone was the industrial edge of the mid nineteenth century and in its place was an unconditional rejection of the machine in favour of regional domestic arts and handcrafts.

Although Fleming and Marian Twelves launched the Langdale Linen Industry in 1883, it was the Keswick School which established the first revival-associated exhibition in 1885, shaping what would become a familiar format of the regular display of locally made, hand worked, traditional regional arts and crafts. In 1886 Arthur Simpson began his annual exhibition, establishing the first combined local arts and crafts event which became similarly successful as a means of promoting and selling locally made 'art' products. Simpson's exhibition also proved to be one of the most effective methods of publicising unity among Lakeland's Ruskinians, providing a much-needed focal point for the increasing amount of arts work being produced locally under their and Ruskin's influence. In 1900 even Annie Garnett was inspired to hold her own exhibition of her prize-winning fabrics at Bowness, declaring her success as a national exhibitor, but also her recognition of herself as first and foremost a Lakeland craftswoman. In the same year the Coniston exhibition was launched, designed at first as a celebration of Ruskin, then moving on to become an annual celebration of local arts and crafts, the majority of which were directly associated with his presence in Lakeland. Elsewhere in the region, various one-off exhibitions were organised to celebrate the return to regional arts and crafts in, among other places, Milnthorpe, Levens, Ambleside, Silverdale and Penrith.

With the adoption of the local village shows after 1883, which had been held across the region for many years, local arts and crafts had never had so many opportunities to promote their existence and the belief of their creators in the value of regionalism. Throughout the period from 1885 to 1920—and even just beyond—there was a concerted effort not only to exhibit revival-associated work, but for those at the forefront of the revival to attend in person, to take a chief organising role, and often to give inaugural addresses, lectures or closing speeches. Two of the last regional events to include traces of the revival were the 1921 Grasmere exhibition and the 1927 Hawkshead exhibition, both of which revealed the decline of the Lakeland Ruskinian revival as an active movement. At the Grasmere exhibition Ruskin was still a gentle presence, albeit chiefly in the form of The Spinnery, The Handicrafts, and the Keswick School. But changes were clearly already under way, with younger exhibitors who had no obvious associations with Ruskin in Lakeland taking a more prominent position. The work of outsiders, including the artist Frank Bramley and the needlewoman May Morris, was mingled with embroideries from Wiltshire and locally produced knitting, quilts, samplers and embroideries which had no direct relation to the textiles produced as a result of the revival. Perhaps more significantly the *Westmorland Gazette* reported that 'There is a remarkable shortage of woodcraft considering that the Lake District has at one time excelled in that work.'[1] This comment revealed that regional crafts were once again on the wane, their triumph over mass mechanisation and its apparent disregard for regional identity and individuality all but over. At the 1927 Hawkshead exhibition Alfred Willink, one of the revival's most enthusiastic participants and supporters, delivered an opening speech which brought a temporary (but final) reminder of what had happened locally in previous years, particularly noting the success of the 1891 Kendal exhibition. Still convinced of the need to seek design inspiration from nature, and to pass on traditional arts and crafts, Willink's only obvious allies on that occasion were Rigby and Colling-

---

[1] *Westmorland Gazette*, 23 July 1921.

wood, both of whom exhibited Lakeland landscape paintings, but died only a few years later.

The two most important events held in south Lakeland between 1880 and 1920 were the 1891 and 1899 Kendal exhibitions. The 1891 exhibition was by far the largest gathering of local artists, craftsmen and craftswomen, and the largest single public forum for those who had instigated the recent and already immensely successful revival of local arts and crafts under Ruskin's direct and indirect influence. The initial idea—inspired by the success of earlier smaller exhibitions in south Lakeland, including Simpson's annual display and the Penrith exhibition—came from W.T. Ravel, a Kendalian with no obvious Ruskin connections. Ravel put forward the idea for a larger event in a letter to the *Westmorland Gazette* in October 1889 and immediately courted the support of the Rawnsleys, Alfred Willink of Burneside, Percy Hibbert of Heversham, Alfred Harris of Kirkby Lonsdale and Arthur Simpson, a strong core of Lakeland Ruskinians. Although the idea did not come from Ruskin or one of his local devotees, it was certainly inspired by other local exhibitions where revival arts and crafts dominated and was immediately supported by all those at the heart of the revival.

Most unlike anything held elsewhere in the country at that time, the 1891 Kendal exhibition was to be an entirely individual exercise, one which Rawnsley enthusiastically urged be made 'open to the whole of the Diocese of Carlisle' and be held 'yearly at different centres'.[1] Initial proposals were put forward in March 1890 at two meetings in Kendal Town Hall, with the mayor presiding over, among others, Willink, Simpson and the Somervells. The meetings were the result of a positive reaction to a circular sent out locally and autumn 1891 was voted the best time to hold the event. It was decided that the area covered by the exhibition would be the whole of Westmorland with a fringe of ten miles open to the members of art schools, including Silverdale, Coniston, Hawkshead, Keswick, Penrith and Sedbergh (but not Lancaster), the district which had felt (and was still feeling) Ruskin's influence most keenly. From the very beginning, therefore, quite definite geographic boundaries were established, the exhibition being an entirely regional effort devised to show the considerable changes in local arts and crafts which had taken place over the previous eight years, principally since the arrival of Albert Fleming and Marian Twelves. The size of the exhibition was similarly dictated by recent events, as was its all-encompassing nature. Amateurs and professionals, men and women, children and adults,

---

[1] *Westmorland Gazette*, 29 March 1890.

rich and poor, were all invited to submit work, with all abilities, classes and ages taken into consideration. Local businesses were invited to submit locally made products in an attempt to promote all that was positive about the area, enhancing the regional flavour yet further. To reaffirm the value of local arts in the past, twelve of Romney's paintings were chosen for display, a subtle reminder of one of Lakeland's best known artists and an attempt to educate those to whom the region's previous artistic successes were unknown.

By May 1891 a committee had been established with James Cropper, a prominent local businessman, as chairman. The vice-chairmen were the mayor of Kendal, W.D. Crewdson, and Mr Bagot of Levens Hall. Three honorary secretaries, including Alfred Willink, were appointed, together with district secretaries, including Arthur Severn for Hawkshead, Arthur Simpson for Kendal and Percy Hibbert for Milnthorpe. The more notable members of the general committee included Lady Bective, Colin and John Somervell, Albert Fleming and Alfred Harris, revealing the contribution of Lakeland's Ruskinians to the event. The list of guarantors included Simpson, Fleming, Arthur Severn, Arthur and Helen Currer-Briggs (later of Broadleys), Alfred Harris and the Somervells. By that time Ruskin might have been too old and ill to take any direct part, but indirectly his presence would have been clearly felt at every stage through his Lakeland followers and admirers. The exhibition committee selected various Kendal venues including the Drill Hall and St George's Hall for an assortment of celebrations, displays, lectures and musical events which would run throughout the four-week event. Throughout July and August 1891 notices appeared in the *Westmorland Gazette*, during which time a substantial catalogue was distributed for perusal, and the exhibition opened on 27 August.

For south Lakeland the 1891 Kendal exhibition was an extremely adventurous exercise and was significant not only because it had no apparent predecessor—and so can be directly attributed to the Ruskinian changes then occurring in the region—but also because of its size. By July 1891 the number of exhibits had already exceeded the limit of a thousand originally decided on by the committee, and the final number reached almost two thousand. In response to local needs, the exhibition was arranged in a range of categories which were grouped into three divisions. Division I consisted of crafts, Division II of pictures and Division III of an assortment of items including loans. Division I was much the largest of the three and was made up of fifteen sections divided into various sub-sections and classes. Section 1 was Painting (with eleven divisions, including 'Original Painting in Oil—Landscape and Other Subjects' and 'Best Water-Colour Drawing of any Landscape, with

Old House or Cottage'). Section 2 was Drawing (with four divisions, such as 'Architectural Drawing'). Section 3 was Engraving (with three divisions, including 'Proof and Plate of Original Etching'). Section 4 was Sculpture (with nineteen divisions, such as 'Stone Carving' and 'Wood Carving'). Section 5 was Photography (with eleven divisions covering landscape, portrait, reflections, animals, still life and lantern slides). Section 6 was Models (four divisions). Section 7 was Pottery (six divisions). Section 8 was Metal Work (20 divisions covering every aspect from plumbing to decorative wrought-iron work). Section 9 was Leather Work (16 divisions covering saddlery to bookbinding). Section 10 was Needlework, by far the largest with 56 divisions. Section 11 was Woodwork (22 divisions). Section 12 was Basket Work (with six divisions). Section 13 was Hand Spinning and Weaving (five divisions). Section 14 was Collections (seven divisions on nature), and Section 15 was Taxidermy (two divisions).

Division II was made up entirely of paintings by over 70 artists. The majority were local or locally influenced and included W. Collingwood of Bristol and future members of the Lake Artists' Society such as Dorrie and W.G. Collingwood, Hubert Coutts, Harold Moss, Cuthbert Rigby, Arthur Severn, Sydney Scott and Arthur Tucker. The subject matter naturally reflected the aesthetic delights of Lakeland, although not exclusively. Hubert Coutts's contributions included *Early Spring, Windermere*, while Harold Moss showed several studies of Windermere and Cuthbert Rigby six pictures including *Drizzly Weather—Brotheril-keld Farm, Eskdale, Cumberland*. Presented in alphabetical order, each artist exhibited up to eight paintings. In Division III loans on display included paintings of 'historical and local value' by, among others, Raphael, Reynolds, Gainsborough, Constable (Ruskin's favourites) and of course Romney, but also Ruskin, W. Collingwood and W.G. Collingwood, all of whom fulfilled the exhibition's additional aim to instruct those who attended. Forty-one judges, predominantly local, were appointed to award prizes in the various sections, Arthur Severn and Edith Rawnsley among them. Outside judges included T.J. Cobden-Sanderson and W.A.S. Benson, whose presence confirmed that the exhibition was significant enough to win the attention of two highly respected London design figures, rather than any direct association with the Arts and Crafts Exhibition Society, in which they were active.

With no obvious outside influences on which to model itself, the Kendal exhibition was a specially devised, unique celebration of all things Lakeland. As a result, Division I in particular was dominated not only by local exhibitors and locally produced exhibits, but by classes and categories with a deliberately local, regional flavour. In Painting certain categories were restricted to such subjects as 'Best Water-Colour Drawing of Westmorland, Cumberland, or North Lancashire Cottage, with a Bit of Garden or Porch' and 'Five Vignettes in Water-Colour or Monochrome, Bits of Kendal'. In the former category, paintings of cottages in Kendal, Keswick, Milnthorpe, Kirkby Lonsdale, Ulverston and Windermere were submitted, representing most parts of the exhibition district. In Photography categories included 'Best Set of Twelve Views—Objects Within Six Miles of Kendal'. Other sections, such as Collections, were wholly devoted to Lakeland. In that instance subtitles included 'Dried Ferns Found Within the Exhibition Area, Giving Scientific Names', 'Best Geological Collection Found Within the Exhibition Area', and 'Entomological Collection Found Within the Exhibition Area', Ruskin's own example of the careful exploration of the natural detail of south Lakeland perhaps also bearing fruit.

Other categories were open only to those from certain places. In Basket Work one was open only to 'Those Living in the Parish of Cartmel'. In other sections, categories were open only 'to Lady Amateurs of Kendal', 'Children Attending Elementary Schools in the Exhibition District', or 'Pupils Past and Present of Bowness Art School under Mr Dodgson'. Others were open to 'All Living in the Exhibition District'. The distribution of prizes was, therefore, fair, with the very smallest hamlets and the least known amateur local artists, craftsmen, and craftswomen winning something. Even the prizes themselves were donated by local people, businesses and organisations, contributions coming from the earl and countess of Bective, the bishop of Barrow-in-Furness, Arthur Severn, Mrs Bagot of Levens Hall, Mrs John Somervell and the Kendal Photographic Society.[1]

To mark the exhibition's opening decorations were hung in the streets of Kendal and a procession was held. Princess Louise, marchioness of Lorne attended as patroness. During her visit the princess, who stayed with the Bagot family at Levens, received gifts of hand spun linen and an oak panel based on thistles designed and carved by Arthur Simpson. Throughout the exhibition, which ran until 26 September, various lectures were given, Rawnsley's contribution being 'Some Notes on the Industrial Art Movement', which considered the 'hoveldom and haddledom' of manufacturing towns. In detectable Ruskinian tones he concluded that:

---

[1] *Catalogue of the Kendal Arts, Crafts, and Loan Exhibition* (1891) (copy in Kendal Library).

one of the surest ways to make life more cheerful in the country and less possible in our crowded cities was the training of the country people's eyes to see that God had scattered riches over the countryside for their enjoyment.[1]

T.J. Cobden-Sanderson spoke on 'Bookbinding', while, at the request of Simpson, Collingwood gave a lecture on the 'British School of Portraiture and the British School of Water Colour Landscape', with references to Ruskin, Arthur Severn and Kate Greenaway. A letter to Simpson from Collingwood, agreeing to be one of the lecturers, shows that Simpson had some early organisational role in the exhibition.[2] The prizes were presented by the mayor on 12 September, and the total attendance reached 30,000, a mark of resounding success which was undoubtedly aided by the special rates offered by the railways throughout the event.

Given that the 1891 Kendal exhibition was largely orchestrated by local Ruskinians, and was based on revival-associated exhibitions already held in the region between 1883 and 1891, the local Lakeland Ruskinian revival made by far the greatest contribution in terms of exhibits. It was the first exhibition to which *all* those involved with the revival contributed and the first to provide a public measure of the spread and extent of the revival, particularly concerning the numbers involved and its domestic nature. Simpson's and the Keswick School's exhibitions had already hinted in a more public manner that something important and different was happening locally, but the Kendal exhibition was a much stronger voice of solidarity among Ruskin's Lakeland followers and evidence of what was happening, chiefly as a result of a particular set of circumstances arising from Ruskin's move to the region in 1872. Not surprisingly, given the rapid return to regional crafts, the sections devoted to textiles and woodcarving were two of the largest in the exhibition, and were specially devised to cater for the increasing numbers of local women inspired by the revival to take up the needle and the wheel once again, and for the increasing number of local men inspired to take up woodcarving.

So great was local involvement in textiles by 1891, principally as a result of the local revival, that that section had to be divided into Plain Needlework and Artistic Needlework. Plain Needlework was then divided into eleven classes with an additional 24 special categories, while Artistic Needlework was divided into nine classes with five additional

---

[1] *Westmorland Gazette*, 5 Sept. 1891.

[2] AHM, Collingwood to Simpson, 10 May 1891.

special categories and another six classes which covered knitting, shawls, netted d'oyleys, knitted petticoats, children's socks and stockings, and other types of 'fancy' knitting. As a result textiles made by far the greatest statement of a wholehearted return to regional hand work, with 635 exhibits on display. Particular attention was drawn to the Langdale and Ruskin Linen Industries which were then in full flow, with special prizes (awarded by Albert Fleming) given under the heading of Artistic Needlework for 'Piano Back or Centre for Dinner Table, on Langdale Linen' (with a prize of 20s.), and 'Langdale Linen-Embroidered or Drawn' (with prizes of 20s. and 10s.).[1]

All those at the forefront of local textiles exhibited work, including Annie Garnett, Miss Rawson, Winnie Garnett, Mrs Brownson, Mrs Heskett, Mrs Pepper, other female members of the Pepper family, and members of Miss Twelves's Keswick School workshop. They were joined by members of the Stabler family of Levens, several women under the care of Mrs Harris of Kirkby Lonsdale, numerous spinsters and embroiderers from smaller branches of the Linen Industry recently established, and Mary Baxter (a servant) and Miss Lily Severn of Brantwood.[2] With demonstrations of handloom weaving taking place throughout, there can have been little opportunity to overlook the successful restoration of regional textile skills to Lakeland life. Due largely to the influence of Miss Twelves and Mrs Pepper, embroidery of a more decorative or artistic nature made a particularly vivid statement that a new edge had been introduced to regional textiles which was very much in keeping with that adopted some years earlier by, among others, the Royal School of Art Needlework. Local needlework had become an art as much as a craft and, far from being potentially limiting, was making significant strides in keeping up with wider developments.

Woodwork too by 1891 had established an artistic edge proved to be necessary to survival and the Kendal exhibition provided the biggest opportunity yet to advertise local artistic, as well as practical, talents in that field. Such was the response not only in numbers taking up woodcarving but also in numbers contributing to the exhibition that two separate categories were devised. The first covered basic woodwork such as joinery, hand turning and cabinet work, with 47 exhibits submitted, while the second covered more adventurous areas, including furniture making and artistic carving (such as the nature-inspired panels of the type promoted by Simpson), with 84 exhibits submitted. Among the

---

[1] *Catalogue.*
[2] Ibid.

more notable exhibits were several spinning wheels (not for sale) carved by Thomas Scott of Windermere, an illustration of the current revival of wheels in south Lakeland. Other exhibits came from Gatebeck, Milnthorpe, Burneside and Kirkby Lonsdale, as well as from Thomas Dixon of Kendal (one of Simpson's chief carvers), the Keswick School and Arthur Simpson, all of which also spoke most clearly of the local revival then firmly under way. There was a particularly healthy growth evident in the return to a once lost regional craft, the numbers involved by 1891 reflecting an equally healthy interest in what had also been a largely redundant skill only a few years before.

Every aspect of the 1891 exhibition, from Ravel's initial letter proposing the venture to its 'memorable' closing scenes,[1] was reported in the leading local paper, the *Westmorland Gazette*, which had published Ravel's letter proposing the original idea and had kept up a keen interest in the event throughout. A lengthy and detailed report of the opening ceremony drew particular attention to the presence of Princess Louise. Everything from the 'enthusiastic reception' for the princess on the first day of the exhibition to the actual ceremony, and the 'Old Folk's Tea' for 630 local pensioners which followed, was meticulously described.[2] Although less interested in the details of origins and organisation, other local papers, including the *Kendal Mercury and Times*, the *Kendal and County News*, the *Carlisle Journal* and the *Carlisle Patriot*, gave similar coverage of its first day. The *Carlisle Journal* described the street decorations, including the Venetian masts, festoons, shields and banners, and the frieze bearing the words 'Welcome Princess Louise' and the Prince of Wales's feathers which was draped across the Town Hall.[3]

In the lists of those present at the opening ceremony given in all the papers were the names of James Cropper, the earl of Carlisle, the bishop of Carlisle, Lady Bective, Mr and Mrs Crewdson, the Severns (representing Ruskin), Alfred Harris, Alfred Willink, Colin Somervell and J.F. Curwen (a member of another leading local family). Speeches were delivered by local dignitaries, including the bishop, who concluded that 'the progress of Kendal depends very much on the encouragement of arts and crafts among its inhabitants'. In his contribution Lord Carlisle reaffirmed the exhibition's regional flavour and Ruskin basis, noting:

[1] *Westmorland Gazette*, 3 Oct. 1891.

[2] Ibid., 29 Aug. 1891.

[3] *Carlisle Journal*, 28 Aug. 1891.

I have no doubt that the residence in your neighbourhood of Mr
Ruskin—(cheers)—has done a great deal to stimulate this work, as
his written work undoubtedly has had a great part in creating it.
(Applause.) I do not know what share he may have had in
founding the different industries; but I feel certain of this, that he
must, in his old age, feel satisfaction when he reviews the results
that have already been attained.[1]

Not only did that particular speech confirm the deeply Ruskinian nature
of the exhibition and exhibitors, but indicated that the event was by no
means the end of what was taking place in south Lakeland under
Ruskin's influence, with more to be 'attained'. In one of its final
complimentary reviews, the *Westmorland Gazette* reported that the
exhibition would 'terminate its brilliant but all too brief career this
(Saturday) evening', adding that 'its practical and financial success'
ought to be an encouragement to follow it up.[2]

The 1891 exhibition was clearly an immense success, commercially,
financially, philosophically and practically. It increased local interest in
local products, it made a profit, it made a public statement about the
Ruskinian value of regionalism at a time of mass industrialisation, and
it gave everyone the opportunity to display under favourable conditions
what they were capable of producing. No item had been judged too
menial to display, with wooden casks, joiners' tool chests, knitted vests,
ribbed stockings, samples of darning and mending, and sets of horse-
shoes shown alongside Keswick School copper and silverware, Simpson
furniture and Rigby paintings. In his prize-giving speech the mayor of
Kendal expressed the opinion that the 'happiness of life' was in
'successful labour', and that every item in the exhibition 'told of
increased happiness to the person who prepared it'.[3]

The very nature of the exhibition, however, meant that something of
its value was lost outside Lakeland, and little was reported nationally.
The Times devoted a short paragraph to Princess Louise's visit to Barrow
to open a fund-raising event, which took priority over the exhibition that
she also attended. Nor was the event reported in any major art journal,
despite its scale and aims. It was unfortunate that the journals which
became most interested in Lakeland handcrafts had not yet begun
publication. *The Studio* was founded only in 1893, and the *Art Workers'*

---

[1] *Westmorland Gazette*, 29 Aug. 1891.

[2] Ibid., 26 Sept. 1891.

[3] Ibid., 12 Sept. 1891.

Quarterly in 1902. The majority of art journals which were in operation in 1891, such as the *Art Journal* and *The Year's Art*, chose to concentrate mostly on exhibitions of national importance. In terms of what it represented—a celebration of regional arts and crafts in defiance of mass mechanisation—the Kendal exhibition was clearly ahead of its time and outlets for national publicity only appeared some years later.

Rawnsley's desire to repeat the 1891 exhibition annually never materialised. But in 1899, in an attempt to repeat the earlier success and in response to the large amount of art and craft work still being produced in the region (largely as a result of Ruskin's continued influence), the Kendal Exhibition of Pictures and Decorative Art was devised. On that occasion Cuthbert Rigby played a key role as exhibitor and, with Simpson, as honorary secretary. Once again the names of John Somervell (then mayor) and Arthur Simpson appeared in the committee list, whilst honorary district secretaries included Collingwood (for Coniston), the local artist Alfred Heaton Cooper (for Hawkshead), Alfred Willink (for Kendal, Burneside and Staveley), the Rawnsleys (for Keswick) and Percy Hibbert (for Milnthorpe, Heversham, Beetham and Arnside).[1]

Held in Abbot Hall, Kendal, in July 1899, the exhibition was noticeably smaller than its predecessor, but again concentrated on local work. Exhibitors included the Collingwoods, Edith Rawnsley, Arthur Simpson, the Keswick School, J.W. Oddie, the Kirkby Lonsdale classes, Percy Hibbert, Heaton Cooper, Rigby, Annie Garnett and Harold Stabler. Also present, however, was the work of Voysey, Joseph Southall, Lamorna Birch, Godfrey Blount, Edgar Wood and Morton's of Carlisle. Inexplicably, the Langdale and Ruskin Linen Industries were not well represented, Fleming declining to send the usual demonstrator of spinning and weaving he sent to Simpson's exhibition and to the 1891 Kendal exhibition. Of the textiles exhibited only a small number were locally produced, including an embroidered linen book cover made by Marian Twelves's Keswick workshop for Joan Severn.

Although Ruskin attended neither exhibition, he did contribute as an exhibitor. In 1891 an assortment of his drawings and paintings were shown, together with a Ruskin linen cushion owned by him and worked by Mrs Rawnsley, and in 1899 Collingwood's portrait of Ruskin (1897) was exhibited along with several of Ruskin's drawings and paintings then owned by Fleming and Oddie. More references were made to him in various lectures, including Rawnsley's inaugural address:

---

[1] The following is based on the *Catalogue of the Exhibition of Pictures and Decorative Art, Kendal, 1899* (copy in Kendal Library).

After all what was the art movement in our midst but a very serious attempt to get blind eyes to see the beauty of nature all round and about them and to translate that beauty into fact, and in no place better than in the lovely Kendal valley could men perceive and know that beauty, and learn in quiet how to express their feelings about it. It might be said how could that committee, those few gentlemen who had undertaken that laborious task, open the eyes of the blind to perceive and know what true art was. His answer would be that we lived within touch of that great prophet and artist of our time—John Ruskin—and that animated by his spirit much was possible.

He continued by discussing the way

one master had opened the eyes not only of Westmorland and Cumberland but of all the world at the end of the nineteenth century to perceive the truth and beauty of Nature, and the need of close and loving observation.[1]

That speech, more than any other delivered at a local exhibition, clarified the value of Ruskin as a near presence as well as theoretical influence in turn-of-the-century Lakeland. Either directly or indirectly, virtually every item displayed at both exhibitions spoke of that presence and of the impact made across the region by one of the most important writers of the period. Although Kendal staged no further exhibitions on such a scale, local exhibitions continued to run successfully elsewhere in the region, and the local revival was never slow to create opportunities for exhibition. Having developed alongside the revival, however, when the Linen Industry and other classes and workshops began to dwindle, so too did the local exhibition, with little of any note taking place after 1927.

[1] *Westmorland Gazette*, 8 July 1899.

13

OTHER DEVELOPMENTS
IN LAKELAND
ARTS AND CRAFTS

The confusion surrounding the categorisation of events in Lakeland under Ruskin's influence has arisen partly from lack of research but also from the generally complex arts scene in the region in the late nineteenth century. The Ruskinian revival was by no means the only arts activity in the Lake District between 1880 and 1920. Other developments involved both those who were more permanent fixtures in the region but not necessarily connected with the local revival, and those who were more transient figures. In particular, the occasional presence in north Lakeland of several leading figures connected with the Arts and Crafts Exhibition Society has led to a misunderstanding of the nature of the Lakeland Ruskinian revival. A highly influential movement, the Arts and Crafts undoubtedly made its presence felt in south Lakeland, with local architecture still bearing the visual signs of its effects. But it was by no means a dominant force in late nineteenth-century Lakeland. Aside from the revival of once thriving arts and crafts, which clearly and unquestionably dominated south Lakeland between 1880 and 1920, several other prominent local and visiting arts figures made a more substantial contribution to the region's individual arts flavour.

To a degree, the Arts and Crafts—or pre-Arts and Crafts—arrived in Lakeland as early as the 1870s, chiefly in the form of those who would later become the movement's principal exponents, including William Morris, Walter Crane and Philip Webb. Their presence, however, was less to do with a deliberate attempt to establish any particular design style in the Lake District than with their friendship (important in itself) with George Howard, 9th earl of Carlisle, and his wife Rosalind (1845–1921). Philip Webb, a fellow socialist, was particularly drawn to the Howards and along with Morris and Crane spent time at their summer residence, Naworth Castle at Brampton, Cumberland. In 1869–70 Webb designed the Howards' London residence, 1 Palace Green, and in return Howard secured him several commissions in and around Brampton between 1874 and 1880. The most important was St Martin's church, Brampton (1874–8), an early tribute to the architectural simplicity which would become synonymous with the Arts and Crafts. Webb's only church, St Martin's is noticeably devoid of unnecessary ornamentation, but has typically rich Morris & Co. windows, dominated by an august east window consisting of fourteen figures and a central pelican panel. Unfortunately, the project was fraught with difficulties, including prolonged wrangles over costs which took place between Webb and the Brampton parishioners. The tower was completed only in 1905 by George Jack. At around the same time Webb designed two houses at Brampton, Four Gables (1876–8) and Green Lanes (1877), the latter originally intended to be the vicarage to St Martin's. Various other commissions were carried out for the Howards at Naworth, including a clock face (1874) in the castle courtyard, oak fittings and a panelled room for Lady Howard (c.1878), and various family memorials at nearby Lanercost Priory.

Although William Morris completed some minor interior decoration on his visits to Naworth, his presence was more keenly felt in Lakeland through the firm of Morris & Co., in which he was joined by Edward Burne-Jones. Burne-Jones had a long and close friendship with Ruskin, although he rarely visited Brantwood, but did send his wife and children to stay there on several occasions. Between 1870 and 1926 Morris & Co. were responsible for no fewer than fifteen stained glass commissions in Lakeland, all of which, except for two windows made for Lunefield (the Harris family home at Kirkby Lonsdale) around 1870 and a landing window for Ambleside vicarage in 1894, were made for local churches. One of the earliest and most successful was the east window for the Jesus Chapel, Troutbeck, (c.1873), and one of the last was an east window for Armathwaite church (1926), although by that time both Morris and Burne-Jones were long since dead.[1] Henry Holiday, who felt the influence of the Pre-Raphaelites rather than the Arts and Crafts, also contributed to local stained glass to a lesser degree. Surviving examples of his work can be found at St Mary's, Ambleside (north and south aisle windows, 1888–91) and St Michael's, Muncaster (chancel side windows and one south window, 1882–7).

With the increase in wealthy incomers in the late 1880s and 1890s, south Lakeland saw a sudden rash of building which introduced a conglomeration of architectural styles to a region which was more

---

[1] Other Morris & Co. stained glass commissions for Lakeland are listed in the Chronology.

accustomed to the vernacular cottage. Perhaps surprisingly, this did not result in the overwhelming presence of Arts and Crafts, although several major houses which typified the style were built. Although too individual to fit comfortably under the Arts and Crafts label, C.F.A. Voysey was probably the first to introduce to south Lakeland the simplicity which reflected what was happening generally across the country immediately prior to 1900 with his Broadleys (*c.*1899, built for the Currer-Briggs family) and Moor Crag (*c.*1898, built for the Buckley family). Despite his popularity, Voysey made only a minor impression on south Lakeland. Only three of his six designs for houses were realised, and the design of one of those—Littleholme—was probably a joint effort with Arthur Simpson. Voysey's other designs for Lakeland houses were for W.E. Rowley at Kirkoswald, for H. Rickards at Windermere, and for G. Toulmin, also at Windermere.[1] Why the houses were never built remains unclear.

With the completion of M.H. Baillie Scott's Blackwell at Windermere shortly afterwards (*c.*1899), the Arts and Crafts style appeared to be more firmly established in Lakeland, its followers sharing Ruskin's own rejection of heavy ornamentation and decoration in favour of simplicity. Arguably a better interpretation of the Arts and Crafts than either Broadleys or Moor Crag, which speak predominantly of Voysey, the exterior of Blackwell is undeniably economical in decoration. The interior, however, boasts a great hall with a rich peacock frieze, rich stained glass and a white drawing room of which Charles Rennie Mackintosh would have approved. But again the architect made little impact on Lakeland generally, which saw no obvious adoption of Baillie Scott's style or philosophies, even if Blackwell remains as evidence of the breadth of styles employed in south Lakeland at the time of the revival of local arts and crafts. Although Voysey's Littleholme followed around 1910, the Arts and Crafts dwindled in south Lakeland after 1900, as the infiltration of wealthy industrialists into the south of the region also declined.

Again somewhat surprisingly, given that she too enjoyed national success as the epitome of the Arts and Crafts in her work, Gertrude Jekyll (1843–1932) executed only one garden design in Lakeland. Not all those who commissioned national figures were outsiders who had moved into Lakeland—Blackwell was built for a local man and a patron of local arts and crafts, Sir Edward Holt—and there was clearly a

---

[1] *Catalogue of the Drawings of the Royal Institute of British Architects* (1989), 25, 28, 45–6.

willingness to accept changing fashions as well as the seemingly antiquated revival of regional arts and crafts. But few of those living in the region could employ Baillie Scott or Voysey. Arthur Simpson overcame the problem of expense by overseeing the architect's plans, making sure that the house was comparatively small, using local materials, and executing all the woodwork himself. He was also reputedly not charged for the finished drawings.[1]

In the case of Jekyll, who was well known for the labour-intensive nature of her gardens, in 1904 she was employed by the owners of Brackenbrough, a substantial property at Calthwaite which reflected considerable success in regional farming. In 1901 the owners had been able to commission the Scottish architect Robert Lorimer (1864–1929) to design extensions, and three years later Jekyll was invited to add two large herbaceous borders to the garden (which are no longer maintained). Measuring 228 feet and 105 feet in length, the borders were made up of plants and shrubs chosen purely for their colour and flowering period, and bore no relation either to their surrounding landscape or to local traditions in planting. But the mere presence of Jekyll's work in Lakeland reveals that the Arts and Crafts did permeate the region to a minor degree and added to its arts history. The impact of Brackenbrough's garden borders, however, was minimal, and Jekyll did not produce any complete garden design or indeed do any other work at all in the region.

One other outside design force made his presence felt in the region, but slightly later. In 1909 the craftsman Alec Miller (1879–1961) was commissioned to produce a series of woodcarvings for St Mary's, Urswick, which took until 1912 to complete. Woodcarving, of course, had experienced a strong resurgence in Lakeland under Simpson's influence, and Miller was the only major outside carver to make an impression on the south of the region between 1880 and 1920. A member of the Art Workers' Guild, Miller was a leading craftsman in Charles R. Ashbee's Guild of Handicraft and was presumably chosen for the commission on his reputation. The most distinctive and decorative carvings consisted of the organ case, south door, screen, pulpit and pews, whose designs were based on the scallop shell, the emblem of St James, which is repeated around the church. Although Ashbee's guild is also discussed in terms of the Arts and Crafts, Miller's work at Urswick completely defies categorisation, thus adding to the complexity of Lakeland arts at this time. Categorisation, however, is less significant

---

[1] Simpson family archive.

than the date of the work. By 1907 the Guild of Handicraft was suffering heavy losses, which resulted in some guildsmen leaving Chipping Campden, with only a small number—Miller among them—electing to remain. The last meeting of the remaining guildsmen was held in Miller's workshop on 25 January 1919. The Urswick carvings, therefore, were executed by a member of a much depleted group and are among the most significant surviving complete sets of woodcarving by Miller and the Guild of Handicraft. At the time Miller began the Urswick commission, Collingwood was involved in archaeological work on the church and would have been aware of what was taking place inside the building. Despite its national importance, Miller's work again represents only an isolated occurrence in south Lakeland, and no other items executed by either Miller or the Guild of Handicraft have been located. As in architecture, in woodcarving there was no clear, sustained Arts and Crafts influence present in Lakeland in the early twentieth century.

In 1928, however, the Arts and Crafts did appear in south Lakeland on a more permanent level in the form of the craftswoman Ann Macbeth. As a close friend of the Patterdale craftswoman and former Handicrafts pupil May Spence (1857–1957), Macbeth was a frequent visitor to the Lake District at the beginning of the century before moving to the region in the late 1920s after her retirement from the Glasgow School of Art. Born in Bolton, Lancashire, she was the daughter of a Scottish engineer and the granddaughter of artist Norman Macbeth, a member of the Royal Scottish Academy. In 1897 she began studying at the Glasgow School of Art under Francis Newbery. Shortly after she began to assist Jessie Newbery (Newbery's wife) in needlework classes and by 1907 had taken over classes in ceramic decoration and book decoration. By 1910 she had also taken over Mrs Newberry's needlework classes, and became known as 'Professor of Embroidery'. Although her permanent residence began after the period discussed here, she had contributed to Simpson's annual exhibition from at least 1903, when she showed specimens of embroidery and hand-painted pottery,[1] and so was not completely dissociated from earlier events. A recognisable Arts and Crafts figure who broke new ground in needlework, Macbeth had worked at the centre of Arts and Crafts developments for many years, the Glasgow School of Art, influenced by (and influencing), among others, Margaret and Frances Macdonald, Anne Knox Arthur, Jessie King, Jessie Newbery and Annie French. Her association with May Spence and the Simpsons, however, brought a new edge to Macbeth's later work which clearly reflected the

---

[1] Simpson family archive.

influence of the local revival on her rather than that of the Arts and Crafts on south Lakeland. Once based in Patterdale, Macbeth produced a quantity of landscapes in watercolour and hand painted pottery, but also four embroidered wool hangings, the two larger of which vividly represented both her intense Christianity and her years in Lakeland.

The two smaller hangings were based on a bowl of flowers and doves of peace. The former was owned by a local family, while the latter was (and still is) hung in the local church. The two larger works, however, spoke of a clear recognition of what had been taking place in the region for a considerable time prior to her move there. While any personal devotion to Ruskin remained hidden, in *The Good Shepherd* and *The Nativity* she revealed that same admiration for Lakeland expressed by all those at the heart of the revival under Ruskin's influence. She too accepted the region as her own artistically, and in *The Good Shepherd* she skilfully set Christ the Shepherd against a detailed and accurately portrayed landscape of Hartsop, Deepdale, Caudale Moor and Kirkstone—the landscape visible from Wordsworth Cottage, one of her temporary homes in Patterdale. It was her first major artistic study of the region, taking many months to complete, and in 1938 was exhibited at The Handicrafts and at an exhibition of arts and crafts held at Ambleside.

The Good Shepherd later took its rightful place in Patterdale church and still hangs there today, an outcome not shared by its companion *The Nativity*. Measuring a similarly substantial 75 inches by 78 inches, *The Nativity*, which ended up in Glasgow, reflected the same detailed observation of the Lakeland landscape practised by Macbeth's local Ruskinian contemporaries, and showed the same awareness of its unique colours and moods particularly evident in Annie Garnett's textiles. Completed c.1940 *The Nativity* set Mary and Jesus in a vivid Lakeland landscape of Helvellyn and Grisedale with Patterdale village in the background. Although Macbeth completed several minor textiles for Patterdale church after 1928, *The Nativity* was her last sizeable Lakeland work, and one of the last of her lengthy career.

Whether the former Glasgow School teacher made any significant impact on Lakeland is difficult to assess. But she is still regarded in Patterdale as a Lakeland craftswoman rather than as a nationally important design figure, and is remembered chiefly for her friendship with May Spence and the Simpsons, her Lakeland textiles, and her generosity in teaching others—including Jane Simpson—the art of painting on pots. In recognition of her devotion to the region, on her death in 1948 Macbeth chose to have her ashes scattered around Patterdale, close to where she had lived for some twenty years and close to where May Spence was buried nine years later.

The development of Lakeland's highly individual arts personality between 1880 and 1920 was also shaped by a small number of other notable figures not necessarily directly associated with any particular movement. The best known of these were Alfred Heaton Cooper and Beatrix Potter. Neither were Westmerians by birth but both developed that same passion for Lakeland as Ruskin, Fleming, Rawnsley and others, and chose to live out much of their lives there. As a result, their art work developed along the Lakeland theme and brought both into contact with the local revival. Heaton Cooper exhibited his Lakeland paintings at several local joint (as well as solo) exhibitions. At the 1899 Kendal exhibition he showed, among other works, *Evening, Hawkshead*, priced at 15 guineas, and helped with the organisation of the event. Clearly well acquainted with those such as Collingwood, who took an equally active role at local exhibitions, Heaton Cooper was evidently aware of local developments in art, and caught the same mood of regionalism exuded by the Lakeland Ruskinian revival. A more commercial artist, however, he became better known than any of his local contemporaries, producing a large collection of widely exhibited paintings and book illustrations which, for over 40 years, drew national attention.

Of an equally independent nature, Beatrix Potter moved to Sawrey in 1905 after visiting the Lake District for many years. With her internationally known illustrated children's books, she too has become a familiar public face of Lakeland arts and her studies of the natural landscape and of the architecture around her home have brought increasingly widespread recognition for the region in recent years. Although she lacked any strong associations with the local revival, through her father she became a close friend of the Rawnsleys who, after 1905, kept her abreast of developments, at least within the Keswick School. The subject of numerous biographical studies, Potter has been much discussed.[1] She had no special interest in Ruskin[2] and compared Langdale linen unfavourably with cloth made in Scotland:

This hand-woven unbleached (for linen is linen, I believe the bleaching chemicals are the mischief) will last for ever. There were some lumps, but on the whole fine, strong cloth, infinitely superior

---

[1] Including most recently Anne Stevenson Hobbs, *Beatrix Potter's Art* (1989).

[2] Above, p. 101, for Potter's view of Ruskin.

to anything they make in Langdale.[1]

These views probably explain why Potter took no part in local exhibitions, nor made any other contribution to arts developments in Lakeland. On her death, however, she left some 4,500 acres to Rawnsley's National Trust,[2] and was clearly supportive of Ruskinian philosophies towards conservation if not of the man himself.

Also declining to take part in any local exhibitions, yet following the mood of regionalism in Lakeland arts at the turn of the last century, was the photographer Herbert Bell. More openly supportive of Ruskin, Bell was a member of the Ruskin Society at Ambleside (founded in 1882) and spent much of his life producing photographic studies of a Lakeland beloved by Wordsworth and Ruskin and conserved by Rawnsley and others. Echoing the paintings of Rigby, Collingwood, Heaton Cooper and others, Bell's work presented both the natural delights of the region and its pre-industrial way of life, the Ruskinian theme of man at one with his natural surroundings being particularly potent for the local photographer. The true value of his work as a record not only of an era long since gone, but also of the physical background against which the revival of local arts and crafts generally flourished, has yet to be fully realised.

Of more lasting importance to late nineteenth-century Lakeland, chiefly because of their more obvious impact on the built environment and their more marked associations with the local revival, were the landscape architect Thomas H. Mawson (1861–1933) and the architect Dan Gibson. Both men's work survives as clear evidence that the local revival also affected architecture, and shows how its domestic origins influenced a revival of building unique to the region.

Originally from Scorton in Lancashire, Mawson moved to the Lake District in 1885 and, assisted by his brothers Robert and Isaac, established a nursery at Windermere. Mawson was in Lakeland, therefore, almost from the beginnings of the local revival, arriving around the same time that Simpson returned to Kendal. With a lifelong interest in Ruskin, he began to take an active part in local arts developments almost immediately. It was probably his interest in Ruskin that brought Mawson into contact with Joan Severn and it was she who initially helped to establish his nursery, recommending him to a Mr Bridson at Bryerswood, Sawrey, a house designed by the Bolton architect Richard Knill Freeman. Bridson recommended him to others in the area and, as a result, by 1889

[1] L. Linder (ed.), *The Journal of Beatrix Potter* (1966), 275.

[2] *Westmorland Gazette*, 30 Sept. 1944.

Mawson was able to establish a separate landscape business. He undertook larger commissions such as Graythwaite Hall, also at Sawrey, which gave him the opportunity to exert considerable influence over the physical appearance of sizeable areas of south Lakeland (in the case of Graythwaite, for example, six acres). What is particularly significant about Mawson is that, while not wholly committed to the local revival (as were Fleming or Rawnsley, for example), he was a lifelong 'admiring disciple' of Ruskin. Joan Severn played a direct role in establishing his career and he clearly put Ruskin's theories into practice.[1]

Although he studied the works of Humphrey Repton, Edward Kemp and others, Mawson acknowledged that 'the natural result' of his 'passion for the works and views of Professor Ruskin' (on which he lectured) was a concern for local design tradition.[2] Like Ruskin, he believed in 'slavishly' following 'the tradition of any locality' where he was working, and so took up the same basic philosophy which fired the local revival.[3] Rejecting the eighteenth-century desire to change nature to suit man, Mawson took the natural features of each site presented to him and incorporated them into the finished design. So important was the broader Lakeland landscape to a Mawson garden that in one instance he: 'advocated the changing of the entire location of a proposed house on the Westmorland moors; in order that it might have as a site a natural terrace of rock'.[4] He used only local plants, trees, shrubs and materials and always took into consideration regional soil and climatic conditions-an approach which coincided with Ruskin's own practice at Brantwood, but was opposed to Jekyll's approaches at Brackenbrough. His admiration for Ruskin, however, never prompted Mawson to join the Guild of St George, or to work exclusively to the writer's theories.

Over the years Mawson carried out a considerable number of landscaping and gardening commissions in Lakeland and elsewhere which brought him into close contact with those at the centre of local activities, including the revival of arts and crafts. His more prestigious clients included Edward Tygarly, Lady Bective and Sir Edward Holt (for whom he laid out the grounds at Blackwell), most of whom patronised local arts, and he may have carried out work at Brantwood for Mrs Severn. As a friend of Simpson and Voysey, Mawson also designed the garden for Broadleys for Arthur Currer-Briggs, and collaborated with

---

[1] T.H. Mawson, *The Life and Work of an English Landscape Architect* (1927), 26.

[2] Ibid., 64.

[3] Ibid.

[4] Ibid., 93.

Voysey and the Buckleys on the garden for Moor Crag. From Simpson, he commissioned a 'handy and portable drawing-case with fold over lid' so that he might draw while travelling, and his wife attended the opening of Simpson's new showroom in Windermere in 1901, along with Cuthbert Rigby, Annie Garnett and Dan Gibson.[1] In 1899 Mawson also contributed to the Kendal exhibition as both guarantor and exhibitor, showing a photograph of The Corbels and a plan of gardens for Cuerdon Hall, Warrington.[2]

Mawson's friendship with Dan Gibson was to prove the most fruitful for Lakeland, particularly its architecture. Mawson met Gibson when he employed Richard Knill Freeman on his first large landscaping job at Graythwaite Hall, Sawrey. Gibson was then Knill Freeman's resident architect and accompanied him on the commission, completed between 1889 and 1895. Born in Bassingthorpe (Lincs.) in 1865 Gibson was the fourth son of John Gibson, a farmer. During his career he spent time not only with the architect Knill Freeman, but with Ernest George & Peto in London. By 1898 Mawson, keen to show a greater degree of architectural expression in his work, had persuaded Gibson to move to Windermere and establish a formal partnership. Although commissions were carried out far and wide, their Lakeland work very much caught the pervading mood of regionalism, with Mawson producing locally influenced gardens whilst Gibson designed buildings in a similar vein.

Probably under Mawson's influence, Gibson adopted a distinctive style after 1898 which spoke predominantly of the Lakeland vernacular cottage, with the Cumberland round chimney becoming a strong feature of his work. The partnership lasted less than two years, one of their last projects being Brockhole (*c*.1899) near Troutbeck Bridge for W. Gaddum, another of the wealthy northern industrialists who moved to late nineteenth-century Lakeland. While Mawson laid out the gardens, terraces, entrance drives and plantations, Gibson designed the house, incorporating a number of different designs combined with local building motifs. After the partnership ended (most amicably) Mawson and Gibson continued to work together informally, collaborating on two houses, The Corbels (*c*.1899) and Shrublands (*c*.1900), built for Mawson and his brother Robert at Windermere. Both houses 'adhered to the architectural traditions of the Westmorland dales', and were far more indicative of

---

[1] Ibid., 134.

[2] *Catalogue of the Exhibition of Pictures and Decorative Art, Kendal, 1899* (copy in Kendal Library).

what was happening locally rather than nationally.[1] Around the same time, Mawson's second son became a pupil in Gibson's office.[2]

Gibson was so taken with the Lake District and developments there that he established himself independently in Windermere, and, having exhibited at the 1899 Kendal exhibition, became even more engrossed in local activities until his early death in 1907. At the 1899 Kendal exhibition Gibson exhibited several paintings, including *Summer Cottage on Windermere* and *Sketch of Yorkshire Church*, and showed a copper fender worked to his design by Harold Stabler's associate Ll.B. Rathbone. Gibson also lent several items from his extensive collection of antiques, including old Dutch tiles and jewellery.[3] During these years, he designed at least six substantial Lakeland properties, as well as carrying out numerous smaller commissions, arguably the finest of which was Birket Houses (*c.*1904) at Winster. According to Lawrence Weaver, its rooms were designed solely with reference to their 'liveable character and their aspects', Gibson's admiration for the Lakeland cottage revealing itself in the modest size of the rooms, the equally modest staff quarters, and the free use of the Cumberland round chimney.[4]

Although the Keswick School had already helped to revive local domestic architecture in 1894 with its new premises, Gibson's Lakeland work won more widespread approval for the regional style. As Gertrude Jekyll noted in 1912, Birket Houses was a fitting attempt to 'revive the type of architecture proper to the Lake District'.[5] Such wider recognition helped to shape national perception of Lakeland's distinct design identity, and added to its unique personality. As a result of associating with those at the heart of the local revival, Gibson moved into other areas of design, working with Arthur Simpson on a sizeable carving commission for St Margaret's church, Prestwich, begun in 1899. The two had already worked successfully together before that date, with Simpson providing much of the interior woodwork for Gibson's Lakeland houses. At Prestwich, Gibson designed the choir stalls, pulpit, reredos, altar rail, panelling and Rood Screen in Danzig oak, which Simpson completed carving only around 1920.

At his death, Gibson left much unfulfilled in terms of Lakeland

---

[1] Mawson, *Life and Work*, 64.

[2] Ibid., 62.

[3] *Catalogue of the Exhibition of Pictures and Decorative Art, Kendal, 1899*.

[4] L. Weaver, *Small Country Houses of To-Day* (1919), i. 52.

[5] G. Jekyll and L. Weaver, *Gardens for Small Country Houses* (1912), 95.

architecture, and, unlike Mawson,[1] has since been neglected. There are indications, however, that both brought about significant changes in attitudes towards local building (of which Ruskin himself, as an admirer of Lakeland architecture, would have approved), which had far longer lasting consequences than the likes of Blackwell or Broadleys. In 1919 Rawnsley formed the last of his Lakeland defence groups, the Lake District Safeguarding Society, which continued until about 1940. In 1936 the society published a leaflet entitled *An Appeal to Those Intending to Build.*[2] Compiled by the Lake District Advisory Architectural Panel, which included W.L. Dolman, who had worked with Gibson, the leaflet encapsulated everything which Gibson, Mawson, Annie Garnett and the Rawnsleys had put into practice in local building some years earlier. Concerned with the need to preserve local traditions as an important part of the region's heritage, the panel offered detailed advice on architectural tradition and regional traits in existing buildings, and what would 'meet the practical requirements of the District' in new buildings. It recommended that only local materials be used and that new buildings should be in keeping with the district. As late as 1936, therefore, traces of the revival of local traditions and its Ruskinian philosophies were still evident.

[1] G. Beard and J. Wardman, *Thomas H. Mawson 1861–1933: The Life and Work of a Northern Landscape Architect* (University of Lancaster Visual Arts Centre, 1976); H. Jordan, 'Thomas Hayton Mawson 1861–1933. The English Garden Designs of an Edwardian Landscape Architect' (Unpublished London University (Wye College) Ph.D. thesis, 1988).

[2] Copy in CROK, WDX 422/2/8.

14

CONCLUSION

Between 1880 and 1920, and even beyond, the Lake District experienced a significant and sizeable return to regional, domestic handcrafts. At the core of this movement were two key driving forces—John Ruskin and Lakeland—both of which remained its focal points throughout. As a result of these forces, the revival developed a character which remained unequalled outside the region during that forty-year period. Ruskin had a particularly long and intense relationship with Lakeland which undeniably coloured not only his own life and approach to the area and its history, but the lives and attitudes of those whom he inspired to found the revival. Stretching from early childhood until death, that relationship was essential in the pre-revival years (prior to 1883) in laying foundations which ensured a positive response to the realisation of the writer's teachings. From its inception, however, the revival focused just as keenly on Lakeland's distinctive history and character, which was then under threat.

The willingness of the people of Lakeland to accept Ruskin was a major (and in no sense coincidental) factor in the revival's short-term and long-term success. That acceptance began not in 1883, when the revival began, but in the 1870s with what was arguably Ruskin's most public defence of Lakeland—the rejection of its railways. Lakeland's acceptance of Ruskin, therefore, was a long-term and gradual process rather than instant or spontaneous. That personal element of cultivating a direct relationship was instigated by Ruskin's move to Lakeland in 1872, and his immersion in its life and culture, including his defence of its physical attributes in deliberate imitation of Wordsworth. He never sought to return to London and never expressed any regret at moving. That in itself says something of the importance of the region to Ruskin, and that high regard clearly helped to transmute Lakeland's perception of the writer.

The Lakeland revival was inextricably linked to one of England's most prolific and controversial writers. But it was in no sense a sudden or spontaneous development, which occurred when Ruskin arrived in the region in 1872. Rather, it represented the more gradual, definite and definable, and more positive, conversion to Ruskin by Lakeland. While those who headed the revival came from various parts of the country, it was only on arriving in Lakeland that the actual idea of reviving traditional local handcrafts evolved. With varying backgrounds, it was their initial exposure to Lakeland, combined with a more intensely personal relationship with Ruskin, which instigated their realisation of the writer's theories. For Fleming, for example, his contact not only with Ruskin but with Lakeland early in 1883, when he encountered his first Westmorland spinning wheel, activated his realisation of Ruskin and inspired others to follow his practical example. It was the combination of Ruskin and Lakeland—or, it was a very specific set of internal circumstances—which sparked off the Lakeland revival, arguably the most successful reversion to local, domestic handcrafts in England between 1880 and 1920.

Each of the workshops, classes and industries discussed here—each important in its own right as a successful artistic exercise—developed a strong individual personality which resulted from its founder's personal understanding of Ruskin. Just as important, collectively they represented a strong and positive regional arts movement which revitalised metalwork, church art, silk manufacture, embroidery, lace making, jewellery, bookbinding, pottery, furniture, leather work, garden design and landscape architecture, as well as art, decorative woodcarving, textile production and architecture. All this must be seen as the deliberate promotion of northern arts, but also as evidence that Ruskin still had a considerable impact at the end of his life. New heights in artistic production and standards were reached in Lakeland between 1880 and 1920, which were linked absolutely to Ruskin's presence in the region.

The fact that the Langdale Linen Industry in particular has until now remained largely ignored reveals much not only about attitudes towards the arts in the north, but also towards domestic handcrafts and towards women such as Marian Twelves as valid contributors to art and design. But valid contributors they were, and artistic developments clearly did occur away from the recognised centres of London, Birmingham and Glasgow. Lakeland should be recognised as having anticipated the wider return to domestic handcrafts formalised in 1884 with the founding of the Home Arts and Industries Association. Although independent, and contained within specific geographic boundaries, the revival ran alongside broader developments after that date, establishing Lakeland as a forerunner to one of the most widespread domestic arts movements in late nineteenth-century England. Whilst it was never intended to herald a national conversion to traditional local handcrafts (other than to encourage everyone to buy its wares), the Lakeland revival clearly had broader implications for industrial England. A successful working example of Ruskin's theories, the Lakeland movement introduced ideas which openly defied modern developments and demonstrated the possibility of a return to hand production and the domestic arts. Such was its success that the revival did not vanish within a short period, as might be expected with such an open defiance of mechanisation. On the contrary, it continued in a diminished form into the 1940s and 1950s, and the Keswick School survived into the 1980s. It thus long outlived the fashion for Art Deco in the 1920s and 1930s—the effects of which can be seen just outside Lakeland in Morecambe. The domestic revival, by contrast, can still be clearly seen all around the region, and in both homes and churches is still the most easily recognisable phase in Lakeland's arts history.

The revival was an independent—but never isolated—movement which apparently never suffered artistically or financially because of its independence. Rather, its internal driving forces were its greatest strengths, and it survived for so long principally because of them. Certainly in terms of the local spread of ideas, there was a continuous and healthy exchange throughout the 40 or so years in which the revival thrived. At the head of that exchange was W.G. Collingwood who acted as the voice of Ruskin when he himself was no longer able to communicate. The exchange helped to ensure that the revival never became sterile and always moved forward. It is also clear that women played a crucial role in realising Ruskin's theories, carrying out much of the practical side of the revival, as well as expressing their individual creativity on a scale never before seen in Lakeland.

This study challenges previous perceptions of the revival as a minor reaction to wider developments, notably the Arts and Crafts, and reaffirms its individuality, both theoretical and artistic. The size and scale of the revival means that some of those involved, particularly in the early years, will always remain anonymous. Oral testimony has provided many clues but written evidence has failed to identify a number of participants. It has also proved impossible to trace all the work produced between 1880 and 1920 or to identify the makers of some surviving items.

Further research might help to clarify other aspects of the revival. For example, what happened to the movement in the 1930s and 1940s, and what finally finished the revival as the dominant local arts force? What (or who), if anything (or anyone), took its place? The effect of the two World Wars on Lakeland, not only on the local revival, but the arts as a whole, remains similarly unclear. Arthur Simpson, for example, was profoundly affected by the death of at least two of his Quaker craftsmen in the First World War, and The Handicrafts was equally affected by the lack of wood available during and after the Second World War. Local men killed during the two wars must have included some who partici-pated in the revival, suggesting that, to a degree, skills would have been lost again. The Keswick School in particular, with its considerable numbers of male students, may have been especially affected.

Not only do other areas of Lakeland's arts (particularly relating to the eighteenth and twentieth centuries) await more thorough investigation, but so too do other areas of the domestic arts movement of late nineteenth-century Britain. The connections between Lakeland and the Home Arts and Industries Association suggests research into both the association and its exhibitions would help to establish a clearer picture of the nationwide spread of the domestic arts movement. Lakeland was by no means the only domestic arts development of the period and comparisons could be made between the region and other Home Arts exhibitors. Some of the more important included Mrs G.F. Watts's Compton class (G.F. Watts was known to Ruskin personally), Mrs Waterhouse's Yattendon carvers, Mabel de Grey's St Saviour's, Pimlico, classes, and, in Ireland, the Fivemiletown metalwork class. Of more immediate relevance to the Langdale Linen Industry was the Haslemere handcraft industries. Associated with the Peasant Arts Society, Haslemere established several textile workshops some eleven years after the Linen Industry was founded and exhibited at the Home Arts. Closer scrutiny of the Newlyn metalwork class might provide interesting comparisons with the Keswick School metalwork classes, although Newlyn was founded some ten years later.

Between 1880 and 1920 Lakeland saw an astounding development of the local arts exhibition, quite unlike anything which had gone before. The pinnacle of that development was the 1891 Kendal Arts, Crafts and Loan Exhibition, the largest and clearest public statement of Lakeland's independence and unity. While the local exhibition was one of its chief sources of publicity, Lakeland also exhibited at the Home Arts exhibi-tions with considerable consistency. Given the role of women as contributors to the British domestic arts scene generally between 1880 and 1920, an analysis of the part they played in the success of the Home Arts exhibitions would prove useful to any future study of the domestic arts, both in Lakeland and elsewhere. The women of Lakeland made a major contribution to the region's exhibitions, and to those of the Home Arts. But women elsewhere followed their example after 1884 and helped to ensure the success of the domestic arts movement generally. Given that Ruskin was a key figure in nineteenth-century arts, further research into the Home Arts would establish whether there were any theoretical links with the writer, which have previously been largely ignored. His theoretical influence, for example on Laxey, may have been underestimated in relation to other practical endeavours of the nineteenth century. Much has been published on the Pre-Raphaelite Brotherhood and the Arts and Crafts Exhibition Society, both of which were linked to Ruskin. But this study has shown that the strong theoretical and literary background of the Lakeland revival was just as important to its founding and development. To Marian Twelves in particular, that adherence to Ruskin's theories became increasingly important as her work progressed, despite the often complex nature of his writings, and her own lack of formal education. Even in his final years Ruskin had a definite impact on the British arts. Although no less important an example of the realisation of Ruskin's theories than the Pre-Raphaelite Brotherhood or the Arts and Crafts Exhibition Society, Lakeland has until now remained largely neglected as an area of Ruskin's positive theoretical and personal influence.

No comprehensive biographies have been written of Canon Rawnsley, Edith Rawnsley, Arthur W. Simpson, W.G. Collingwood, Dorrie and Barbara Collingwood or Harold Stabler. Only Thomas H. Mawson, a peripheral figure in the revival, has left an autobiography, and even Ruskin's *Praeterita* remains incomplete. Arthur Simpson's notes for his life story remained incomplete due to his sudden death, and the lack of direct descendants of, for example, Fleming and Marian Twelves, has meant that even some family histories have largely vanished. Other minor figures yet to be investigated include the Lakeland photographer Herbert Bell and the Keswick School designer Isabel McBean. Generally, there appears to be a lack of interest in regional artists, craftsmen and craftswomen, or regional writers. Rawnsley's books on Lakeland, for example, have not been reissued, although some of Collingwood's lesser-known Lakeland works have.

It seems most fitting to end with Wordworth's poem *Song for the Spinning Wheel*. Composed in 1812 and published in 1820, the poem epitomises all that fired Ruskin, and those who followed in his footsteps in Lakeland. The region's revival of traditional arts and crafts ultimately lay rooted in what the poet described in his works: the need to retain and maintain Lakeland's identity. For a while, this was done more successfully than could ever have been anticipated:

> Swiftly turn the murmuring wheel!
> Night has brought the welcome hour,
> When the weary fingers feel
> Help, as if from faery power;
> Dewy night o'er shades the ground;
> Turn the swift wheel round and round!

Now, beneath the starry sky,
Couch the widely-scattered sheep;—
Ply the pleasant labour, ply!
For the spindle, while they sleep,
Runs with speed more smooth and fine.
Gathering up a trustier line.

Short-lived likings may be bred
By a glance from fickle eyes;
But true love is like the thread
Which the kindly wool supplies,
When the flocks are all at rest,
Sleeping on the mountain's breast.

APPENDIX

NOTES AND CORRESPONDENCE

16 (I) I Commend the whole of the following letter to the reader's most serious consideration

BROXBOURNE, HERTS, 11th *June,* 1874.

My DEAR Sir,—You are so tolerant of correspondents with grievances, that I venture to say a few more words, in reply to your note about Law Reform. In November next the Judicature Bill will come into operation. The preamble recites this incontestable fact, 'that it is expedient to make provision for the better administration of justice in England.' Now, the two salient features of the incessant clamour for Law Reform are these—1st, an increased conviction of the sanctity of property; 2nd, a proportionate decrease in the estimate of human life. For years past the English people have spent incalculable money and talk in trying to induce Parliament to give them safe titles to their land, and sharp and instant means of getting in their debts: the Land Transfer Bill is in answer to this first demand, and the Judicature Bill to the second. Meanwhile the Criminal Code may shift for itself; and here we have, as the outcome of centuries of vulgar national flourish about Magna Charta, Habeas Corpus, and much else, the present infamous system of punishing crime by pecuniary penalties. Now the spirit of this evil system is simply this: 'A crime is an offence against society. Making the criminal suffer pain won't materially benefit society, but making him suffer in his pocket will;' and so society elects to be battered about and variously maltreated, on a sliding scale of charges, adjusted more on medical than moral principles. No doubt it is very desirable to have a title-deed to your thousand acres, no bigger than the palm of your hand, to be able to

228

put it in a box, and sit upon it, and defy all the lawyers in the land to pick a flaw in your title; quite a millennium-like state of things, but liable to be somewhat marred if your next-door neighbour may knock you off your box, stab you with a small pocket-knife, and jump on your stomach, all with grievous damage to you, but comparative immunity to himself. We are one day to have cheap law, meanwhile we have such cheap crime that injuries to the person are now within the reach of all. I may be a villain of the first water, if I have a few spare pounds in my pocket. From a careful survey of lately reported cases, I find I can run away with my neighbour's wife, seduce his daughter, half poison his household with adulterated food, and finally stab him with a pocket-knife, for rather less than £1000. Stabbing is so ridiculously cheap that I can indulge in it for a trifling penalty of £1. (See Southall's case.[1]) But woe be to me if I dare to encroach on my neighbour's land, prejudice his trade, or touch his pocket; then the law has remedies, vast and many, and I shall not only incur pecuniary penalties that are to all effects and purpose limitless, but I shall be made to suffer in person also. These two things are exactly indicative of the gradual decay of the national mind under the influence of two schools. The first teaches that man's primary object in life is to 'get on in the world'; hence we have this exaggerated estimate of the value and sanctity of property. The second school teaches that love can exist without reverence, mercy without justice, and liberty without obedience; and as the logical result of such teaching, we have lost all clear and healthy knowledge of what justice really is, and invent a system of punishments which is not even really punitive, and without any element of retribution at all. Let us have instead a justice that not only condones the crime, but also makes a profit out of the criminal. And we get her; but note the irony of Fate: when our modern goddess *does* pluck up heart to be angry, she seems doomed to be angry in the wrong way, and with the wrong people. Here is a late instance (the printed report of which I send you):–

William Hawkes, a blind man and very infirm, was brought up, having been committed from Marlborough Street, to be dealt with as a rogue and vagabond. On being placed in the dock, Mr Montagu Williams, as *amicus curce,* said he had known the prisoner for years, from seeing him sitting on Waterloo Bridge tracing his fingers over a book designed for the blind to read, and in no instance had he seen him beg from those who passed by, so that he was practically doing no harm, and some time ago the late Sir William Bodkin had dealt very mercifully with him.

---

[1] (A police court case of the time.)

Something ought to be done for him.

Mr Harris said he could corroborate all that his learned friend had stated.

The Assistant-Judge said he had been convicted by the magistrate, and was sent here to be sentenced as a rogue and vagabond, *but the Court would not deal hardly with him.*

Horsford, chief officer of the Mendicity Society, said the prisoner had been frequently convicted for begging.

The Assistant-Judge sentenced him to be imprisoned for four months.—May, 1874.

The other day I was reading a beautiful Eastern story of a certain blind man who sat by the wayside begging; clearly a very importunate and troublesome blind man, who would by no means hold his peace, but who, nevertheless, had his heart's desire granted unto him at last. And yesterday I was also reading a very unlovely Western story of another blind man, who was 'very infirm,' not at all importunate, did not even beg; only sat there by the roadside and read out of a certain Book that has a great deal to say about justice and mercy. The sequel of the two stories varies considerably: in this latter one our civilized English Law clutches the old blind man by the throat, tells him he is a rogue and a vagabond, and flings him into prison for four months! But our enlightened British Public is too busy clamouring for short deeds and cheap means of litigation, ever to give thought or time to mere 'sentimental grievances.' Have you seen the strange comment on Carlyle's letter of some months ago, in which he prophesied evil things to come, if England still persisted in doing her work 'ill, swiftly, and mendaciously'?[1]. Our export trade, for the first five months of this year, shows a decrease of just eight millions! 'The newspapers note with a horrified amazement, that the continental nations decline dealing any longer at the "old shop," and fall back on home products, and try to explain it by reference to the Capital and Labour question.' Carlyle foresaw Germany's future, and told us plainly of it; he foresees England's decadence, and warns us just as plainly of *that;* and the price we have already paid, in this year of grace 1874, for telling him to hold his tongue, is just eight millions.

Yours sincerely,[2]

---

[1] (A letter on 'Capital and Labour' in *The Times* of January 28, 1874: see the Introduction to Vol. XXVII. (p. xlv.), where extracts from it are given.).

[2] (The writer was Mr Albert Fleming.)

17. Next, or next but one, to the *Fors* for the squires,[1] will come that for the lawyers.[2] In the meantime, can any correspondent inform me, approximately, what the income and earnings of the legal profession are annually in England, and what sum is spent in collateral expenses for

FORS CLAVIGERA: VOL. IV

---

[1] (Letter 45.)

[2] (Letter 47; the points suggested by Mr Fleming's letter were not, however, touched upon there (see below, p. 201), being reserved for 'subsequent consideration.')

BIBLIOGRAPHY

ARCHIVAL SOURCES

Cumbria Record Office, Kendal
WDX 515: A.W. Simpson and W.G. Collingwood papers.
WDB 76 and WDB 86: Thomas H. Mawson papers.
WDS 73 and WDS 0116: Langdale Linen Industry papers.

Cumbria Record Office, Carlisle
DB 111: Keswick School of Industrial Arts papers.

Sheffield Archives
GSG 21: Guild of St George papers.

John Rylands University Library, Manchester
Ruskin papers.

The Ruskin Library, Lancaster University
Ruskin papers.

Kendal Library
Papers and exhibition items.

Abbot Hall Art Gallery and Museum, Kendal
Annie Garnett, Langdale Linen Industry and Keswick School of Industrial Arts papers.

Armitt Library, Ambleside
Local history items.

Ruskin Museum, Coniston
Papers and exhibition catalogues.

The Ruskin Galleries, Bembridge, Isle of Wight
Ruskin papers.

Huntington Library, California
Letters and other Ruskin material.

Yale University Beinecke Library
Ruskin letters.

Private collection
A. W. Simpson papers.

EXHIBITION CATALOGUES AND LEAFLETS

Benjamin, F. A., *The Ruskin Linen Industry of Keswick* (Cockermouth, Michael Moon, 1974).
Blake, Marguerite, *Revival of Spinning and Weaving in Langdale* (1976).
Catalogue of the Annual Coniston Exhibition (1900–19) (Ulverston, William Holmes).
Catalogue of the Kendal Arts, Crafts and Loan Exhibition (Kendal, Titus Wilson, 1891) (Copy in Kendal Library).
Catalogue of the Kendal Exhibition of Pictures and Decorative Art (Kendal, 1899).
Crosthwaite Parish Magazine (1883-1910).
Davidson, Eleanor, *The Simpsons of Kendal* (University of Lancaster, 1978).
Garnett, Annie, *Plants and Seeds, the Spinnery, Bowness-on-Windermere*.
Holder, Julian, *The Home Arts and Industries Association* (n.d.).
Collingwood, W.G. (ed.), *Catalogue of the Ruskin Museum* (5th edn, 1919).
Simpson, Arthur W., *Observations on Woodcarving by a Craftsman* (*c*.1910).
Twelves, Marian, *The Ruskin Linen Industry, Keswick* (Keswick, T. Bakewell, *c*.1900).

NEWSPAPERS AND JOURNALS

Architectural Review (1896-1900)
Art Journal (1883-1911)
Art Workers' Quarterly (1902-6)
Blackwood's Magazine (various years)
British Workman (1894)
Cabinet Maker and Complete House Furnisher (1918)
Carlisle Journal (1891)
Carlisle Patriot (1891-94)
Cornhill Magazine (various years)
Country Life (various years)

Daily Chronicle
Daily News (1900)
The Friend (1922)
Huntington Library Quarterly (1989)
Keswick Guardian (1890-91)
Manchester Guardian (1887)
Pall Mall Gazette (various years)
Punch (1876–1930)
Ruskin Reading Guild Journal (1889)
Sheffield Arts Review (1993)
The Spectator (1900)
Standard (1883)
The Studio (1893–1930)
Sunday Chronicle (1894)
Sunday Companion (1901)
The Times (1891)
West Cumberland Times (1891)
Westmorland Gazette (1883–1930)
Woman's Agricultural Times (1899)
The Year's Art (1891)

OTHER PUBLISHED WORKS

The place of publication is London, except where indicated.

Adams, Anthony (ed.), *Barbara Hepworth* (Moonraker Press, 1970).
Beard, Geoffrey, and Wardman, Joan, *Thomas H. Mawson 1861-1933: The Life and Work of a Northern Landscape Architect* (University of Lancaster, Visual Arts Centre, 1976).
Bottomley, Gordon, *Poems of Thirty Years* (Constable, 1925).
Bruce, Ian, *The Loving Eye and Skilful Hand* (Carlisle, Bookcase, 2001).
Burkett, M.E., and Sloss, J.D.G., *William Green of Ambleside* (Kendal, Abbot Hall Art Gallery, 1984).
Callen, Anthea, *Angel in the Studio Women in the Arts and Crafts Movement 1870-1914* (Astragal Books, 1979).
Collingwood, W.G. (ed.) *Transactions of the Cumberland and Westmorland Antiquarian and Archaeological Society*, xiv (1914), xvi (1916).
Collingwood, W.G., *The Life and Work of John Ruskin* (Methuen & Co., 1893).
Collingwood, W.G. (ed.), *The Poems of John Ruskin* (George Allen, 1891).
Collingwood, W.G., *Ruskin Relics* (Isbister & Co., 1903).
Cook, E.T., *Studies in Ruskin* (George Allen, 1890).
Cook, E.T. and Wedderburn, A. (ed.), *The Works of John Ruskin* (George Allen, 1903–12).

Crawford, Alan, *By Hammer and Hand* (Birmingham Museums and Art Gallery, 1984).

Crowley, David and Taylor, Lou (ed.) *The Lost Arts of Europe: the Haslemere Collection of European peasant art* (Haslemere Educational Museum, 2000).

Dawson, John, *Torver* (Phillimore, 1985).

Eeles, F.C., *The Parish Church of St Kentigern, Crosthwaite* (rev. edn) (Kendal, Titus Wilson, 1974).

Evans, J., and Whitehouse, J.H. (ed.), *The Diaries of John Ruskin* (Oxford, Clarendon Press, 1956–9).

Fleming, Albert, *In the House of Rimmon* (Partridge & Cooper, 1873).

Fleming, Albert (ed.), *Hortus Inclusus* (George Allen, 1887).

Garnett, Annie, *Notes on Hand-Spinning* (Dulau & Co., 1896).

Garnett, Annie, *Spinnery Notes* (Chiswick Press, 1912).

Garraty, J.L., and Sternstein, J.L., *Encyclopedia of American Biography* (2nd edn) (New York, Harper Collins, 1996).

Gebhard, David, *Charles F. A. Voysey, Architect* (Los Angeles, Hennesey & Ingalls, 1975).

Graves, Algernon (ed.), *The Royal Academy Exhibitors* (Henry Graves & Co., 1905).

Griffith, Leonard, Meisel, Louis K. and Meisel, Susan Pear, *Clarice Cliff. The Bizarre Affair* (Thames & Hudson, 1988).

Hewison, R. (ed.), *New Approaches to Ruskin* (Routledge & Kegan Paul, 1981).

Hobbs, A. Stevenson, *Beatrix Potter's Art* (F. Warne & Co., 1989).

Huish, Marcus B., *Samplers and Tapestry Embroideries* (New York, Dover 1970; originally published in 1913).

Jekyll, Gertrude, and Weaver, Lawrence, *Gardens for Small Country Houses* (Antique Collectors' Club, 1988; originally published in 1912).

Linder, L. (ed.), *The Journal of Beatrix Potter* (Frederick Warne & Co., 1966).

Lindop, Grevel, *A Literary Guide to the Lake District* (Chatto & Windus, 1993).

Mawson, Thomas H., *The Life and Work of an English Landscape Architect* (Richards Press, 1927).

Murphy, Graham, *Founders of the National Trust* (Helm, 1987).

Prickett, Elizabeth, *Ruskin Lace and Linen Work* (Batsford, 1985).

Rawnsley, Eleanor, *Canon Rawnsley. An Account of his Life* (Glasgow, MacLehose, Jackson & Co., 1923).

Rawnsley, H.D., *Sonnets at the English Lakes* (Longmans Green & Co., 1881).

Rawnsley, H.D., *Ruskin and the English Lakes* (Glasgow, James MacLehose & Sons, 1901).

Rawnsley, H. D., *Edward Thring, Teacher and Poet* (T. Fisher Unwin, 1889).

Renouf, Jane, *Alfred Heaton Cooper Painter of Landscape* (Grasmere, Red Bank Press, 1997).

Roberts, Elizabeth, *A History of Linen in the North West* (University of Lancaster, Centre for North-West Regional Studies, 1998).

Royal Academy Exhibitors 1905–70 (E.P. Publishing, 1981).

Royal Institute of British Architects, *Catalogue of the Drawings of the Royal Institute of British Architects* (Gregg Publishing, 1989).

Ruskin, John, *Praeterita* (George Allen, 1886).
Ruskin, John, *On the Old Road* (new edn) (George Allen, 1899).
Ruskin, John, *Modern Painters* (new edn) (George Allen, 1897).
Ruskin, John, *Deucalion, Arrows of the Chace* (Boston, Dana Estates & Co., n.d.).
Ruskin, John, *The Two Paths* (Smith, Elder & Co., 1859).
Satchell, John, *The Kendal Weaver* (Kendal Civic Society & Frank Peters Publishing, 1986).
Warner, H.H. (ed.), *Songs of the Spindle and Legends of the Loom* (N.J. Powell & Co., 1889).
Waterson, M., *The National Trust: The First Hundred Years* (BBC Books, 1994).
Weaver, Lawrence, *Small Country Houses of To-Day* (Country Life, 1919).
Williams, W.E. (ed.), *Wordsworth* (rev. edn) (Penguin, 1988).
The Works of William Wordsworth (Wordsworth Editions Ltd, 1994).

UNPUBLISHED THESIS

Jordan, Harriet, 'Thomas Hayton Mawson 1861–1933. The English Garden Designs of an Edwardian Landscape Architect' (University of London (Wye College) Ph.D., 1988).

INDEX

237